Since his retirement, The Secret Footballer has been given the opportunity to continue playing football in America and India. He has received offers to become the manager of a League I club, chief scout and assistant manager for Championship clubs and the Director of Football for a League I club. He declined every offer.

And today? That'd be telling.

www.thesecretfootballer.com

Also by the Secret Footballer:

I Am the Secret Footballer
Tales from the Secret Footballer
The Secret Footballer's Guide to the Modern Game

THE SECRET FOOTBALLER

ACCESS ALL AREAS

First published in 2015
by Guardian Books, Kings Place, 90 York Way, London, N1 9GU
and Faber & Faber Limited
Bloomsbury House, 74–77 Great Russell Street
London WC1B 3DA

This paperback edition published in 2016

A CIP record for this book is available from the British Library

ISBN 978-1-78335-060-5

Typeset by seagulls.net
Printed and bound by CPI Group (UK) Ltd, Croydon CR0 4YY

*Publisher's note: Some identifying features have been altered in this
book to protect The Secret Footballer's identity.*

2 4 6 8 10 9 7 5 3 1

For 'Scott'

The mate who very nearly made it through the madness and
the bullshit and never asked for a fucking thing in return

CONTENTS

TSF shows little interest in his classes and has a limited desire to engage in subjects in which he doesn't stand out. The one exception is English where he is extremely adept at telling us that he just wants to play football.

SCHOOL REPORT CARD, 1996

People call them 'rats' because a rat will do anything to survive; isn't that right, Mr Hill?

LAWYER FOR THE PROSECUTION TO FORMER NEW YORK MAFIOSO TURNCOAT, HENRY HILL, NEW YORK, 1980

FOREWORD

By Mrs TSF

People often ask me what it's like to be a WAG; but I don't consider myself to be a person who is defined by an acronym made up by a journalist – even if I do know what they mean. In his early books my husband, the Secret Footballer – an idea that he came up with – lifted the lid on how the world of football really works. I read those books and, personally, I came away feeling that they were only the tip of the iceberg – but then apparently I don't understand brand building. Although the first books are certainly informative about the real workings of the football world, and a lot of fun, they are to my mind, given what I've witnessed, pretty tame, and I told him that. So he said he'd write the book that I wanted to read, and reveal all the things he said he had protected me from: the things I was better off not knowing. I'd just have to deal with it once it was released.

When people ask me what it's like to be a WAG, it doesn't even occur to me that what they really want to know is how many pairs of shoes I have, what car I drive, how many bedrooms there are in my house, and what Coleen is like (I don't know, by the way). I tell them to read this book. If you really want a snapshot of what it has been like to be married to a footballer, wondering whether he is going to be on the front page of the *Sun* on Monday morning rather than the back, worrying if some people are going to turn up at our front door because he has got in the way of a deal somewhere, read this book. This is the book that will really open your eyes to what I have been dealing with for 15 years: the violence, the threats, the women, the debauchery and the intense mood-swings. This is the book that I wanted him to write from day one. It isn't pretty – in fact, it's everything that I thought it would be and ultimately dreaded – but it is this book that gives me closure.

I think the most impressive thing is that he got out alive. As I stand here today I can honestly tell you, with my hand on my heart, that there were a couple of occasions when I went to bed and I really did not expect to see him ever again when I woke up the next morning. Everything about the game seemed to add to the toll for him rather than improve the situation. Every time a new experience came along it seemed to ratchet up the pressure on him, because he was always the player that the club used as its poster boy.

And then there are the injuries. Since the introduction I wrote for his last book he has managed to crack another rib and put his tooth through his top lip. I don't know if you've ever seen anybody with their tooth sticking through their top lip, but it's one of those curious things that is both horrifying and humorous at the same time.

It has never been the case that he thinks he's right about everything. It's more that, if he does something then it will be his way or no way. This isn't because he has an unshakable belief that his way is the right way – rather, he has an unshakable belief that teaching and training primarily serve to restrain a person's natural instinct for the way that something should be done. And there is a naivety in that belief which manifests itself in a creative output that ensures his uniqueness, honesty and integrity. All of his coaches in football told him that they couldn't coach him because he played in such a way that seemed to galvanise the entire team – he'd play passes or take up positions that were not like anything you'd ever coach a player who had come through a youth team or an academy.

And when he started writing his columns for the *Guardian* it was the same. I can remember Paul Johnson, the deputy editor of the paper, saying to him, 'It's a different style of writing. You'd never train a journalist this way, that's what makes it so good.' He lives for comments like that; he loves the fact that he can turn his hand to something and hold his own. That's how he feels about football: he's an outsider coming in and he's actually doing it, in his own way, as well as anyone else, while everyone else is left scratching their head asking, 'How?'

When he signed for his first big team, an ex-England player who was already at the club did an interview, with the local paper no less, in which he said that if the club wanted to do anything significant then it should not be signing players from the lower leagues.

He probably won't thank me for telling you the story because it's so well known, but a few years later when that player had retired and become a pundit he inevitably had to cover his former team – football always throws up uncomfortable scenarios like that. At that point my husband was having a great season and the club were on the verge of making history. My husband's ex-teammate came running up to him in front of all the Sky cameras and all the people who hang around the tunnel on a match day and tried to hug him, as if they were long-lost friends. My husband stepped back, looked him dead in the eye, and said, 'I think you might be beneath me, I'm afraid.' It was a metaphor for what each had achieved during their time at the same club. My husband left as one of the best players in the club's history, his head held high, untouchable by any player before or since – but not just for his prowess on the field; it was the respect for the way he led the fans into battle. They felt that they were following him; everybody did. As long as my husband was walking out of the tunnel on to the pitch, then the club had a great chance of success. That's how he felt, and people all around the city bought into him. And, ultimately, he ended up pulling off that faith in the most spectacular way.

As with all people who are on the edge, just about in control of themselves, he has crossed the line and done some things that he isn't proud about. He regrets calling Dietmar Hamann a Nazi (he then swapped shirts with him, something that he holds Hamann in the highest esteem for), but he doesn't regret calling Michael Ballack a Nazi because he's convinced that Ballack continually tried to elbow him after an argument that he'd had with another player. Though, as it happens, I feel like I should apologise for what he said to the other player too.

But when the Secret Footballer is over, it won't have been for him, or me, or our children, or our bank balance. It will have been for you. It's entertainment. Give the public what they want, entertain them, that's what he wants. That's how he was as a player. He could have played in the Premier League for 10 years, but he hated it and decided that he'd be happier writing books about it. You have to admire that: there aren't many people left who will forfeit riches and fame for entertainment alone.

But deep down I know that he loves football. He has loved football all his life in some capacity. I remember when we first met and we talked about our schools. Our mothers both worked as school dinner ladies and I remember asking him what his favourite dinner was. He said that he made his mum put him on packed lunches so that he could eat it in class before the break and have the full lunch hour to play football.

If you contrast the innocence of that to where a life of playing football would eventually take him, the difference is night and day; but even in those moments it was a journey, an adventure for me, something that none of the people I grew up with have ever had the chance to experience – and I'm a better person for it. The Secret Footballer has a way about him that can infuriate and exasperate, but everything that happens to us as a result of the things he does is a life experience that is a thousand times more interesting than what happens in the town where I grew up.

And from the moment he began playing professionally, I was only ever interested in what my husband was doing on the pitch. The curious thing for me is that it wasn't like that for the other wives and girlfriends. At his first big club I'd sit with the WAGs and they'd be pointing to the pitch and saying, 'Thierry looks good today.' Or, 'Oh, I heard a story about Rio,' before they'd all start gossiping about it. That never made any sense to me. Our husbands were out there playing, running themselves into the ground, putting their teeth through their lips and so on, and these women were talking about the other team. In fact, I don't think I ever heard one reference to anyone on our own team until one of them scored – and then, depending on the goalscorer, the wife would get up and strut around the executive box like a peacock.

During one game a big player was sent off for the other side after a bad tackle, and one of the wives turned round to me and said, 'Oh my God, did you see that?' And I said that I'd missed it because I was watching my husband. 'But the ball was down the other end of the pitch!' she replied, incredulously.

That tells you everything you need to know about how we live our lives and how my husband approaches football. I have absolutely no interest in the ball, because the ball only ever does what it's told. And where's the excitement in that?

INTRODUCTION

- -

Night-time. A stadium. The PA crackles into life. 'Ladies and gentlemen, we all know why we are here tonight ... [a tsunami of cheers] so please, please, please, because he is our leader, because he is the one that José calls "Special", and because he is one moody bastard, please give it up for ... the Secret Footballer.'

Delirious standing ovation. Faces shining and upturned. A cult at boiling point. A man appears on stage. In silhouette, but ripped and buff. You can tell that he is the essence of sex. Raw power.

'Thank you! Thank you! Now stop! Please take your seats, ladies and germs. Enough with the cheering and the clapping. Enough. The bouquets? Really? What about my allergies? Fuckers ...

'Now listen. Throughout the life of the Secret Footballer you have always had the truth [more cheering]. You've had a perspective on football that nobody would ever have given you in a million years.'

Standing O. Stewards uneasy.

'There are three reasons for that: one, the players who have the most to say generally don't need to say anything thanks to the wages that they have been earning ...'

'Amen to that,' say the crowd.

'Two, they simply wouldn't have come up with the idea, and even if they had they couldn't have executed it.'

'Praise the Lord,' say the crowd.

'And three, they don't want you to know a fucking thing about their life, and especially the shit that they've been up to throughout their career.'

'*Hallefuckinglujah!!!!*' Crowd erupts. Stewards lose control. Thousands of mobile phones carrying pictures of lit candles are held aloft. The Secret Footballer turns his back to the crowd, takes a quick selfie of secret self with the cliff-face of candles behind same self, then leaves the stage one last time.

Don't mourn.

The Secret Footballer will live on thanks to the website that I've set up. I will write about football because I am resigned to the fact that I will never get away from it, and it will never get away from me. When all is said and done and the pot that I used to piss in has been carted off and melted down for scrap, I actually know what I'm talking about.

A great manager once said to me, 'TSF, do you know what the best thing about football is? Everybody gets a chance to express his own opinion about what we do ... And do you know what the worst thing about football is? Every one of those arseholes can't wait to tell you what that fucking opinion is.'

Let's go back to the beginning and the education that makes TSF the only other infallible footballing deity outside the Neville family.

When I was a non-league footballer, my manager at the time told me that he'd got me a trial with Millwall. Non-league managers do that. They know that the best young players have absolutely no clue as to what is going on above their heads and, as a result, they will swallow any old rubbish fed to them by their manager. In my case, I was told by my manager – a former player – that he'd been on the phone to everyone telling them that they had to come down to watch this kid who was doing really well in non-league. The rumours had gone to my head, and in one game I had taken a black marker pen and written '£10m' on my chest on the off-chance that I scored and could whip my shirt over my head during the game.

The reality was that Millwall had been watching me for a while and had approached my manager to ask who represented me. Obviously at that level nobody was filling the role of an agent, and at the time I was earning £30 a week. Even though I was 'on contract', some of my teammates were earning £100 a week but, of course, I didn't know that. My manager took it upon himself to represent me, and I went to Millwall on a week's trial.

Before I'd even got there, things didn't go well. I was given two phone numbers. One was the number of a fellow player with whom I'd be travelling and staying in north Bromley, which is where you will find Millwall's training ground, and the other number was that of the Millwall manager, Mark McGhee. I was told to ring the number of my fellow player so that we could agree our travel arrangements. Tragically, I got the numbers mixed up and rang the wrong person, twice. I repeatedly abused what I thought was the father of the other player when he refused to put his son on the phone, claiming that nobody by that name lived at the address. I thought he was taking the piss out of me.

Twenty minutes later, and with me scratching my head at why the number I'd been given hadn't married up with the person I'd been led to believe would answer, my phone rang. When I answered, a voice said, 'Hello, TSF, this is Mark McGhee. I think you've got off to a very bad start, don't you?'

My arsehole fell out and rolled across the floor. Keep in mind that for a kid who had yet to arrive on the professional scene, this was a man who had won the European Cup Winners' Cup with Aberdeen by beating none other than Real Madrid in the final 2–1. He had, I later learned, set up the winning goal with a cross from the left. The following season, he won the European Super Cup, against Hamburg, scoring in the second leg.

He hadn't won any Mr Congeniality contests though. This was football, but at a level that I'd never dreamed I'd need to comprehend.

Because of that balls-up I was on the back foot the moment I got to Millwall. McGhee hardly talked to me, and his coach, Steve Gritt, who had organised my arrival and accommodation, was little better. Someone I did see from time to time was Ray Harford, a local legend with Luton and a fella who was trying to play the role of coach but couldn't help telling you everything he knew about the game while being a thoroughly decent guy in the process. He died of lung cancer not long afterwards, aged just 58.

Just prior to Ray's passing, Millwall were a very decent team. They had great wingers such as Paul Ifill and Steven Reid, and hard men like David Livermore and Matt Lawrence, while their centre-halves – Stuart Nethercott, Sean Dyche and David Tuttle – had been around and knew their stuff. None of them wanted to talk to me – none of them except one player, a friendly Ozzie by the name of Tim Cahill. Cahill was something of a fans' favourite and he'd invite me out to lunch or to play snooker when training had finished. Sometimes we'd just hang out and play video games – he beat me at snooker by the way, and I formed the impression that he played a lot of it. He was maybe lonely, being as he was so far from home, but even so he was a top man. I made a point of shaking his hand every time I played against him thereafter. Those occasions included games in which we both tried to leave a mark on each other. Still, they almost always ended in an embrace. Tim Cahill is a gentleman and someone I would have a beer with any time – especially if he ever invites me to New York.

The Millwall team was supplemented with decent young kids from the Millwall youth team, and the New Den, as you can imagine, was hostile. Up front, Millwall had a player called Neil Harris, who was scoring goals left, right and centre. Neil

Harris wasn't allowed to train in case he got injured, which I now know is a ridiculous notion.

Neil was my first motivational tool. He was probably just high on confidence and safe in the knowledge that the fans loved him, but his demeanour, his face, everything about him made me want to knock him right off his fucking perch. He looked like a fat accountant who didn't know what he was doing, not at all like a footballer. He spoke as if he owned the fucking training ground, and he told stories that weren't funny – not to me, anyway, but everyone else laughed at them wholeheartedly. They called him a 'bubble wrap' player, somebody the manager didn't want injured at any cost. I now know that bubble wrap players are as rare an occurrence as Martin Keown saying something insightful on *Match of the Day*. Harris is probably a good lad, as far as I know, and he certainly knew where the goal was – he seemed to score without trying, which is an art in itself. But from that first day, he became the establishment in my mind, somebody to take on.

Needless to say, I didn't get the gig at Millwall, but another team had shown an interest. That team would go on to sign me because my non-league manager and the manager of the league club knew each other and had no doubt come to an arrangement. That's not uncommon at all. Indeed, it's how nine-tenths of the deals from non-league to league football happen. I didn't care, of course. I was in, and I was determined to make sure that, in as quick a time as possible, everybody knew my name.

When you are naive about something, be that football or anything else, you can only approach it in a very rudimentary, basic manner. That's how I approached professional football, and I played the game in exactly the same way as I did in the streets where I'd come from. I played the game in the way I had played it with my friends. No rules. No education. No etiquette. Best player wins.

Then a curious thing happened once I was signed by my first professional club: my fellow footballers, my teammates, laughed at me. I wasn't a kid. But when I ran for every ball and tackled anything that moved, and kissed the badge (yes, I did kiss the badge from time to time) they talked about me as if I was a teacher's pet who had no idea how to play 'proper' football. I wouldn't last five minutes. Some of them tried to bully me, until they realised that I bit back. One particular crowning moment came when we were eating our pre-match meal in a hotel. I was wearing a beanie hat, and one of the older pros, sitting on the older pros' table, told me to take it off at the dinner table. Everybody on the table stared at me. I kept it on. He kept telling me to take it off. Soon the whole squad was looking at me. It was their idea of banter – let's see if we can get this guy to do what we tell him. I looked him dead in the eye and told him to come and take it off my head. For most people around me, it was the first thing I think they'd ever heard me say, and it was a big, big moment. We carried on eating our dinner. My beanie hat stayed where it had been when we first sat down.

Stupid stuff. Sometimes they'd pose a question out loud. I'd answer and that would piss them off. If they had ever wanted to know the answer they certainly didn't want to hear it from me. In dressing rooms you never stick your head up above the parapet like that. If a senior player is asking a question out loud he is merely demonstrating that this is a question that nobody knows the answer to.

But I wasn't even trying to be clever. I just happened to know the answer more often than not. I'd shout it out, and the conversation would continue as if nobody had heard anything. I vividly remember the squad sat down to dinner in the canteen one day, staring at the one TV that we had hanging off the prefab wall. It was always tuned to Sky Sports News, and back then adverts encouraging you to take loans out – even if you'd been turned down before – were rife. During one such advertisement, the captain asked nobody in particular, 'What the fuck are CCJs?' Without looking up, I replied, 'County court judgements.' I recall that he looked at me – an upstart – with utter contempt, and for a time my life got harder. I wasn't being clever, and I don't consider somebody who knows the answer to a lot of stuff about life as being particularly intelligent. Knowledge back then was born of necessity – if you didn't understand certain things that affected your class then you were fucked. But it made an immediate impression on everybody in the room. I was different. I'd been somewhere before – they weren't sure where, exactly, and that made them nervous.

I realised that the ritual was about keeping me in my place, but I wasn't interested in playing along. They'd call it 'paying your dues'. I hadn't paid my dues in professional football. Fine. I'd call what went on a short-sighted, half-arsed form of bullying, really.

Let me tell you the run of the before, the during and the after of that early football education. At first they laughed. The thought of a new nobody coming into their dressing room and into their team was so strange to them that their only response could be to laugh. Then when the 'nobody' did well on the pitch it wasn't so funny. They became jealous. This was counter to everything they had been taught when they started out in the academy, not long after they were potty-trained. His dues! His dues! He hasn't paid his dues!

I kept doing well. Then they resented themselves for not being the first among the squad to spot a player in their midst. There would have been dressing-room kudos on offer if one of them had seen the point of my existence. The jealousy congealed into disdain. What was worse was that they had to answer honestly when the media asked them to comment on how well I was doing.

I could feel their pain. There are few things worse than a journalist who wants a soundbite from the main man about a kid he has absolutely no interest in drawing attention to. It dents the ego. Ambushed by hacks with tape recorders, they would listen to a chorus of, 'What about this new lad, this TSF? He looks like a player, doesn't he?' The older pro wants to scream, 'No, he isn't a real player, he fucking scampers after the ball the whole time and he chases every tackle like a dog after a stick – and listen, why are you asking me about him? What's he done? He's just a fucking kid. I'm the guy standing in front of you. Let's talk about me again. Remember that goal I scored six years ago? Let's talk about that one again. Fuck him. Anyway, between you and me, he hasn't paid his dues – and he's a big fucking know-it-all.'

They couldn't say that, though. With no other choice, they had to be the professional: 'Yeah, he's settled in really well. The lads really like him. He's got a long way to go, but if he keeps working hard … blah, blah, blah.'

When I was sold to a much bigger club I deliberately lost contact with them.

Forgive your enemies, they say.

Keep their addresses and keep the notes you made, I say.

In the years that followed I would, of course, bump into some of those guys here and there. They all, to a man, asked me to help them out or to be associated with them in some way. Some just wanted me to follow them on Instagram; some asked if I could do a presentation for their kid's youth team. Others offered me discounts for products from businesses that they had started or worked for, usually jewellery or cars. I remember conservatories being a product I was urged to invest in for humanitarian reasons.

And each time I declined. The worst offenders I even strung along for a little while – just for a bit of added vengeance.

Yes, go on, say it. The bigger man would extend his hand and let bygones be bygones. I hear you. But the world doesn't work like that, I'm afraid – and the football world certainly doesn't run on love. I can be a horrible bastard. I made my bed long ago. I'm quite prepared to give everyone a chance. In fact, my downfall in the past has been as a result of giving too much of myself in return for nothing at all.

I didn't forget those guys, and I didn't make myself feel like a hell of a guy by shaking their hands and hugging it all away years later. What I did instead was refuse to pull the ladder up after myself in whatever dressing room I went into. I gave advice and help to any young lad who wanted it.

It's like this. I don't care if you played football with me once upon a time. I don't wear the same rose-tinted glasses as you. I don't go in for nostalgia like you. Banter isn't a defence for everything. It's about the person you were, not the jersey we wore. (With the possible exception of Tim Cahill, of course.) Just because we hugged when you scored or when we won a match against a rival, it doesn't mean anything. You felt like I was a burden to you at the time when, in fact, I was learning about the type of people I needed to avoid. In the end you didn't get me, motherfucker. I got you.

So keep ringing the doorbell trying to sell me your double glazing. And I'll keep gazing down from my ivory tower. After all, you earned it for me.

All this isn't as bitter as it sounds. It comes back to the education. It comes back to these books. Up until the Secret Footballer series was born, I felt that the canvas upon which football memoirs were constructed was overtly safe. That is to say that most football books involved the same stories of drunkenness, gambling and memories of certain games. They showed a side of football that people knew existed but which didn't offer any insight into how football was really played. There was a formula, a one-size-fits-all approach to books on football, and none of them actually touched on how the bloody game was played or how players actually live. Everybody you ever played with was 'a great lad'. Everybody worked hard and played hard. Here's a few harmless, disinfected stories. That'll be £16.99 please. I read most of what was on offer and thought, 'Bullshit.' To me, football wasn't like that. Robbie Savage wasn't a great lad, John Terry wasn't a great lad, Frank Lampard wasn't a great lad. They were all different but, to me, all three had different traits about them that made me want to snap them in half on a football pitch.

But it didn't end there. Sky TV wasn't the big ugly monster that people thought it was: its money hasn't ruined football; it has actually enhanced it. Sky TV is, in fact, a great product. And some of the most trusted pundits on our TV screens actually do know what they are talking about. But so much crap had been spoken on a weekly basis that people just think every pundit is full of shit. Today, when I listen to Gary Neville give his expert opinion, I can hear the telltale signs of somebody who knows his stuff, and I hear him talk about the game in a way that I wanted to get across in my first book. He's brilliant, a breath of fresh air – just goes to show how much shit was out there before.

In my time, some of the tactical nous that went into winning football matches was unlike anything that had ever been heard before; the analytics and the budget were incredible. The way the academy was taught was eye-opening to say the least, and the way that coaches were hired and fired was unlike anything I'd ever read in a biography before. Even the way we partied – if that's what you really want to hear – was so fucking nuts that we made the bankers look like a kindergarten class, because, ultimately, unlike people in professions who know what they're doing, footballers have generally given no thought as to whether or not their pension is in place. Or at least when I played, nobody gave a fuck.

When I saw that gap I went for it.

Be honest. Tell it like it is.

From the first moment I wanted to show that a series of books about football could be written in real time, as the player played the game, incorporating how the game evolved and how the player at the centre of the books was dealing with the things that the game threw at him in his personal life.

Accept that premise and there is a perception that football books don't have to be safe any more. All the old ways of doing things should be null and void; and, if you want to write a football book, you'll have to come up with something pretty special, because stories of getting pissed three minutes before kick-off are not what people reading football books want to hear any more. George Best did it years ago and it seems we haven't moved on. People now want to hear about tactics, and talent and genuine insight. Moreover, the name of a top player appearing on the cover is not going to be enough to guarantee the book getting in the charts automatically. Ashley Cole take a bow.

If the Secret Footballer books had been written by a named footballer they'd have won every award going. But how do you put on an expensive awards show where the winner doesn't turn up and kiss the arses of those who have never written so much as a sentence on professional sport in their lives? You don't. I know that.

And that is why I've sent every award back that I've ever won. In some cases the local media took photos of those awards in the bin, in their own office. They wanted to make me look bad. That's not the idea of an award, is it? And there is no constitutional law that says I have to collect an award. The awards were just bait to get me into the open.

But, at the end of the day, I haven't written these books for any awards, or individual glory. I wrote these books for you – for readers, for football fans. Authenticity is the key, and without it I'm nothing. This stuff you have in your hands isn't for show; it's for real.

So I rose, I peaked and when I came out of the Premier League after a fucking whirlwind that made your head spin, I decided to pit my wits once more against the great and the good of lower-league football. First in the Championship, and then lower and lower. And, the funny thing is, when you come down from the Premier League you find that players in the pre-match line-up will shake your hand ridiculously hard, just like a little kid does when you turn up to a shitty school and they dare each other to shake your hand extra hard. I shake the hands of both the lower-league footballer and the smart-arse kid as hard as I can in return – it surprises them enormously and hurts them too. Bonus.

So I walk down the line and it's always the same players, the 24- or 25-year-olds playing for this shitty League One or League Two club, just smart enough and old enough to realise that they are stuck here, who want to shake your hand as if to say, 'Welcome to my world. No one gets out alive.' They pretend it's my fault that they never left this ghetto of the game. I just stare at them. I stop the whole procession. I hold everything up. I look at them dead in the eye, even though they are now looking at the next player, until they look back at me. And as soon as they look back at me I know I have them. I know it's all a ruse. They are bluffers. Semi-tough and stuck with it.

When I walk off the pitch 90 minutes later they are the same guys who ask for my shirt. I give it to them. Am I a fool? No. It serves a purpose. Trying to break my fingers was a misplaced gesture of respect. The next game I have more respect from them, and it's different from before. They have asked for my jersey. Submission. Admission. They rolled over to show me their soft tummies. I won. Giving my shirt away is the equivalent of taking a scalp. Knowing that my shirt hangs in their lounge is a feeling that gives me perverse pleasure.

In my house, there isn't a single shirt that hangs on my wall. Not one. I gave them away long ago.

I am the Secret Footballer and all bets from here on in are off.

1. WINNING

In the last home game of the greatest season in history we were able to climb the stairs that run through the directors' box at the stadium and continue halfway up the main stand. Let me tell you something, there is nothing like that in football. As a young kid growing up in the eighties I was used to seeing clubs that won trophies on big nights go and parade them to crowds that assembled below them – the team first forming a knot of glory halfway up the main stand. I loved that. It's the way to do it. Whether it was Graeme Souness lifting the European Cup among a sea of people, or an FA Cup win after the sun had gone down, the fans draping scarves and hats on their heroes as they wearily ascended those famous stairs. I loved it no matter who won. I vividly remember Maradona lifting the 1986 World Cup in the middle of a huge terrace in Mexico.

Then it changed, and my dad and I would both groan at the TV during big games, as we saw them building a makeshift stage on the hallowed turf, with tacky sponsor logos everywhere. 'Oh, bloody hell,' we'd say, 'it's an on-the-pitcher!' I ask you, how would you rather celebrate after winning something? Behind a Budweiser advertising board? Or up on high, holding the trophy over the whole stadium, amongst your own fans? Fucking Budweiser.

But winning is winning, and after doing just that, our team were booked on an open-top bus ride through the city the following week. Really, I just wanted to go away for the summer, but that's how I am. I prefer to keep the good moments to myself; I don't feel the need to go out with everyone and rip the town up – I've done that before. But on this occasion a mass celebration was unavoidable and so I went along with my usual head on – I was the kid on the back seat, asking, 'Are we there yet? How long is this going to take? And when can I get home to do my own thing. I'm bored.'

We got on the bus at the old depot and we waited for the stragglers. Finally we set off, at a snail's pace, and crawled towards the main road, which had about two dozen fans scattered along the side. The disappointment among the players was obvious. The route was a good 10 miles or so, and at this rate there was going to be some very uncomfortable waving and a few awkward silences. There were only a few seats on the top deck. We had to stand. I could feel my back stiffening up already.

But in the distance, as we crawled along, we began to hear singing – the kind of chorusing that you only hear in a football stadium; the kind of chorusing that only comes from a vast sway of people all in unison. Eventually, when we rounded a corner and headed towards the city centre, the singing grew louder and louder, until the bus reached the top of a hill and lurched between two tall buildings on either side of us. As we straightened out the buildings did an incredible job of funnelling an unbelievable noise from the throats of what must have been 10,000 fans. They were rammed into every side street and spilling out of the main square, which at the same time framed them perfectly. The roar that went up was unlike anything I've ever experienced before, and as the fans caught sight of us and us of them, a burst of flag-waving and scarf-throwing erupted from every angle. My spine is tingling as I sit here writing, some time later.

Along the way the streets were filled with the colours of our club and crowds that were perhaps 20 or 30 deep in places. Everybody wanted to have their own personal photographs of the bus, and especially the trophy, as it flickered in the summer sun at the front of the old vehicle, carving its way through the crowds like the prow of a boat cutting through the ocean. The parting crowds were desperately trying to touch the bus while calling out for mementoes to be thrown overboard.

The security men must have saved at least 100 people from being run over that day, and in the end I succumbed and threw my tracksuit top overboard to a man who looked as if his whole life had been leading up to that moment. Nobody, in this city, ever thought they'd see such a day, and they certainly never could have imagined in their wildest dreams that this trophy would be won in such style, with such outright arrogance and swagger. We had literally swept everybody aside with total authority. For the moment at least, the footballing world was focused on this part of the UK and, I have to be honest, it felt fucking good. I never said it at the time, but I knew it was the culmination of a life's work, my life's work. That may sound a little easy to you, but it's true. I never wanted to be a celebrity; all I wanted was to achieve footballing excellence in the kind of way that nobody, anywhere in the world, had seen before. And now I'd done it.

The open-top bus ride finished at the stadium, and there had to be at least 100,000 people lining the streets and roads into the stadium. We were told that we'd be introduced to the fans in the stadium one at a time from the tunnel, in a pre-determined order. I was at the back. The players were received fantastically by the fans. Some of them were recent additions, only having arrived at the club in the last couple of years. I had been there for a little longer, and in the seasons that hadn't brought success I'd shown what could be achieved. Since coming to the club I'd had a Player of the Year award and I had become a fans' favourite. I gave my all when I played, and I'd had the injuries to prove it. That year, my contribution had reached new heights, and the rest of the club had decided to join the party. When my name was read out, the stadium erupted. I'll never forget it. Sometimes, when I'm feeling really down and things aren't going well, I'll play the DVD of that day at home. Forget the hairs standing up on your neck, this is the real deal; this is what football means to people, and this is what football can do for you, if you're lucky enough to play it and win something. I sometimes hear the top, world-class players quantifying success in terms of relevance to the world at large, and it fucking pisses me off, because I know what it takes to win and how it feels and, believe me, whatever you win is just as hard-won as the next man's triumph.

On the way out of the stadium we walked down the stairs and into a large area at one end of the stand with a bar. The place was swollen with fans, and as they saw me coming down the stairs the whole place broke out into the song the fans used to sing about me during matches. It echoed around the concourse and applause followed, along with chants of the name of the club. I remember my dad shouting, 'Wow, listen to that.' My mum started crying. I knew we'd conquered a summit, but if I'd known then that it would never get any better than that, I'd have retired at the bottom of those steps.

Once or twice over the ensuing years, Mrs TSF and I took the time to smell the roses. I remember one Christmas, in particular, I was dragging the world by the tail. Happy. I'd sit in the hot tub with my wife, sipping champagne. We'd watch the fireworks going up all over the city, lighting up the stadium as they went, and in turn lighting up the huge picture of me in the club's new kit, draped down one side of the stand. I was 50-foot tall. In my prime.

I don't know why I became a footballer, but as a reward this was beyond my dreams. I went from a £30-a-week part-timer to a £600-a-week lower-league player, to this. Almost by accident.

In those moments, of course, you know life is pretty good – but you also know those moments are fleeting. You can barely grasp them before they vanish. They melt away, even as you reach out for them. And you recall that the hard work that goes into getting anywhere near a moment like that is phenomenal. It doesn't *just* happen.

It is true to say that, in most circumstances, you don't know what you've got until it's gone. For example, when I was playing for that team that swept everything before them it was often difficult to see exactly how good I had it. I lived three miles from the training ground, and three miles from the stadium. In fact, I could see the whole city from that hot tub in the back garden, and there were nights when I felt like I was king of that city. I was at that club for a long time, and I had some great moments – but when you are so hell-bent on being successful it is almost impossible to dwell on the enjoyment of winning a particular game, or breaking records. I was always looking at what was next, and so were most of the other players. There were a few moments that we were able to savour before we moved on. But for most of us moving on was a mistake, although that makes the sentiment about that magical season all the sweeter.

• • •

It must never be forgotten that winning is partly a product of the wages that a club pays its team staff, which is comprised mostly of the playing squad. Winning is great, but money helps.

I know a guy, a good guy, whose name might vaguely mean something to you. He's a centre-half in the Premier League. Not one of the great clubs. Not one of the great players. One of the great humans though. Good guy. He gets paid £55,000 a week. Basic.

Are you happy for him?

Let me help you. On top of that £55,000 a week, my friend earns somewhere between five and ten grand for an appearance. In other words, he is a footballer who gets a bonus when he plays football.

Do you want to tweet him your best wishes?

Luckily, he is a defender who goes up for corners so his agent has negotiated another five thousand or so a goal on to that.

You want to celebrate every goal with him, don't you?

They are your staples as a footballer. Basic, appearance, goal and win. At this time I imagine his win bonus would be around five grand a go. I should have mentioned that. He gets a few bob extra if his team wins also.

On top of that there is a team bonus sheet that has to be signed and submitted to the FA before 1 August each season. The club will say to the first team that this year there is maybe £2 million to be split. They might do it pro rata. Or just divide it evenly among the group. Or, if you are in the top three or four in the Premiership on any given weekend, then you might get ten grand a game for winning. If you are in the top four the win bonus goes down a little. It doesn't kick in during the first month. If you win the first game by a big margin you are on top, so you agree a rate that the bonus won't sink below, and then in the second month your proper bonus system kicks in.

'Of course,' you say, 'that is great, you motivate the whole team that way.' Not really. Most players want an arrangement whereby if they play, they get the pay. Like if you are the first-choice keeper week in week out, why would you want the same share of the pie as the third-choice keeper who is 17 and will, in all likelihood, never play a game for the club as long as you both shall live. Fuck him.

So the team bonus money goes mainly to my mate, and the others who earn the most and play the most. Of course it does. Did you think my mate was a communist? Did you think he was busting his gut playing football just because he liked it? He's a professional footballer.

It is hard work keeping professional footballers happy. I have been that footballer. Fifty-five thousand pounds a week. That didn't guarantee a smile from me.

For some reason, although the commerce of it is obvious, a lot of people have a problem with the money footballers earn. These are usually the same people who feel that foot-ballers should be role models. Bullshit.

William Goldman, in his great book *Adventures in the Screen Trade*, traces the history of the cinema star and his or her wage packet. Once upon a time studios wouldn't divulge the names of actors. They knew it made sense to keep the actors down. So for a while the most famous actress in America was known only as 'the Biograph Girl' because the Biograph film studio virtually owned her. But when her contract was up with Biograph she 'transferred' to another studio and negotiated that movie credits would feature her name, Florence Lawrence. In 1912 she became the highest paid movie star in the world. She was making $250 a week.

A year later Mary Pickford was making $500 a week.

By 1916 Charlie Chaplin was earning $10,000 a week.

And then in 1921 Fatty Arbuckle became the first star to make $1 million a year. Fatty put backsides on seats. The studios always knew that and tried for a long time to wriggle out of paying Fatty and his comrades their due.

Now, nobody has a problem with what money movie stars make and nobody tells them to be role models. But footballers, most of whom leave home in their teens and have their education in a dressing room, are supposed to be pillars of society, and the money we make for encouraging people to buy subscriptions to watch us on TV, or to come through the turnstiles to watch us in the flesh, is resented.

The £55,000 a week my friend makes. Who should get that money instead of him? Some fat shareholder? Rupert Murdoch? My mate took a huge risk leaving home and leaving school to become a player. On any given Saturday his career could end with a bad tackle or an awkward twist that snaps a ligament, and people would say, 'Ah, that's a blow. Still, at least he has his insurance.' Not the fucking point. He's earned it. And his time for making a lot of money will be short. I've learned that.

You only know how good it all was when the circus moves on without you. You only miss it when you realise that it doesn't miss you. Today, somebody else's picture hangs 50 feet from the stadium roof.

I'm on LinkedIn now, since I retired. Every day I am swamped by a tsunami of financial services people. 'Hi, TSF, who looks after your portfolio?' 'Hi, TSF, is your money safe right now?' 'Hi, TSF, need some help with those accounts?'

The answer is: I don't fucking know. Leave me alone for now. Let me get my head around all this. Fatty Arbuckle never had to take this shit, did he?

2. LOSING

I may have misled you in the last chapter. Normal service resumes. It's not all fireworks and hot tubs. It's not all beer and skittles. Even with all the money and all the fame, football can piss you off. It can suck your enthusiasm away. I'm smarter than the average bear, but I made a couple of wrong turnings in my career and got lost in the woods. Properly lost. The lessons I remember were the hardest ones to learn. You say to me that in a world where everybody is making so much money there are bigger tragedies than an unhappy footballer.

There are worse things, but a footballer has a small window in his life in which to make the most of the talents he has been given and the skills he has worked on. An athlete in his prime, regardless of the money he earns, is a beautiful thing. A happy team full of such athletes does what it says under the Shankly statue at Anfield. It makes 'the people happy'.

One wrong move, to a club with a vindictive manager, say, and it can take away your best years. It can rob you of all the joy. You walk away with the taste of shit in your mouth.

A true story. A football story, believe it or not.

A friend of mine, a player, takes a call one day on his mobile from a newspaperman of his acquaintance. 'Hi, it's me,' says the newspaperman. 'Are you on your own and able to talk?'

'Yes, mate, there's no one here. What's up?'

'I've got something for you that I've been working on. It concerns your manager, and it's got him bang to rights. One problem: my paper won't print it, it's just not what we do. But the *News of the World* will. Are you interested?'

'Yes, mate, of course.'

No high moral tone about the *News of the World* from my mate that day. You see, my mate had fallen foul of his gaffer and his career hadn't just been parked, it was on the way to the wrecking yard. My mate was being kept away from the first team. He felt like he had a disease and was in quarantine. He trained and played with the kids. He had been the victim of a few shocking outbursts from the manager, who seemed determined not just to drop him and humiliate him but also to break him.

My friend has talent and a fan club within the game. He could play for another club tomorrow, but at this point he had been told that wasn't going to happen. Things had got to the stage where player and gaffer literally hated each other. And the manager held all the cards. Until now ...

An hour later the player and the hack were huddled over extremely average lattes in a service station. The small talk was brief. There was only one reason why the player was there. He told the journalist to tell him exactly what he'd found.

'Do you know that your club balance sheet is hugely dispro-portionate in terms of wages and transfer fees compared to the rest of the Premier League?' said the journalist. 'There is a lot of money going out and not much coming in, and the players who are coming in aren't world-beaters. The transfer fees seem to be inflated. Now, that has probably been happening in almost every case, but what I've got is specific information for two players that your club signed last August.'

'Tell me more,' said my mate.

'You might remember that those players cost your club something like £5 million and £6 million each. The first one wasn't out of the ordinary, because he fits in with the type of football that you play, but the second one was bizarre, not the type of player that your manager goes for and completely against the way you guys play football. You might also remember that they arrived from a club that had just been relegated. That club were on the verge of some pretty heavy legal proceedings regarding payments that needed to be made to creditors – in short, they had to find £5 million very quickly. Your club bid for the first player and agreed to pay £2.5 million upfront and the rest in a year's time, so the selling club were still £2.5 million short of what they needed. So they subsequently went back and asked your club if there was anybody else that interested them. Your club came back and struck the same deal for a second player, £2.5 million upfront and the rest in a year and, hey presto, there's the £5 million that the selling club desperately need.

'Now. Here's the rub. Knowing how desperate the selling club were, your manager introduced an agent to the deal. It was ridiculous, because the selling club wanted to sell and the buying club wanted to buy, and the two players already *had* agents. Both of those players wanted to move club. It should have been the easiest deal in the history of football, so why the need for this independent agent? At first the selling club protested and there were the usual phone calls back and forth to try to remove this agent from the deal but, of course, the selling club was desperate, and in the end they had no choice but to accept the deal and make the payment to the independent agent, who it was said was acting on behalf of your club. The payment that was made was £500,000. That's £500,000 for nothing. The selling club was livid, but it couldn't do anything because it desperately needed the money to pay the creditors. And do you know who the agent introduced to that deal was? Your manager's agent.'

My mate trusted the journalist and had known him for some time, but he still asked how good this information was. It turned out that it wasn't just good, it was fucking great.

'The manager of the selling club is a very good friend of mine. It came from him. He was furious at the situation. Here, let me show you how furious ...' And with that the journalist took out a bunch of papers: copies of the contracts from the deal for the two players, and a copy of the contract signed, on behalf of the selling club, by the agent in question, my mate's manager's agent. It turned out that the manager of the selling club had passed this information on in the heat of the moment; in fact, this situation is widely credited with costing this manager his job at the selling club, even though his hands seemed to be completely tied.

'By the way,' said the hack, 'when I rang the chief executive of your team for a quote his exact words were, "We're aware of that and he's been slapped on the wrist. That's all we've got to say." And then he hung up.'

'Jesus,' said my mate, 'that's fucking dynamite.'

'Correct, so do you want it?' he asked.

'Oh, yes.'

So my mate left the motorway services with copies of everything the journalist had brought, but no real idea what to do with it all. His problem was that if he passed the info to the tabloid he could end the manager's career, but if word leaked about where the information had come from he would end his own career too. Nobody in football touches anybody who is capable of something like that.

So he just sat on the info for a year until another friend (not me) urged him to make contact with the *News of the World*. The paper asked for a couple of extra details, such as the identities of the actual agents of the players in question. They asked my mates, did they want money? No thanks. The journalist they dealt with told them that the story would run on the opening weekend of the season. The fuse was lit. They sat back and waited. And then BANG!

The *News of the World* went pop.

Faced with a shit storm of bugging scandals, payments to police, and all the hacking that reached right to the very top of

News International, the decision was taken to close the *News of the World*. Everybody in the story moved on unscathed. Life resumed as normal. Until my mate got another phone call. This time from another player badly scarred by life under the demon gaffer: 'Mate, you know I live on the same estate as the gaffer?' he began. 'Well, I've been seeing him walking in and out of his house for a couple of months with a bird.'

'Yeah?' my friend said. 'Not his wife, I take it?'

'No, mate, definitely not his wife.'

This was different. It was home-front stuff. By now there was almost a little committee of aggrieved players hoping for my mate to swing into action – a year is a long time in football when you're not playing.

The voice on the phone already had a plan. A private detective. 'Sam' would sit near the manager's house and photograph enough comings and goings until there was a file just fat enough to fit into a brown envelope. He would use this envelope as a lever to engineer a move away from the club. The friend would get his transfer and freedom. The manager would get the only copies of the photos. So, a few days later, a well-known footballer turned up at an office in central London and rang the buzzer. The private detective came downstairs and took the footballer into a small side room. He was wearing a cap and he had a rucksack over one shoulder. It was early morning. The footballer assumed that he had arrived just as the PI was getting into the office.

'This room is secure,' said the PI. 'Tell me what's on your mind and then we'll go upstairs.'

'Sam' was retained at a rate of £4,000 a week, but he couldn't start work until the following spring. At this time Christmas was fast approaching. But again fate saved the manager. In the weeks that followed, his team began to lose – stumbling at first and then lurching into freefall. The word from inside the dressing room was that he'd changed; he'd lost his fight and he'd lost his hunger. It was clear that he knew his time was now limited. He wasn't fighting any more; he was in the palliative care stage, hoping for a dignified exit. That made the private detective unnecessary. As soon as a new manager came in those who were desperate to escape could either go or see how things worked out under a new regime. As the club flirted with relegation the private detective was put on standby and eventually stood down. The manager moved on. The club recovered. My mates still hate the man. In football, class isn't the only thing that is permanent. Enemies last a lifetime too.

I know. I've had a few myself. As I say, that's a football story. The money is great and the highs are wonderful, but humiliation and bullying and bad management are the same no matter what you earn. Every player starts out just wanting to play football, and then, as we say, it starts going wrong.

When it comes to footballers and their freedom, don't be fooled by the shit you read in the newspapers. My agent used to peddle his bullshit in the *Sun*'s rumour column because he wanted to flush out a deal with another club. The way it works is very simple. I, as TSF, want or need to move clubs. My agent rings Sky Sports or the *Sun* or the *Guardian* and says, 'Here's a story for you.' Desperate for a bit of bullshit these media outlets publish the story and the people who read it (that's you, folks) never spot the ulterior motive behind it. And why would you?

In my case I had three Premier League clubs that were vying for my signature during one particular summer. Two of them I didn't want to sign for, and one I did. The club I wanted to join was Aston Villa (this is when Villa were a very good side). In order to flush out an offer from Villa, my agent put a story in the press. The story alluded to the fact that another club had made an offer to sign me, which was actually true. In a transfer window a player's name will appear somewhere on a list of preferential signatures. Unfortunately, at Villa, my name was third on the list. The idea is that as time ticks down, and the list shortens as players make their preferred moves, those of us who don't have that luxury are snapped up by our preferred clubs.

Only this time, there was an unexpected twist in the tale. My agent came back to me. 'Villa are definitely interested,' said my agent. 'They want to pay £24,000 a week, but they also have one name remaining on their list that usurps your name.' 'Fair enough,' I thought, 'that's football.' But time was running out. There was a week of the transfer deadline remaining and I was in limbo. That in itself is not uncommon, but that summer my wife had given birth to our first child, and we were more concerned for the future than usual. Then a curious thing happened. The manager of a club that up until now had never shown any interest in my signature called me at home. Presumably I had moved up somebody's list. He did his best to sell his club to me, but he came over as a complete control freak. He wouldn't let me get a word in on the phone. He bashed me over the head with what he wanted to do at 'his' football club, and that we could all share in the history together.

I now know that he was selling me his legacy, way before it had even happened. At the time I didn't see it. I was a Premier League footballer who needed a team. As is the etiquette, I rang my agent immediately and told him that a Premier League manager had been on the phone and that he should call him to get to the bottom of this new interest.

For my part, I completely disregarded the call. I didn't want to go to this team. When I played for my first Premier League team I used to sit next to my best friend on the coach, and when we rocked up at certain stadiums we'd always look at each other before one of us said, 'If ever I end up having to play here I'm gonna fucking kill myself.' Then both of us would fall about laughing. I'd always said that about two clubs in particular, and he'd always said it about two other clubs. His clubs, as I recall, were Hull and Sheffield United.

My agent rang back. 'The club is offering you a three-year deal with the option of a fourth, starting at £30,000 a week and rising each year,' he said. I signed the following day, and it was the biggest footballing mistake I have ever made.

In fact, the story gets better. I signed on deadline day. During negotiations I got a call from a club in the north east. Very interested, they said. My agent was with me. I let him know. He pointed out that if we left this club now and drove to the north east the exact opposite of the bidding war I was imagining would happen. It would be too late to go anywhere else. The north east could name its price.

The gentlemen we were dealing with, however, sensed some unease since I had taken the phone call. They proposed a break and the chairman said he would show me the club's trophy room by way of a little tour. The trophy room was bare, as it turned out. A few photos of the club's greatest player. Nothing else. The chairman excused himself briefly and disappeared. When I went to leave the trophy room I discovered the door was locked. It took over two hours to find a locksmith who could free me. By the time I was freed, on transfer deadline day, there was no time to consider any other offers. I signed with a heavy heart. What a magical start.

And guess what? Things did not go well. Not long after signing, I was dropped, with my new club struggling in the Premier League. I had 'scapegoat' tattooed on my arse.

Let me skip forward now ...

Years later I had a 'where were you when Kennedy was shot' experience. It happened that I was in a club – but not a football club. My mate was coming out of the toilet. Some intriguing stripper act was about to start on the stage. I was in London, for design week in Clerkenwell, with a friend who owns a high-end furniture business and has to show his face at these events. Unsurprisingly, the world of office furniture is starved of 'celebrity', and so my friend liked to invite me down because the industry is full of middle-aged men who once saw me play and who, rather bizarrely, seemed to delight in hearing the odd football story while asking me if their heroes were really as good to play against as their rose-tinted memories would have them believe. Strangely, my mate wasn't interested in any of that, the trade show, or the dodgy club we'd ended up in. He was grinning and pointing at the television. I turned around to look. Kennedy hadn't been shot. Much better news. Flashing across the breaking news bar on Sky Sports News was the message, 'TSF's ex-manager to leave Premier League club with immediate effect.' To put the story into context, I'd waited a fucking long time for this moment in the hope that it would end as acrimoniously as possible, maybe with a training-ground tragedy or even a mafia-style hit.

My career had descended into the realms of bullying. I was being told to come in on Sundays and train with a couple of youth team players. He made me play pre-season games with the youth team instead of the first team, and played me out of position to try to make me look bad. On one occasion he made me captain, just to rub it in. Go in for the toss there, big shot. He then took to the media to hammer me, and one interview he gave cost me my reputation. I should have sued him for defamation of character, I really should have. And I really, *really* fucking wish that I had, now that I look back on it. Players bullshit a lot when they retire from the game; they look back with rose-tinted glasses at an immaculate career and they say things like, 'I've got no regrets.' Bullshit again. Every player has a hundred regrets when they finish playing, and the one above would probably make my personal top five.

Years later, when I was trying to get a new club, I found out that he'd bad-mouthed me to every single manager who had expressed an interest in my services, whether they sought his opinion or not. He'd actually phoned them and said, 'Listen, if you're thinking of signing this guy, don't bother, he's trouble.' Fucking idiot.

And that was part of the reason my career was curtailed at the top level – that, and the fact that I just felt I had more to give elsewhere. I can't tell you how hard it is to watch players playing at a level higher than me, who are obviously inferior in terms of ability.

I have this manager to thank for letting me experience all that.

But now he was gone. It was a huge story, both for me personally and in the wider football world, and within seconds my phone went crazy with messages from family and friends, but mostly from players, past and present, saying how happy they were with the news.

By this point everybody in the place was looking at the TV and talking to me about the manager in question. There was only one thing for it: I bought the whole place a round of drinks and held a toast – it was a moment of celebration.

So what was he like?

He'd do stupid things for no reason other than to piss off the players he didn't like. He'd do anything in order to maintain control, through fear and bullying, among the weaker players – of which there were many. An example of his crippling vanity came when we were once launching a new kit at the stadium. It was a big deal, with a major kit manufacturer and a big sponsor, and the club had invited fans to watch a kind of catwalk show. There was a big screen that played a couple of videos, one of which was a montage of the highlights of the previous season; the other a collection of goal-of-the-season contenders which the crowd could vote on. Now, I'm not particularly fussed about seeing myself on the big screen, but during the previous campaign I had lost my head and hit a shot from miles out that had somehow flown into the top corner. It was the undisputed goal of the season according to anyone who saw it, but after the 10 goals were flashed up my strike was nowhere to be seen. I already had an inkling as to why, but I didn't really give too much of a shit, to be honest. By this point my relationship with the manager had been reduced to talking through an interme-diary. He used to walk towards me and pretend to be on his phone; he'd get it out of his pocket even though both of us knew that it hadn't rung.

During a break in the catwalk proceedings I went for a pee and bumped into the club's 'head of media communica-tions'. He was a good guy, very genuine, and his department had put this day together. I couldn't resist a dig: 'Mate, you've missed the best goal out,' I said. He laughed. 'Jesus, mate, do you know the bullshit I've had to put up with this week off the back of your goal?' he said. I asked him what he meant. 'It's been a nightmare,' he said. 'We had the whole presentation ready – goal of the year, the highlights video – then the gaffer came in and told us to take out every clip with you in it. Even the clips where you were celebrating somebody else's goal. It's been a fucking stressful 24 hours, mate.' Apparently the manager had requested a preview the day before the show and had made his request immediately after seeing it. The re-edit had caused the department to go into meltdown.

This is how shallow the man was. Probably still is. You don't grow depth, do you? He inflicted a lot of misery on so many of his players, even the ones who had served him so well over the years. If you can get an honest answer out of the players who played under him, you won't find too many of them who have a good word to say about him.

He ruled by fear. He preached the gospel of shit football and he had the media in his pocket. He survived for so long thanks largely to a lack of expectation at the club and a chairman who backed him with crazy money. He signed some big-name players purely to say that he was the manager who had signed them for the club. His ego was out of control and he was fortunate to have his chairman by the balls right up to the point where he finally went too far and almost got his team relegated. When he 'left' the club, I sent him a text that said simply, 'How does it feel?' Unsurprisingly, he didn't reply.

I haven't seen my old manager since we parted ways, and I'm not quite sure what I'd do if I ever did. However, my friend has bumped into him and, bizarrely, the manager offered his hand and asked him how he was. My friend walked straight past him and carried on looking forward. That's impressive restraint on his part.

It is certainly true that you have to be very careful about who you make enemies of in this game. You never know who will come back to bite you on the arse. I told my manager that very thing on the day I left his club. Word on the street is that he left two jobs in the Premier League with no payoff whatsoever and, let me tell you a fact right now: nobody leaves a Premier League managerial job with no payoff unless they are either dead or have days to live.

This manager was not dying or dead. He simply got found out and exposed by his boss. In short, they had the shit on him. Twice, I begged the clubs in question to divulge; twice, both parties entered into non-disclosure agreements with the manager in question. One day the truth will out.

To be blunt, I hate the man, and I am disappointed in myself for hating anybody. And I dread how I will feel if I guide one of these kids into an organisation run by this man or anybody like him.

• • •

A friend and myself have set up a fledgling agency. On the books is one of the most exciting kids in the Football League. He's a kid who doesn't seek out stardom but knows it will find him simply because he is a footballer who can excite crowds of people. It's also worth noting that I didn't seek him out, he came to me. He asked me to help him after the club offered him a professional contract and he had no idea what to do because he couldn't get hold of his current agent, who was busy with one particular Premier League player.

Within a couple of months I had set a plan in place that cited his current agency for breach of contract. This is pretty easy to do, but it takes brains and foresight. You ask the kid to make consecutive phone calls and send emails over the course of two weeks. You get him to record the times and dates of those calls and emails, and the subsequent lack of response. You pay the legal bills, serve papers on the current agent citing breach of contract, and *voilà*, the player is yours.

At the same time I devoted great chunks of my time to coaching this kid in the things I knew he'd need to know in order to succeed at the highest level. Come rain, wind or snow – and it did fucking snow, several times – we were out there on our own, me coaching, him listening intently.

But when I sit with the dad of this talented kid I'm representing, and he daydreams out loud about a bigger agency taking on his son, or about us making easy money from quick deals, or getting to the Premiership overnight, I think of this manager and the hole he put in my career. I tell the father that he hasn't got a clue what is lurking in the woods out there. One stupid move and your career might never recover.

I moved to that club because I thought, in the culture of football, that 'I needed a move'.

You don't know what you've got till it's gone.

• • •

When the January transfer window opened, a top club immediately put in a bid for my friend – the one who was frozen out, training with the kids. Understandably, he was very keen to go. But the truth gets around in football circles very quickly, and the manager did not want him to go because he knew the details of their bitter relationship would come out almost immediately, as soon as my friend did his first interview. He knew that by keeping him in the building he could eventually butter him up, or at least keep a lid on things.

The plan the manager eventually came up with to prevent the transfer was a good one, in fairness. He used a manager he was very tight with at a north-east club to put together a phoney offer for my friend. The genuine offer on the table was from a London-based team, but his current club could reserve the right to sell him to whichever club was putting the most money on the table. You can guess what happened next. The offer from the London club, where my friend wanted to go, was £2.5 million. The offer that came in from the north east was, of course, £3 million.

The north-east club had absolutely no intention of signing him, and on transfer deadline day my friend was in a hotel room at the wrong end of the country, purely so that he couldn't get to London for a medical. Surprise, surprise, as the window ticked down the club in the north east withdrew its offer, even though my friend's representatives had never actually seen an official offer to start with. My friend's manager couldn't even leave the deal with the London club alone and leaked a story to the media that the deal had broken down over personal terms. This was utter bollocks – personal terms had never been discussed because the manager had no intention of giving my friend permission to talk to the London club. Without that permission, you can't discuss personal terms.

Just to make sure that the deal with the London club never got off the ground – as if sending my friend to the other end of the country wasn't safe enough – the chief executive and the manager both turned off their mobile phones and refused to take calls from my friend and his representatives. Remember, this is a Premier League club on transfer deadline day. That just doesn't happen.

And I'll tell you why I know that it doesn't happen. The chief executive reported back to my friend, his agents and the media that no offer had been received from a London club. But unbeknownst to him, two days earlier, the chief executive had been recorded on the phone by the London club declining their offer. So then, in order to keep up appearances, on transfer deadline day my friend's club sent a text message to the London club finally accepting the same offer. But at that point there were just two hours left of transfer deadline day, and not enough time for my friend to get from the north east to London to complete a medical, let alone fax all the documents required and negotiate a contract. So, as far as the media were concerned an offer had been accepted and my friend's club pushed the line that the player had failed to agree terms. This led to the media branding my friend 'greedy'. Which is about as far away from the truth as it's possible to get. The whole thing was a complete stitch-up. My friend stayed in the building for another six months at least. Those who stuck up for him were shipped out to other clubs.

That is how football really works, I'm afraid to say. It is genuinely cut-throat, and when you sometimes read stories about greedy players in the newspapers, just stop and think for a second before you rush to judgement. Now and again, that story might be the result of somebody else's selfish motive.

To a certain extent I have become the bitter old pro that I always hated and dreaded turning into. But as I say to my mate, who soldiered on through those bad times too, at least I'm not vain. That would be worse. My friend had a clause in his contract that his manager had to bring him off if he scored a hat-trick, purely so he could get a standing ovation. He also had a £10,000 goal bonus. Nice work.

'That's what professional football should be all about,' I think to myself when I remember the good times. A hat-trick, a standing O from a roaring crowd, money in the bank and no clouds in the sky. Unfortunately, there are sharks out there looking to ensure that it is them, not you, who gets the standing ovation.

I remember the famous Rodney King quote in situations like this: 'Can we all get along?' And then I remember my best mate in football talking about his manager, and putting it much better: 'Mate, he's such a cunt that hell will probably turn him away when he gets down there.'

I can see that. Definitely.

3. RETIRING

It's quiet today. Whatever day today is, well, it is quiet. Too fucking quiet.

I'm an ex-footballer.

There's no action any more. No rattle. No hum. No stir. No sir.

People used to follow me down the street asking for pictures and autographs.

Hey, remember what I just told you? My profile once slid down the side of a 10-storey stadium, 50 foot across, looking out over the city where I was a bona fide hero.

In my head, I'm still 50 foot tall. It's the football that got smaller.

Now I'm just a curiosity. I'm a former pro.

'Was he any good?'

'Dunno.'

'Heard his knees went or something.'

'I think I remember the name?'

'My dad says he was trouble.'

'He looks fucking harmless now anyway.'

'Did you see Messi's goal last night?'

I tried sitting in meetings trying not to fall into the canyon, just for something to do. The canyon opens up just after I say, 'Can we try to get this boxed off by Friday latest, please?'

I float over the canyon just daydreaming on a cloud. I try not to fall asleep. The far side of the canyon is reached when I say, 'OK, just to give you all a heads-up as regards the upshot of Thursday's meeting as to whether we can in fact install a suggestion box on the first floor. The answer is, no. Any other suggestions? No? Good.' I look around with an expression suggesting that anybody who has any other business can face death by a million paper cuts.

For the briefest of time, I moved through a world full of people who have settled for the safe option. These people scare me. I don't care how 'real' they are or how nice. To me they reek of decomposing dreams and Greggs. One of them smelled of Lego.

I reminded myself of something every day. My words to live by. I would rather have jumped off a high fucking bridge than see out my days eating cardboard sandwiches and talking about the football from the weekend. I'm not a water cooler kind of guy. To my surprise I miss the buzz and the chaos and the noise of the old life.

Transfer deadline day passed last week. Quietly for me, thank God. It was the first transfer deadline day of my retirement. As I said, I have a few players to represent these days, but the summertime is when I want to see action: the players in my agency stable are growing and there are important people at a few well-respected clubs who are saying some nice things about a few of them. Yes, the summertime is when the action kicks in and you don't want to be left out, no matter how much you're looking forward to a break at the end of the season. Most agents and managers feel that way, but then the hype and hysteria kick in and people make those silly moves that leave everything tasting a little sour.

So, two questions, TSF: if you are so smart how come you ain't so rich? And, if it was all so bad how come you're getting those little violins ready to cry me a river about how it's all over now? Just fuck off and play.

Well ... it's complicated.

I always thought that I would play until I was 30. When the move I spoke about earlier turned to shit the thrill was gone. I knew I would never catch up to where my career should have been. I knew that by the time I was 30 my head would be toxic from everything I had seen and done. I would quit at 30 and go into some sort of decompression chamber till I recovered.

I would quit on my own terms.

And I tried to. I retired. I really did.

And just when I thought I was out, they pulled me back in ... Three times I tried to retire but there has always been a market for a 30-plus footballer who knows where both goals are. Footballers are slaves to the market.

The first of my would-be retirements came at the end of a spell with a club that was undergoing a tumultuous period of administration. We players caught some shrapnel. My car was the subject of target practice from the 'faithful', who saw me as the antichrist. I was deemed to have been stealing money from the club by generally doing what the players before me had been doing, albeit on significantly reduced wages. I was getting paid for playing football for the club. I told my wife that I'd retire as soon as the club paid me what it owed. In the end, I settled on a fraction of the actual figure. Hey, whatcha gonna do?

I retreated down an alley firing shots as I went.

And so I was shot full of lead but I was retired.

I bought a rocking chair, sat on the porch and thought, 'So this is life after football?'

Then the phone rang.

I agreed to abandon the rocking chair, travel to a club a long distance away, and take the place of a player who, I was told, was taking some kind of sabbatical from the game and would be back at some point later in the season. Mental illness was my guess, but I didn't like to ask. Still don't.

The deal came about because, as it turned out, my neighbour knew a guy who owned a football club that was desperate for a bit of cover on the cheap. I had totally fallen out of love with the game and was very happy waking up with nothing to do except wonder how a wanker like Jeremy Kyle could make it so big.

I was beginning to suspect that I couldn't exactly afford to contemplate the sorrowful mystery of Jeremy Kyle day after day and ... badda-bing. The call came. Back in again.

As the club was at the other end of the country I agreed to sign until Christmas, by which point the player on sabbatical would make a hero's return and I'd be left walking to the cab trying to say my goodbyes to the backs of thousands of fans all cheering hysterically while craning their necks to get a look at their idol. 'So ... um ... bye then ... er ... thanks for having me ... guys?'

But he didn't come back.

I stayed on for a while longer. Again, I worked on the cheap. And then that was me done again. Pretty happy with my football career and unbelievably happy to be out and alive and with one thing that I've always wanted to maintain: my own teeth.

I set about plotting my retirement again. I was more serious this time. There would be cruises and bingo nights, chats with the postman and windows of opportunity to watch porn while the missus ferried the kids around.

And then my goombah agent rang. He does that. No respect.

His pitch was simple enough. Would I meet a manager who was desperate to sell his club to me based on the fact that what he really needed was a marquee signing and a bit of know-how in the changing room. I declined. Goombah rang again. And once more, I declined. And on it went for at least two weeks.

Then one morning he rang while I was dropping the kids off at school – which is not a metaphor for taking a shit, as it is in most changing rooms. He said that he was at the training ground and asked whether I could drop in for a chat. Twenty minutes later I was standing in front of him, convincing myself that it was almost too easy not to do this.

So I signed a deal and went home to tell my wife to cancel the two weeks in Barbados that weren't ATOL protected. I told her to keep the kids in the school where the parents looked at us like we were dog shit, and I tenderly advised her to bid farewell to every weekend that she had planned for the next two years. Naturally, she was thrilled. Absolutely 'let's renew our vows in Vegas now, baby' thrilled.

In that first season we narrowly missed out on promotion, but, as you might have guessed, there was a reason for that. Halfway through the promotion push the club announced a 'mutual deal' to end the reign of our manager. If he had stayed we may well have been promoted, but the club felt the urgent need to fend off success. Owners do that sometimes. On a serious note, it is a little known fact that some clubs actually make decisions to avoid promotion because they are not well equipped to cope with the financial strains of going up. Sounds ridiculous, I know, but it's absolutely true. You'll find it extremely common practice in the Conference, and it happens with some League Two and League One clubs where the extra cost of policing isn't covered by any great rise in tickets sold. Five-year plans aren't all about up, and up and up.

Anyway, as soon as the manager left, the club started taking on water and before long we drifted on to the beach. A shiny new manager was found and he stood before us and tried to stick his flag in the sand in an authoritative manner. He needed our respect and co-operation. His flagstick might as well have been a flaccid length of celery.

Not long afterwards, though, I faced a novel new challenge. The manager alluded to the fact that I wasn't wanted. You gasp, but it's true. No professional with Premier League branding ever thinks that such a thing will happen to him; we assume that our connections with the upper echelon make us bullet proof. If it's true for Richard Scudamore, then why not for the rest of us?

Under the previous regime I had been valued and pampered to the extent that I was even able to get a few days off here and there. I had asked for that at the outset and the previous manager had agreed. The older, venerable pro is allowed to get away with those sorts of things as long as it's under the guise of 'not being able to train due to being older (but while I'm in Dubai I will, of course, be thinking about you all every second of the day and drying myself down with an official club shop towel)'.

That looks like good management, and maybe it is. The reality is, you can do it and get away with it because you've played in the Premier League and nobody else in the squad has. There are some players who won't stand for that sort of thing, but I'm not one of them. It's because I'm worth it, I say.

But then my new manager wanted me to leave. He didn't want to give me time off; he wanted me in the ranks of the disappeared. I would just be a question in the 'where are they now?' part of pub quizzes. I'd always played on my own terms; now I was being asked to stop playing on somebody else's. Never happening.

Although, oddly, I kinda fancied retirement. There were circumstances, though, that made it impossible.

Firstly, I am a contrary bastard.

Secondly, I am a contrary bastard.

Third, I had a contract with 18 months left on it.

Also, the lads liked me and the fans came out to watch me. These were facts.

Mainly, though, I was wounded, and there was one thing the manager should have known: cut TSF and he bleeds contrary type O. I was the highest earner at the club and I didn't have to leave for anybody, and, above all, I could still play. I could do things that nobody else could do. Yeah, I was showing the telltale signs of old age. I was experiencing some creakiness, and I knew my best score at *Countdown*. But ... Fortunately the football gods decreed that it wasn't my time and the manager was sacked at the end of the season. It was as I had wished for. Then the gods reminded me to be careful about what I wished for. They gave me a free weekend preview of hell that was contingent on me perhaps buying a timeshare and moving there. At the end of the season the chairman who had brought me in asked me if I'd like a role in the club, grown-up stuff. At one point, when the first manager was sacked, he offered me the assistant manager job – something I declined. Soon the owner had sold the club to a consortium of businessmen. It wasn't a problem; it was actually exciting at the time. I should have realised that consortiums are seldom as deferential as individuals.

In the summer, shortly after we'd busted our arses all morning in pre-season training, there was an announcement. I remember it vividly. It was an announcement with a drum roll. The players were sat down eating lunch together when our communications officer (press guy) called our manager outside into the heat of the day. Two minutes later our communications officer (press guy) came back in followed by our manager, who now looked as if he'd just been told that his family had been killed in a horrific fairground accident. He was somewhere between the 'how?' and the 'why?' stages of grief.

At our tables we nudged each other. Trouble at mill ...

Then, two other men walked in. Both were dressed very severely, but they seemed to like their look. They stood next to the press guy who addressed the players with a statement. As I recall, the statement went something like this:

'All right, lads, this is really difficult, but I've been asked to read the following statement: As you know, for the past month the club has been the speculation of a takeover in various media outlets. I can confirm that this morning ********** was sold to a private consortium and ***** ***** has been relieved of his post.'

I promise you that our manager never saw it coming. None of us did. He had taken training only that morning; this shit was fresh and hot off the press.

'The club will be run on a day-to-day basis by ****** who will operate in the role of chief executive and ***** who will become the club's new chairman.'

The next part is the stuff of legend because it ultimately determined the course of my life. 'The new owners would like to thank ********* for his efforts at the club but have decided to go in a new direction for the club. Starting on Monday the club's new manager will be ***** *******.'

Holy shit.

I don't know why but there seemed to be a huge gap between the start of that sentence and the name of the new manager at the end. The gap filled me with dread. I knew it would be bad news. I knew the name at the end of the sentence would loosen my bowels. I just sensed that this would be bloody awful. Subconsciously, I think I willed it because I wanted to retire even though it was obviously already a done deal. When the press guy said the name, I howled on the inside and I laughed on the outside. That's how quickly your life can change as a footballer. The chairman and chief executive clocked my reaction, and I knew the game was up. The manager in question and I had previous. It's either a very small world or we are very big people.

He didn't like me, and I didn't like the fact that he didn't like me. I'd have been willing to forgive and forget, but he had been a wanker to me, and my fellow teammates, at a previous club. I felt that I'd let him off too cheaply. He knew that. And in football you always assume the worst of people.

He knew he had more coming. He knew that if he pushed my buttons, given the age I was now and that I had nothing to lose, I would hang him.

I've since hammered him in public and rightly so. When he was the manager of a previous club that I played for he'd told the players that we were all in it together, that we were one and that no amount of negative press could infiltrate the changing room or get between us. Just as long as we stuck together, he said, and watched out for one another. A week later he had a job offer. He snatched the offer out of their hands and left the rest of us in the fucking shit. Not so much as a pleasant 'go fuck yourself' did we hear from him. He knew that most players would think, 'Well, that's football.' But he also knew that I was the sort of player who would think, 'Well, if we ever cross paths again I'm gonna fucking make your life hell.'

He knew and he was right.

So next the new chairman stepped forward. 'Um ... I've got some contacts at Formula 1 and if you're all good footballers [he did actually say that] I can arrange it so that you can practise changing the tyres on a Formula 1 car.'

Holy fuck! I quickly formed the opinion that this posh boy had more money than sense and had been living in la-la land for too long. It was a hunch that would serve me well.

For our younger readers some tyre-changing may sound pretty cool, but for those of us who have lived a bit, it was clear here was a man who wasn't just content to be the village idiot, he had to expand his influence. You'd think with the new chairman being so completely out of his depth it mightn't be long before the new manager would bail out. He wouldn't, though, because this was his last shot.

Monday came and I walked out on to the training pitch. At that time of the year the pitches are rock hard, and I heard the manager's little footsteps running after me way before I saw him. I didn't turn to look. The game had started. Let me show you how getting paid off in professional football works.

'How've ya been?' he asks.

'Fine,' I say. 'Looking forward to the start of the season.'

Total bullshit and we both know it.

The mistake the new owners had made when they took control of the club was a mistake that so many small-time owners make. They tell everyone how much money they have. Rookie error. The agent of any player who's likely to sign for the club will ask for top wages. Any club loaning or selling a player asks for top money. A player being sold … the buying club asks for a cheap transfer. And any player that the club wants to see the back of – namely, me – will ask for every single fucking penny that the club owes him on his contract. It's nothing against the club; it is just business. If you tell the world that you have all the money in the world, and that you intend to spend it, then I for one am going to take note of that. I'm very clever that way.

'So, what do you want to do this season?' the manager asks.

In terms of an easy payoff the correct thing to say is that I am looking forward to another season, my last as a professional, most likely. I know this will piss him off, but I'm an honest man. I want my cake too, and I believe that I can have it. In fact, I will have cake instead of changing tyres. My answer also saves us four to six weeks of posturing and beating about the bush. And my father always taught me never to beat the bush while posturing, it's ungentlemanly.

'Well, I don't want to work with you,' I say. 'So why don't you just pay me off?'

He wasn't in the least bit shocked; he knew me well. He knew that I was going to be difficult and that I wouldn't let him off the hook. He knew that I would get more fun out of hardballing the situation than simply accepting the standard 50 per cent payoff. Also, so far as he was concerned, I was a millionaire. But that played into my hands, bizarrely: OK, you don't need the money but, at the same time, you're in no rush to settle either.

After all, why leave? I lived round the corner. I had nothing else to do. I could come around and bust the manager's balls every morning for the next season and collect a decent cheque for doing so.

This went on for a few days until the manager finally got so pissed off and frustrated that he passed my case over to the chief executive. I have to tell you that I fucking live for shit like this. I live for winning negotiations, especially when I know that I can be a real prick in the process. There are no other footballers like me. Not one. Not one footballer can do his own negotiation in this situation. I know that; they know that. It scares them to death because they know that some of my best friends are in the media, and I don't just know where the bodies are buried, I'll be fucking telling Rupert Murdoch exactly where to dig.

I'm Lassie in Rupert's yard.

'What is it, boy?'

'Woof.'

'Bodies?'

'Woof.'

'You think there's bodies buried in the creek?'

'Woof.'

'You think ******** FC put them there? Can you lead us to them, boy?'

'Woof. Just get your fucking Zimmer frame.'

The chief executive rings me and he is perfectly pleasant but I happen to know that for the past 10 years, in various Premier League roles, he's been a full-time wanker. That means that he's good at his job, and that makes me even more determined to dig my heels in. 'Listen,' he says, 'you want to see the club move on, don't you?'

'Not really.'

'You don't need the money,' he says, 'do you?'

'Not the point,' I say. 'You owe me the money, regardless of whether I need it.'

Then it changes. Different tone.

'Listen, we don't want to have to go down the road of you training with the kids, do we? You don't want to travel the country playing in reserve games. That would be embarrassing for you.'

I point out that I've been with the new manager at a previous club. I know things about him that he doesn't even know about himself yet. I can put him on the front page of any newspaper in the country.

'We can do that too,' he says.

'You're missing the point,' I say. 'I don't care, and you've just bought a football club.'

'Well, what would you say to 60 per cent of your net contract?' he asks.

'Not good enough. I want 100 per cent. Or I'm staying put.'

I'm never getting 100 per cent. We both know that much, but I know that they are on the ropes, because the usual negotiation to sever a player's contract starts at 40 per cent. These guys really do have more money than sense. I also know that the club is in a transfer window and needs to comply with FFP rules. They need to make a statement to the fans with a decent signing, and right now that's proving harder than they ever thought. And don't forget that there are other players in the same boat. Those players will eventually crumble, of course – that's what they do – but it will still have eaten up the budget for new players. Meanwhile, time is ticking.

On Tuesday the chief executive comes back to me. 'Seventy per cent,' he says, 'and that really is the final offer.'

I tell him that I'll see him on Thursday after the universal footballers' day off that is Wednesday. He seems oblivious to the fact that he's found an extra 10 per cent of my net wages during the course of one sleep. I reason to myself that at the very least he has another 10 per cent in him, notwithstanding the fact that I am still, essentially, refusing to negotiate. These are all offers. There has never been any hint of a negotiation on my part. Right now, I am holding every single fucking ace that has ever been printed in the history of modern cards. 'It's a shame,' I tell myself, 'that I'm not playing for Real Madrid,' where the offer of a payoff at this point would be around £3 million and I'd be expecting to achieve at least £5 million. But that is to forget the fun that I'm having with these idiots on a personal level.

Predictably, on Thursday the chief executive makes a full and final offer: 80 per cent of the net value of the contract, enough to see me through for another two years, at least. I reluctantly agree. Whenever you agree to any severance in football you need to make sure that it's reluctant – never, ever, be seen to be desperate or grateful. The sum of money is agreed, but there is a sticking point on when it should be paid. The club are saying that it would really help them if the payments could be spread – half now and half in April; this will help them with their tax year. I don't give a shit about helping them with their tax year, but it's nice to have the manager think that I can afford to wait. I'm wearing my poker face to the end.

Finally, when everything is done and the lawyers have agreed the financial aspect of the deal, we move on to what is known as damage limitation. This involves both parties not wanting to lose face in public – that is to say that I have left the club with a year left on my contract and the club has removed one of its most well-respected and talented players, no matter if he is getting on in years. Both sides want to win this one. The club says that it will put a statement together. They do this, and when I read it I go mad. It says that I have found pre-season too much to contend with, that I can't keep up and that I am better off pursuing other interests. In reality, I'm about to leave the club as the fastest player over 10, 20 and 30 metres, as recorded by the club's own sports scientist. Fair enough, I am dead last in the long-distance running but, then again, I always have been last in the long-distance running since I was 20 years old.

I'm not happy. I tell the chief executive that this won't fly. If I'm to leave the game then it won't be because someone who knows less about football than I do has cited me for ill health. I redraft the statement and send it back to the club. This version alludes to the fact that I recognise that the club needs to move forward and that I can free up my wages to help that happen, voluntarily, of course. It works for everybody and we agree to the terms. But when the contract is emailed over to me, there is a clause that allows the club to hold on to my registration. Without this I can't play for anybody. Fairly standard procedure if you're about to sign for Barcelona from Manchester United, but this means that I can't play anywhere – non-league, pub football, nowhere.

That just wouldn't be fair to the great soccer public. What father doesn't dream of being out walking with his young son one Sunday morning and pausing on the pathway to watch a match on some muddy field. And then ... 'My word,' he says. 'Look there, son, the one that's just scored the goal. Well,

I'm blowed if that's not old TSF himself. Crikey, the years have been kind to the bugger. Text your mum to hold off on the Yorkshire puddings. We'll not be done till this one's over and we've shaken the great man's hand and asked him for a dozen selfies ...'

Could happen. Anyway, if I'm about to retire I might still want to play for a local team for no other reason than I enjoy playing football.

I have the club sign over my registration, and the deal is done and dusted.

Not long after my last training session for the club I happened to bump into the squad on a night out. I was with a friend discussing which players Chelsea should buy when the staff of my former club came wading into the bar we were sitting in. I didn't blink. I just made it as uncomfortable as I possibly could. I put my card behind the bar and told them to order whatever they wanted. I told them I was trying to get rid of money. I still have the pictures on my phone of me sticking my middle finger up behind the manager's back as they left the pub without offering to buy me a single drink in return. Childish and pathetic, I know, but I'd had about two dozen gin and slimline tonics by that point, and it was a once in a lifetime opportunity that I can't wait to publish in the picture section of my autobiography. One day. How does the song go? Freedom's just another word for nothing left to lose ...

Stay classy, guys.

Back when I had my first wobble about retiring too early I spoke to my great friend, the *Sunday Times* journalist and four-time Sportswriter of the Year, David Walsh, on the subject of retirement. For those of you who are either illiterate or living on the moon (how did you get this book by the way?) David Walsh is the man who exposed seven-time Tour de France champion, Lance Armstrong, as a doper, a fraud and a cheat. After 13 years of pursuing his man, David proved that Armstrong had cheated his way to victory, but not before Armstrong's lawyers had sued the *Sunday Times* for £1 million in damages.

Eventually, however, David's accusations found a few kindred spirits, and those people began to testify against the all-American hero – and David was vindicated and recognised in the most deserving way.

Many years later, when we met in Dublin to catch up on old times, I asked David what he thought had been Lance Armstrong's personal motivation when mounting his 2009 comeback having won the Tour de France seven times. What possible need was there for him to surface after such an 'illustrious' career? David's answer was typically brilliant: 'Lance came back because he couldn't stay away. Why couldn't he stay away? Because it's like the oldest theme in Hollywood that you've ever come across: the jewel thief, the bank robber, the assassin, they do their jobs brilliantly, they win every time, they kill all the people they should kill, they get all the jewels they should get, they get all the money from the bank they should get. Somebody comes and says, "One more job? C'mon, just one more little turn of the carousel." And they can't resist. Because that was them living like they'd never lived before, or they would never live again.'

I'll defy any footballer who reads those words to say they don't think of a comeback. Forget that Lance Armstrong is the greatest cheat in the history of sport. It is just so sad, as much as anything else in this world is sad, to imagine having nowhere to go and nothing else to do. Retirement is a little death.

Lance was a cheat and he was wrong, but when it ended for him it ended like it does for most of us. He retired and walked into a vacuum. I can't identify with the needles and the pills, but wanting the rush of excitement? Yearning for the thrill of it? Yeah, that haunts me some mornings.

Imagine, though, that you can't live without having your ego stroked. That's not going to be my fate. I want to move on. As stunning and vivid as David's summary of Armstrong's motivation is, I always held the belief that my playing career wouldn't be my grandchildren's first and only question when they sat on my knee and asked what I had done with my life.

There will be more for me. Once you finish one thing, that's it. Leave it behind. Why bother going back?

My very first non-league manager had a beautiful saying that he would use to describe how his team should step up and take the game by the balls. He'd shout at us, very often at halftime, 'You know when you see those poncey fucking cricketers get bowled or caught and they're out, and then they stand there for a few minutes practising the shot that they should have played, yeah? What's the fucking point? You're out, you fucking idiot. Fuck off!'

And that's me. When I'm out, well, I'm out.

Of course, football couldn't leave it that way. The saga couldn't end there. During my last year as a player some of the young players at the club had come to me asking if I'd represent them as an agent. I didn't want to do it, to be honest. I had more pressing things going on, which the club didn't know about but which had hastened my retirement and made the decision easier. But some of them were good players, really good, and, after all, I knew all the chief executives and scouts at the clubs who would be interested in these 'kids', as we call them, even though they are 17 to 20 years old.

There was one deal in particular that pissed me off. The club signed a player who I am convinced is a great player. He was 17 at the time and the new regime had just got him 'over the line' for £200 a week. Disgusting. They knew how good he was and they had stitched him up completely. It was a five-year deal; he would be 22 by the time he could renegotiate. £200 per week. Keep in mind that 15 years earlier, I signed my first professional contract for £600 a week, having never come through a professional youth team. I saw red. I set up an agency immediately and, though I missed this great player, I signed up as many other youth team players at that club as I could, and all but crippled the club's FFP plan.

Out of that youth team came a little crop of three players who will play in the Premier League. One player in particular will play wherever he wants – Bayern Munich, Madrid, Barcelona, Arsenal, Manchester United, Milan – he's that good. People laugh when I tell them that, but I always keep a straight face. I'm serious; he's that good. As with all kids, it will depend on his progress and how he deals with the bullshit around him. I was told that when the manager caught wind of what was happening at his club he got his sidekick, the analytics expert, to ask each player to tell him the name of his agent. I'm told that when the manager saw my name he roared, 'Is TSF having a fucking laugh or what?'

That is the strangled yelp of a man who has just lost millions of pounds, because there is no way that I'll let my players sign new contracts with the club while he remains manager.

It is a lovely position to be in but, that said, my agency work is limited. Outside of signing the best youngsters, agency work revolves around making sure that young players have the latest boots with their name on the side. Supplying them with cast-offs that have the name of a top Premier League player written on the side will not impress them. This actually happened to one of my young players. He got from his former agent a box of cast-off Nikes with a Premier League player's name stitched into each boot. Nice touch. And yes, we have served the offending agency under breach of contract.

What is needed for any retiring player is something for the soul, something to call his own: a passion, a vocation, something that he's good at and where he feels useful; something that isn't beneath him. That's important.

Essentially, he needs a job. I'm starting to get a view of what is next for me.

4. AN A-Z OF AWAY DAYS (WHICH ENDS AT W)

ARSENAL

Arsène Wenger. The genius.

Wenger is this constant point. The man on the hill. Day after day, alone on the hill, the man with the foolish grin is keeping perfectly still ... He is waiting for the football world to come around to him again. He is waiting for beauty and thinking to be the things that matter. He isn't chasing anything else. Mourinho is out there somewhere in the rough and tumble. Whatever way teams are playing this year, Mourinho has his team playing that way, only better.

But Wenger isn't down and dirty. Wenger doesn't see that he needs another Vieira. He will wait for a time when teams don't need a Vieira. Mourinho wants Robben? He sees he needs a Makélélé to protect him. 'Show me what you have in the line of a Makélélé.' Done.

Wenger will wait.

Wenger said recently he tried to sign Ángel Di María when he was 17 years old (Di María was 17, not Wenger). The

Argentinian couldn't get a work permit. Years later Wenger won't pay Manchester United-type money for the player: £67 million or whatever the fuck it is. The thought makes him sick. It should make Di María sick too. He would have grown at Arsenal. But maybe £60 million of that £67 million has gone off to Spain now to make Real Madrid stronger, to make it more insanely expensive to catch Real Madrid. Manchester United think they will catch Real Madrid?

Wenger sees the senselessness of that game, and he stands still and waits for the game to change. He discusses his thinking, and nobody listens. Every now and then the know-nothings in his own ground get together and sing, 'You don't know what you're doing.' I am a Spurs fan and that embarrasses *me*. Here is something that can't be said too often, and I make no apologies for saying it again. Arsène Wenger is a genius. Get out of his grid and leave him be. He knows what he is doing. It's just a pity that the flak he has taken from sections of his own fans has bled into the media, though I guess that was unavoidable. And it is even more of a pity that some of Wenger's most intriguing comments are routinely thrown away by journalists who are unwilling or unable to engage with the same footballing firmament he inhabits.

When Wenger leaves Arsenal behind they should build a library dedicated to him in north London in the style of dead American presidents. We could then take our time analysing his thoughts and influence instead of being bounced about by tabloid headlines.

Earlier this year the headline WENGER'S RED HERR-INGS appeared in a national newspaper the day after a press conference in which Wenger had given one of the most impressive and pinpoint articulations of not only why foreign players come to this country in such great numbers, but also why certain countries are prone to producing a collection of strikers or defenders in the same generation. Most managers now know this to be fact, but only because Arsène Wenger had pointed it out.

Wenger has reached an age where it must frustrate the hell out of him that the footballing world has not yet understood how he views the game. He started out his managerial career giving nothing away, and has latterly dumbed down for the idiots in the media who simply don't possess the in-depth knowledge of football required to understand just how deep you have to go to be successful. Despite the numerous deconstructions of Wenger's footballing philosophy, most of those same journalists still stick to the business of pointing out that the spine of Arsenal's team is weak. The spine of Arsenal's team is anything but weak.

It used to cause much amusement among the footballing fraternity, and equal consternation among journalists, that whenever Patrick Vieira was sent off for Arsenal his manager always claimed to have had his gaze concentrated elsewhere. Wenger's straight bat to interviewers over the years regularly antagonised the media, because Arsène Wenger doesn't miss much; his observations on the game are as sharp as they are intelligent. I enjoy the musings of the Frenchman very much; he digests football and the ramifications of social demographics around the game in a way that feels like a breath of fresh air – even if, at the age of 66, he is anything but new to this.

His comments on the art of defending came almost at the expense and dignity of his own defenders. 'Maybe because our societies are less aggressive in the football education system you cultivate less than intense desire. It's more about the quality of the technique and maybe that creates less defenders,' said Wenger in response to a reporter at an Arsenal press conference who questioned why it has been so difficult to recreate the solid Gunners defences of days gone by. 'I believe as well that young boys practise well on quality pitches,' he continued, 'whereas before it was muddy and you could tackle and throw your body in – it created opportunities for defenders to work naturally on their defensive techniques. Today it's all more standing up. There is less physical commitment because the quality of the pitches is much better.'

For reasons known only to themselves, the media didn't buy that. For me, though, it was an insight, the like of which most managers would never make public. Previously Wenger had made some shrewd remarks regarding the trend for South American strikers in today's game – remarks that all but went under the radar. But I was very taken with them, not only because I'd just written the *Guide to the Modern Game*. Wenger said, 'Look across Europe and where are the strikers from? Many of them, at least 80 per cent, are from South America. Maybe it's because in Europe street football has gone. In street football when you're 10 years old, you want to play with 15-year-olds; then you have to prove you're good, you have to fight and win impossible balls. When it's all a bit more formalised, it's less about developing your individual skill and fighting attitude. We've lost that a bit. Not every South American has that, but if you go back 30 or 40 years in England, life was tougher. Society has changed. We're much more protective than we were 20 or 30 years ago. We have all become a bit softer.'

For me, those comments were gold dust. They were an acute observation of football colliding with social demographics, both at home and abroad. They opened a window on to the level of detail that successful football clubs need to employ. Arsenal signed Alexis Sánchez as a direct result of that thinking, and he proved to be the best player in the squad in 2014–15. At the same time Wenger was turning that shrewdness to his defence and, once again, he was dismissed. But the new approach explains the Belgium central defender Thomas Vermaelen's departure from Arsenal. Despite the fans pointing out that his departure left the squad short-handed, it was the right decision: given his style of football Vermaelen should have been playing in Spain all along, where the league is slower.

Despite being bound by his mantra 'we buy quality, not players to fill up our reserve team' (something that is incredibly easy to do), I absolutely believe that Wenger is finally about to unveil the Arsenal team that so many pundits and fans have been asking him for.

Regarding Wenger's views on the trends that can some-times dictate transfer dealings at the top level, a journalist once asked me why it was that certain types of players come out of certain countries, almost at the same time. In partic-ular he wanted to know why it was that in recent times, given its size, a disproportionate number of top defenders have emerged from Serbia – players like Nemanja Vidić, Branislav Ivanović, Aleksandar Kolarov and Matija Nastasić. Could it be, he wondered, that the war which preceded the break-up of the former Yugoslavia had hardened players coming from the region?

He never did write an article on such a 'red herring' though.

And Wenger never wanted to talk about Vieira's dismissals because no good could come of it. He has always preferred to talk about football at a level that few people understand, and so they dismiss it or ridicule what he says. 'Professor Wenger' they call him, winking at each other like fools.

Two weeks after my own column, musing on red herrings, appeared, Arsenal signed the Brazilian centre-half Gabriel Paulista from Valencia for £13.5 million. Rocket science it is not.

All that aside, and despite Wenger's brilliance, as Totten-ham fans, none of my friends ever wanted to come to watch me play against Arsenal. The first time I invited them was when we played at Highbury. The Spurs fans in the group said that they'd rather throw themselves under a train than go anywhere near Highbury. And it is vicious. I've been at Tottenham v Arsenal derby matches and the hatred is intense. As a player I don't identify with it, but the fans do.

I only see 90 minutes of action, but for the fans the game is only a small part of the overall package of derby day football.

The first time I went to Highbury, it was obvious they needed a new stadium – the changing rooms were all white tiles and wooden benches, and even though the pitch was immaculate, the place was tired. What did surprise me was that the Highbury library failed to materialise – the fans behind the goal sang for 90 minutes while swinging red and white scarves above their heads.

The Emirates is totally different. It can be fairly noisy, but there is an air of expectance in the crowd – exactly the same as at Old Trafford, where the fans are waiting impatiently for the first goal, and the cheers that follow are those of dulled-down inevitability. Don't get me wrong, on the big European nights the place is obviously rocking, but I always felt for the Arsenal players that they never really had that every week. Certainly at the teams I played for our fans were rocking every single weekend, and that's why I played football. When I score I want the fans to go nuts, not stand up and politely applaud me.

But that is a little unfair and certainly not limited to Arsenal. The Emirates is a beautiful stadium but nonetheless it is *just* a big football stadium, just like the Etihad. When I played at both stadiums it was hard to make a distinction between them. In terms of character, they morph into one another. The difference behind the scenes is that the Emirates changing rooms are huge, built to host the Emirates Cup, where four teams inhabit the changing rooms at once and play one after the other. The walls move to make four changing rooms, but when you're the only team in there and you're effectively sitting in a changing room big enough for two squads and their staff, it's surreal. Managers get nervous in big changing rooms; they feel like the architect has designed this cavernous space specifically to intimidate them, so they make the squad bunch up into a corner while they give the team talk. Which is not like the Etihad, where the changing rooms are surprisingly small and a stand that runs above them cuts a right angle off one side of the room.

Despite the fact that it's very hard to win at the Emirates, I did enjoy a fair amount of success when they played against us away from home. In one away match that I played, Arsenal destroyed us with one of the greatest teams ever assembled. I watched the DVD of that game for a long time and learned so much from what Arsenal did, the way they moved the ball up the pitch. It's easy to find patterns and correlations when you watch football in this way. You realise that when the left-back moves forward, the holding midfielder moves round and the winger runs inside, which then pushes both centre-forwards up so that an advanced midfielder can fill the space. It is the simple movement of the full-back that allows the front players to occupy the entire back four of the opposition. In reality, it hastened the onset of counterattacking football, because at the end of the day most teams are incapable of playing Arsenal at their own game; they need an antidote.

But one manager who I played under came up with a second antidote. It wasn't pretty, it didn't change the game as we know it, and we had plenty of critics, but ultimately it worked. In short, the manager decided that we should kick the fuck out of them.

In the games that followed, Arsenal were beaten before they arrived, they were beaten again when they lined up next to us in the tunnel, and they were beaten again by our fans when they walked out on to the pitch. This was true for Arsenal at a handful of grounds, but with us they were beaten the moment the first tackle went in. As players we all get away with the first tackle – maybe the first two tackles on a good day – but it has to be the right tackle: you can't stamp, punch and kick, but you can turn a 50–50 into a 70–30 against an Arsenal player because the Arsenal players will invariably stay on their feet, which means that, as you slide through the ball, you will slide right through the player. I once heard Aaron Ramsey moaning to the ref about the tackling. The ref replied, 'Well, why don't you try tackling too?'

Good answer, ref.

People often asked me if we practised how to rough up the opposition. The answer was no. As footballers we know what roughing up means and how to do it legally. We'd be waiting for the moment our manager gave us the nod in training during the week. He was subtle in how he'd get the message across. We'd be practising set pieces, usually a corner, when he'd say, 'Right, let's get right into these on Saturday, lads. We've got to go after them from the off.' That would be it, that's all it was. Then when the corner came in he would tell the two centre-halves to run towards the near post and the middle of the goal, and tell a striker to run to the back post. He'd say, 'If the ball misses you then at the very least you make sure that you take somebody into the goal with you.' Then he'd say to the second centre-half, 'If you miss it, you do the goalkeeper.'

That 'philosophy' became the mantra for the game. Arsenal hated it and lost, regularly.

I hated it too. It was hard for me to play football like that because I'm a bit of a purist at heart and, well, even if I am a Spurs fan, if Arsène Wenger ever writes a book, I'll be the first in the queue to buy a copy. I made eye contact with Wenger many times while these games were going on and, maybe I'm imagining it (though I'm sure that I'm not), but his seemed a look that said, 'I didn't think that you of all players would stoop this low. I hope your parents are proud of you.'

But out of all the games that I played against Arsenal I have one standout moment. It happened in those great big changing rooms, where the chairman of a club that I used to play for had a penchant for introducing his friends, the rich and famous of TV and film mostly, to each player before the match.

The team bus usually pulled up at 1.30 p.m. and the players would get off, put their bags in the changing rooms, pick up a programme and a bottle of Lucozade, and wander out on to the pitch. We used to do that to check the pitch and see which studs we needed – then all the pitches became like carpet, and so we'd amble around, allowing time for the kit man to hang up the kit. But these days the kit man has his own vehicle and goes on ahead, so the pre-match standing around is now nothing more than a tradition and a chance to upload pictures of an empty stadium to Instagram. Anyhow, afterwards we'd wander inside and the manager might give a little speech (or not) before the players began getting changed. It was at this point that our chairman brought in a very attractive young actress who had starred in a multitude of Hollywood blockbusters. Not that I noticed.

I was as naked as the day I was born, fiddling around with something in my bag, when I heard, '... And this is, TSF.' I spun around to see a beautiful actress with her hand outstretched, ready to say hello. There was a cheer from the lads, who had seen that I hadn't noticed she was in the room, and a couple of pictures were taken by a player keen to capture the moment on his phone. I sometimes wonder what happened to those pictures.

I didn't know what to say. Our chairman had caught us all completely off-guard. Fortunately, she broke the silence. 'Oh, my,' she said, which I thought was great. She was faced with an awkward situation and kept her dignity and remembered who she was. I forced myself to believe the notion that her reaction was instinctive as she saw my enormous knob, but, these days, just like the Arsenal fans, I'm much more of a realist.

Oh, and this isn't a story I would tell Arsène Wenger on a night out.

ASTON VILLA

I like Aston Villa. Somebody has to. They are a real, city-based team, with real fans and a proper stadium, complete with listed bits to boot. At Villa Park they can always boast that they are one of the founding members of my football education: growing up in the eighties as a football-mad kid Villa were always a decent team. I used to try to recreate Tony Morley's run and shot over the field, where you either had to trim the length of the initial run so that you'd hit a fence with the shot, or use a different area of the park and take a bit of power off the shot so that it didn't run too far down the hill.

Aston Villa have played a part in my life ever since. The first time I arrived at Villa Park to play a Premier League match, Villa had a decent team – Gareth Barry, James Milner, Gabriel Agbonlahor, John Carew, Ashley Young and Stiliyan Petrov. They were a strong side, for sure, but they were beatable too, because the club, at that point, was viewed as something of a stepping stone for various players.

That's how I saw them too when, out of the blue, my agent rang and informed me that I was to be part of a deal that would see a player leave Tottenham to join Manchester United, who would then be replaced by a player from Villa who, in turn, were going to replace him with me. My agent agreed everything with Villa – the wages were £24,000 per week – and I was ready to go. I knew that Villa was the perfect club for me in terms of how they played football under Martin O'Neill.

Then two things occurred. In what was a massive coincidence we happened to be playing against Aston Villa the following weekend, and I had the words of my agent ringing in my ears: 'If at the end of this season you've only had one good game, then make sure it's this bloody game.' Twenty minutes in, I was knocked out cold. Stupidly, I played on and was as shit as Villa were dominant. Fortunately, it turned out not to be the deciding factor in the deal because as the dominoes began to fall and the player from Spurs moved on, his replacement from Villa stubbornly refused to budge. And that was the end of that.

But that wasn't the end of my dealings with Aston Villa. I can remember winding Gareth Barry up when he was taking a penalty against us – 'Gareth who? Never heard of you, pal. Why have you got your first name on the back of your shirt? Have you come through the youth team? Is this your debut? Good of them to let you take penalties – help get your confidence up, won't it? Ever scored one, out of interest?' He very nearly missed the stadium with the resultant spot-kick.

I remember losing a few games of my career after chasing down Gabriel Agbonlahor, putting in a nicely timed sliding tackle, before he landed on my shoulder. That incident led to me enduring three weeks of steroid jabs in my shoulder with a nine-inch needle about as thick as a baby's arm. At least that's what it felt like. Steroid jabs are a last resort for ligament or muscular pain that simply won't go away. They are painful and effective. I've had them all over my body, including my knee, where the doctor felt compelled to tell me everything that was going on – 'OK, can you hear that scraping noise? Yes? Well, that's the back of your kneecap, shouldn't be too much longer' – before I realised the shoulder is the place for any doctor looking to inflict maximum pain on a player.

But I like Villa. Villa and I could have been very happy together, I think. And in spite of the fact that I've never played for them, the club seems determined to remain a part of my life, albeit always on the periphery. Recently I – along, I suspect, with most of London's financial institutions – was approached by somebody within the club with the idea of putting a consortium together to buy Aston Villa Football Club. In football terms you will know, if you read *Tales from the Secret Footballer*, that the corporate side of the game is where my particular interest lies these days. Coaching has never appealed to me, because you have to cut your teeth with the youth team on £22,000 a year while working 14-hour days wiping arses. Management is the same sort of thing, except you are changing adult nappies. And then there is scouting, which is something I love, by the way, but it pays even less than coaching. In fact, if you're a scout at most clubs outside of the Premier League, I'd advise that the best way to actually make a profit at year's end is to fiddle your expenses.

Also, it has always been a little dream of mine to buy a football club – or at least use somebody else's money to buy a football club – and install myself as chairman. Aston Villa offered the faintest possibility of that becoming a reality, and in my book (and this is my book) that's good enough. In a situation such as this, there is only one man to call, a man who has been there and done it and managed to get out the other end alive. I rang a couple of Irish players I know. They told me where I could find the former Sunderland chairman and all-round legend, Niall Quinn.

Just outside Dublin I spent the afternoon talking to Niall about the consortium that he had led into Sunderland. And I hung on to his every word. What became immediately clear was that his deal could have fallen apart at least a dozen times but for a little luck, some good timing and absolute balls of steel from various members of the takeover group. The most important thing that Niall told me was to make sure that I had the very best commercial lawyer I could afford, but also to make sure that he was only paid in the event of a successful takeover. The commercial lawyer had to then 'get under the bonnet' of the club and find out where all the skeletons were hidden.

The reason for the commercial lawyer is simple. There are so many ways to buy a football club, so many ways to structure a deal, but all of them hinge on one thing: the definition of 'value'.

The commercial lawyer gave me an example. Every football club is for sale. You might be able to buy Manchester United for £5 billion, and the reason the fee would be so high is because it would be a hugely reluctant sale. But if you went to Bolton, where times are harder than they ever were, you might get the club for nothing and simply inherit the serviced debt. Other clubs are even harder to put a value on, particularly those clubs that have been in the hands of one owner for a long time, and who has pegged the football club to land or property. So, a club that owns its training ground, its academy, and perhaps has a hotel bolted on to the stadium – and maybe even parcels of development land or commercial buildings all over the city – might be worth as much, in terms of 'real market value', as £100 million. The problem is, if the club is in League One or the Championship, nobody is going to pay £100 million. So the minimum negotiation becomes about the stadium and the playing staff; even the training ground isn't a given in the first round of negotiations.

The ownership of football clubs does have its victims. Mark Goldberg thought he was buying Crystal Palace for £30 million but could only raise £22.8 million through a combination of his own money and the money of various backers. Ron Noades, at the time the incumbent, then suggested that Goldberg could buy the club but not the stadium for the new figure, at which point Goldberg should have run a mile. Instead he told Noades that he only had £18 million. Rather than calling off the deal Noades actually offered Goldberg a £5 million loan to help complete it. Again, Goldberg should have run a mile, but he didn't; he completed the deal and ended up with nothing more than the club crest and a group of players. With the club relegated from the Premier League, his backers withdrew their support and Palace was eventually placed into administration in 1999. Mark Goldberg lost his entire fortune in that Crystal Palace takeover and was declared bankrupt in 2000. When you're buying a football club, it's always worth remembering that story, because it highlights the ability that sport has to rule the heart and ignore the head. Ultimately there is only one thing worth remembering when buying a football club, in much the same way that there is only one thing worth remembering when buying any business: does the deal stack up?

There are ways of finding the right deal. These days nobody is willing to pay over the odds for a football club, but people still want to own one. At which point, the negotiation becomes staggered with a deal for the stadium and the playing staff. If the club is in League One and is promoted to the Championship, then certain parts of a deal would kick in – this could include the buying of the training ground – and if the club is promoted to the Premier League then the new investors may be bound by the initial contract to buy, say, the hotel and the remaining assets of the club. All of this is covered by the income generated at various stages of the club's rise up the leagues, with as little as possible of the new owner's money used in the process.

Although these deals can take a while to conclude, given the separate negotiations for various assets, they tend to work out pretty well for everyone involved. Unfortunately, though, Aston Villa was – and remains – not one of these deals. You either want the club lock, stock and barrel, or you're not getting any part of it at all. Randy Lerner has said so. And this is the problem with buying football clubs. The definition of 'value' is flawed because it is so hard to quantify the difference that a little investment in the playing staff or management might make. It isn't like buying a factory where if X amount of money is invested in production then the number of widgets coming off the line is quadrupled and profits go up. In the case of Aston Villa the definition of value is as wide as the Villa Park pitch.

Our consortium was quoted £120 million, all in cash, upfront, no negotiation, with further payments made over a five-year period. Which is not quite as steep as the price Jeremy Peace, the chairman of West Brom, quoted a broker friend of mine. He's after £140 million upfront for the Baggies. Fully expecting a negotiation to break out, we told Villa where they could go and waited by the phone. And waited. But no negotiations were forthcoming, and when we let our poker faces down and got in contact we were told in no uncertain terms that we'd already been given the deal and there would be no change for as long as Lerner owned the club. The truth is that Lerner has been completely blown away by just how competitive the Premier League is. He spent heavily under Martin O'Neill and got nowhere, and now he has changed tack to survival mode. He wants his money back, drip-fed if necessary.

In the Championship we have looked at a number of clubs. Leeds United is an obvious choice because of the huge fan base, but the stadium, especially inside, is crumbling and the playing staff is average at best. Don't even get me started on the debts. There are two clubs we have identified that really tick the boxes but are unfortunately owned by unrealistic people. All such people care about is finding the best club with the most assets, and the best planning permission for the best price. These clubs have lost their

Premier League status but are being sold on the basis that the potential remains enormous; one of the clubs still has its parachute payments in place, which I suspect will be creamed off before any sale occurs.

It has proved to be that way at a number of clubs we've looked at since Aston Villa, and even though Randy Lerner is the main man for now, and our consortium has no interest in paying top dollar for a struggling Premier League club, I suspect it won't be the last I'll see of Aston Villa Football Club.

AFC BOURNEMOUTH

What can you say about Eddie Howe? Talk about sticking to what you know paying off, both for him and for the club. At the age of only 29, Howe was given the job of youth team manager at Bournemouth before taking the top job in 2008. He guided Bournemouth to promotion to League One in 2010, despite a transfer embargo being in place, before leaving for Burnley, where things went wrong. There are lots of managers who say Burnley is like managing a south coast club in the north, in that the fans expect tough tackling and, above all, effort. I don't really see that in Bournemouth, and in 2012 Howe returned to the club, where he achieved promotion to the Championship in April 2013.

Don't be fooled, though. There is a shitload of money behind Bournemouth. A friend of mine, who also happens to be the chairman of a rival club, told me that he paid his manager £100,000 a year. Eddie Howe, he told me, earned

£750,000 a year; more than most Premier League managers. In fact, when my friend's PA phoned Bournemouth to ask where the visiting manager could park his Range Rover, he was greeted like a long-lost brother: 'You have a Range Rover? Park it next to the other Range Rovers [of the board members] here, it will look great; we have a Range Rover gang here.' I ask you. I didn't write that anecdote before because it just sounds like bullshit, but it's true. Russians really are that vain.

I hope Eddie makes it with Bournemouth in the promised land. As impressive as Howe's tenure with Bournemouth has been, I'm afraid that the nature of the modern game means that, as a manager, you barely get a moment to digest a success before people begin dissecting your next move. Bournemouth's monumental rise to the Premier League is as sensational as it gets.

I've played against his sides – it has been painful in the way that they keep the ball and make experienced players look inferior. To play against them is the stuff of nightmares – like playing against Swansea or Arsenal is a nightmare. They are a team of footballers, rather than 11 meatheads calling themselves footballers (which is actually easier to handle). Eddie Howe wants his side to play the game in the way that I also believe the game should be played. His Bournemouth project is built on a passing and moving style of play and a determination to dominate the ball and attack from all areas of the pitch, depending on where the overload rears its head. So far it has been too good for the three divisions that

Bournemouth have left in their wake, and could easily ruffle feathers in the Premier League.

It's a huge step up, but they will catch out a few Premier League teams because of that style. Nobody in football likes playing against passing and moving sides, mostly because the average distance covered for, say, a midfielder goes up from 10–11 kilometres to 12–13 kilometres, as you run after the ball before being too tired to attack once you win it back. Since you ask, the greatest distance I've achieved in a match is 13.3 kilometres, and while I can vividly remember looking at it on the player noticeboard at the training ground – a tactic that managers use to create competition among the players – I can't for the life of me remember what club it was against.

Given that even great managers like José Mourinho will sometimes change tack and shut up shop against certain teams, it will be interesting to see what Eddie Howe does against the big clubs when faced with the same problem. Yes, he's a purist; yes, his team can play. But to approach the game in the same way against the biggest sides in the Premier League is dangerous. Right now, Eddie Howe's stock is sky-high – nobody ever thought that Bournemouth would win the right to play in the Premier League – but, as a manager, you sometimes need to allow yourself to be influenced by what has been proven to work elsewhere.

The danger is that Howe's men will suffer a couple of heavy defeats against the big clubs by playing the way they do, and then lose faith in their approach against the teams where it is highly likely to be successful. There is nothing wrong with sometimes setting up not to get beat, rather than going all out for the win. Howe is shrewd, he knows that; it's just how far he's willing to push the boat out in terms of showing the world the way he believes that football should be played.

And don't think that Howe's team is lightweight in terms of mixing it with the best of them. Teams that play a lot of football are sometimes wrongly labelled as being in some way physically weaker. Try going shoulder to shoulder with Giroud, Arteta, Wilshere, Ramsey or, in Bournemouth's case, Harry Arter, and see how you get on. Bournemouth have come through the Championship, a league in which teams start matches from a position where they know that, at the very least, they will have to fight first before working out what else they need to do tactically to win the game.

I can recall a match against Bournemouth in which a teammate and I put in a couple of really heavy challenges on Harry Arter, who our manager had earmarked as the player who made Bournemouth tick. The idea was that by taking out the playmaker, we'd stop the flow of Bournemouth's game. To an extent it worked. Bournemouth weren't nearly as fluid by virtue of the fact that the fouls disrupted the rhythm and flow of the game. But they still dominated the ball for long spells in between, and Arter shrugged every single one of those challenges off physically.

Just before halftime the Bournemouth midfielder received the ball and went to turn out to play a pass to the opposite wing while one of our players chased him. Unfortunately he turned squarely into me. For a second it looked to be one of those delicious moments when you know that you can make a perfectly legal and fair tackle while also making a decent fist of crippling the other player in the process. You've heard of the term 'hospital pass' before? The pass that Arter received was a glorious example. As I went in from my side, my team-mate went in on the other – unnecessarily, I thought, but then he was under instructions from our manager – and the result was that Arter was reduced to a heap on the floor. The truth was that there had been a running battle for most of the game up to this point, and Arter had had too much to say for himself in our view. There comes a point in some games where that spills over into physical abuse.

When the whistle went for halftime we were walking off the pitch and Arter was abusing me and my teammate and any other player that came near him. I kept reading his name out to him from the back of his shirt, '"Arter"? Never heard of you, pal. Have you been playing long?' Over and over again. He responded by calling me a 'manic-depressive cunt' and telling me to 'go and take another antidepressant'. As we came into the changing rooms he punched the door and, in fairness, hit it so hard that it smashed the wall to the side and looked as if it was going to come off its hinges.

For a long time I was adamant that he was actually crying, but he may have just been sweating profusely around the eyes. In the second half he was extremely committed to winning the game but ineffective as we shut up shop, and

Bournemouth duly lost despite dominating the ball for long spells. I still get a kick out of it to this day, thinking back to that game, but the caveat to that entire anecdote is that Arter is a very, very good footballer and integral to the way that Eddie Howe wants his side to play football.

5. THE INBETWEENER

Talking of Arsène Wenger reminds me of something else – a lesson I learned years ago. There is a huge difference between speaking with cynicism and living cynically. TSF loves the gangsta swagger of talking dirty and mean in a world where machismo and money are the things which maketh the man. Talking hard and fast with a good crust of cynicism crumbled into the words is ironic and funny, especially if you know me.

But living cynically and fucking people over? To be honest, it's not my thing.

Michael McIndoe. Have you ever heard of him? Every footballer from the Premier League down has. He played nearly everybody. And won.

McIndoe is the former Doncaster Rovers, Wolves and Coventry City midfielder who is accused of persuading 300 people, many of them footballers, to invest in a scheme that is now being investigated by police. The sheer scale of the alleged fraud is, to my mind, evidence of how easy it is to separate footballers from large amounts of money. And I write as somebody who once bought an apartment in the

Middle East by accident and forgot about it for over a year. So I am hard to impress.

In fact, when it comes to soliciting cash from footballers, I used to think that I was the king. Then McIndoe came on the scene. Don't get me wrong, I never set out to solicit money from players. It just happened as a by-product of having business plan after business plan sent to me that I'd then dissect on the coach, or in the changing room, or in the bath at the training ground or wherever. And always the same thing happened. One by one the players would come to me and ask, 'Anything decent, pal?' And I'd reply either yes or no. I'd never explain why they shouldn't get involved if I felt it wasn't worthwhile. I protected them. If I thought I had a good one then I'd tell them why it was good, and always the question once I'd finished speaking was, 'Can you get me involved?'

Now that isn't because I was the world's greatest salesman – I could not 'sell you this pen'. But I had something that any wolf of Wall Street would die for, and that was the absolute belief from my peers that because I was 'one of them' I would never deliberately try to defraud them or put them into something I knew to be utter rubbish.

Pretty quickly, though, I had my moment of clarity. It went something like this: 'Why the fuck am I helping these players? I'm doing all the work here. I'll offer to raise the money for the company too in return for equity [shares in the business].' So that meant that as soon as I knew I wanted to invest in a company to the tune of £30,000–250,000, depending on what the business was and what round of funding they were at, I could essentially raise all of the money in return for a fee, but I could then transfer that fee to stock, thus achieving my investment with the company's own money. That sounded good to me, and I have done that since for at least half a dozen companies.

And I'd always tell the players, 'This is your investment, this is your money. It's a gamble, it could go wrong, and if it goes wrong, it'll be your fault. I'm not telling you to do it.'

They always wanted in, though. Then as soon as their investment was in, they treated the company as if it were mine. To them, I was the CEO, I owned the whole dog and pony show – it was mine and they'd given me their money. They wanted to know when they would be getting it back off me with their profit. The number of phone calls I got asking me, 'How's that business? When's it selling? What's it worth?' … The truth was, I didn't know the answers until I got a shareholder update, the same as them. Not good enough. It was seriously painful at times. Sometimes, just having to play football for a living could act as a great relief from all that.

McIndoe didn't think so, though. He recruited people insatiably. As I sit here writing this, he has already entered bankruptcy and has debts approaching £3 million, having built up his scheme to an alleged £30 million.

As a player, Michael McIndoe was just always, sort of, all right. He made a couple of panels for Scotland and drifted around clubs in the second and third tier – always worth a punt but never indispensable once he arrived. He had a certain level where he was able to perform well, but beyond that he just wasn't equipped to cope.

I remember him best at Doncaster Rovers, where he twice made it into the PFA Team of the Year. I can also remember that my team tried to sign him from Doncaster Rovers, and I must confess that when I heard we were interested in him I couldn't place his face and somehow got him terribly confused with James Coppinger, who I thought would be a great signing. Either way, McIndoe's reluctance to sign for us probably means that a lot of people I know dodged a bullet. Or a machine gun spray of bullets.

I remember exactly when McIndoe's scheme hit our dressing room. I remember exactly where I was, the people who were there, and who told me about it. We were in the changing room when a midfielder who loved to invest, indeed had invested via me in a number of third-party companies, came to me and said, 'Mate, have you seen this?' He was extremely excited but, then, he always was. He was a bungalow investor – solid, but nothing upstairs. He got a real buzz from investing, which is both nice and dangerous.

In 2011 McIndoe told my friend that his money would go to a company that invested in gold, property and stocks, all of the things that players like as investments. They are the gold, frankincense and myrrh of footballers' get-rich dreams. They've heard of gold, property and stocks. They've read good things, maybe seen them on TV. They know they work sometimes, so they don't even ask questions. My friend told me that McIndoe then advised him to put in £20,000 as a minimum amount so that he could see how it worked. This is where you build up trust. Exactly as McIndoe had said, my friend told me he received nearly £30,000 two weeks later. Hey fucking presto! It was that easy. A profit of almost £10,000, in only two weeks.

I told him to stop. I said take the money and don't tell anybody where it came from. If people ask then tell them that you won it at the races.

At the time of going to press, nothing has been proven in court about McIndoe's particular scheme – it's all allegations. But there is a history of dodgy investment schemes that footballers should be aware of. You may remember Bernie Madoff, the American investment advisor who defrauded clients of $18 billion over a 30-year period from the 1980s. In 2009 he was sentenced to 150 years in prison. His name has become synonymous with Ponzi schemes – investment operations where the operator pays returns to investors from new capital paid to the operators by new suckers, rather than from profits earned. The schemes are simple. You put your money in and a few weeks later you get your initial investment back with a large profit on top. Typically, that might be something like 20 per cent, as was reported to be the case with McIndoe's scheme. Once you've seen it work with your own eyes and you're holding a big bag of cash, you then get greedy for more.

The scam is older than the man it was named after. Charles Ponzi ran a famous scheme out of Boston in the 1920s, but as long ago as 1844 Charles Dickens was describing a classic

Ponzi scheme being run by the character Tigg Montague in his novel *Martin Chuzzlewit*. From Dickens to Ponzi to Madoff to McIndoe is some journey – and long enough to prove that greedy people are very slow learners.

Madoff wasn't alone in his scheming. In February 2009, another American financier, Allen Stanford, was charged with running what the US Securities and Exchange Commission called 'a massive Ponzi scheme' and in 2012 he was sentenced to 110 years in prison. This was all very fresh in my head at the time, but understandably it perhaps wasn't to anyone else sat in the changing room.

There are pictures taken in 2011 of Michael McIndoe in Marbella – all shades, cigars, champagne and a gang of tanned hangers-on partying on the beach. All looks pretty dodgy, but for a lot of footballers those photos might as well have been the cover of the investment brochure. If they saw those pictures they'd have said, 'Yes please, sign me up for some.' In 'Marbs' (yes, everyone calls it that in football too), McIndoe is reported to have lived a life that would make the sharpest Ponzi scheme operator envious. Former players tell stories of a £2 million mansion, hired at a cost of £27,000 a week, as well as spending sprees totalling £40,000 for champagne at a beach club party. For the sake of context, lots of players, including myself, have spent similar sums, but at least that was our own money.

Back in London, McIndoe is reported to have lived at the May Fair hotel, where he paid £4,000 a week for a suite. Around the corner in Belgravia, it is alleged that he rented an apartment for an (upfront) £150,000 annual fee. Opposite the May Fair hotel is the revolting Funky Buddha club, where McIndoe is said to have thrown lavish parties. There are even reports that he hired the pop star Alexandra Burke to perform at a party, while at the same time he was struggling to cope with a gambling problem, allegedly involving the running-up of a million pounds' worth of bets in just one year with a single bookie.

Unfortunately my friend didn't listen, and nor did three others in our squad. They each put another £50,000 in and duly started their own personal relationship with the Vodafone voicemail service. I called them all the names under the sun when they told me, even when they were adamant that they were shortly about to receive a great big bag of cash in return. The way I saw it, that was £200,000 that could have gone into any one of a number of legitimate companies that I had been asked to raise money for at the same time.

McIndoe has told the London bankruptcy court that he has no income, but when faced with questions from creditors about whether they will ever see any of their money back, he ran out of answers: 'I have nothing to say, I cannot comment about this,' he said.

A few years ago I heard the noted intellectual, Robbie Savage, on the radio saying that his biggest grievance against the Secret Footballer was that I'd gone against the changing-room culture of brotherhood, the unwritten code that says we're all 'in this together' – and I understand where he's coming from, to a certain extent. But my anxiety is that when dodgy investment schemes come into our changing room we discover that we are too entrenched in that 'all for one' way of thinking to step out of it and raise the alarm.

I was concerned about McIndoe's scheme the moment my friend opened his mouth back in 2011, and yet I didn't call the PFA, nor did I call the FA. Perhaps I do have a little of that changing-room mentality in me, after all – or maybe I am just a selfish individual who knew full well that he wasn't going to make that investment and didn't care if anybody else did. I'm not sure I know the answer. But what I do know is that for the right business I could raise the money in an instant with a series of phone calls to footballers up and down the country. Credibility is the key, combined with a great idea. And to my mind, buying the rights to Michael McIndoe's story is an absolute no-brainer because it is a number one bestselling book and a blockbuster film. It ticks all the boxes: young, famous people pissing away loads of money through the alleged fraud of a number of high-profile footballers; the Costa del Crime; copious models and champagne running right through it ...

So while you're thinking to yourself, 'What a great idea. Who do I know who can get the money together to make an offer to the bankrupt McIndoe for his life story?', I've already raised the money and I haven't even had to make a phone call.

That's how easy it is to solicit money from footballers!

And we are supposed to be role models?

No wonder retired footballers have such a bad time of things. Statistically, there is a 33 per cent chance that I will be divorced within a year of retirement. There is a 40 per cent chance I will be bankrupt within five years – and I don't even know Michael McIndoe. Then an 80 per cent chance of osteoarthritis. And odds that I don't like to look at concerning addictions.

Still, I talk cynical but try to live better.

So come to where I've worked for the last 14 years or so. Remember this is us at work. There shall be no mention of what we do with our spare time and easy money. This is the world we eject from when we retire.

People say to me that, being retired, it must be great to catch up with so many of the great names and characters I shared a pitch with? Those friendships, forged in dressing rooms from League Two all the way to the Emirates, they are for life, aren't they? Those friendships are *what it's all about* at the end of the day.

No.

I mean, for a young lad setting out on the road of the professional footballer. He knows that he will be part of some merry band whose loyalties to each other are beyond question?

No.

It's a brotherhood, isn't it? You played together and then you stay together. You shared a dressing room and forever you will walk the earth like a band of brothers?

No. That's sentimental bollocks. You make the same number of friends in football as you would have if you spent the years working in Carphone Warehouse. You are left with some good buddies, and you know a huge crop of tossers.

And before you ask, no, I don't play golf. I'm still sexually active.

People argue these points. Footballers are rich and room together and holiday together and are always having the banter. Surely they retire and go and live in gated communities together and play golf every day while their wives lunch for charity and get group rates with plastic surgeons?

The truth is that on the outside nobody really understands the banter inside the changing room. Banter is our lubricant. It's how we mingle at the cocktail party of professional sport. It's the madness that stops us from going completely mad. If we are obnoxious enough to each other then we can't dislike each other for being obnoxious. Because it's banter.

That's all it is, though. It isn't brotherhood. It doesn't translate out into the real world. Within those four dressing-room walls anything goes. I can be as racially abusive, homophobic, sexist and generally revolting as I want to be. The only thing that will happen is that other players will either laugh or they won't. Nobody will tell anybody on the outside. First rule of banter? No talking about banter.

Aside from the most degrading kind of banter, if that's what you want to call it, the changing room can be a very witty place where sharp minds and acid tongues joust for position. But, after 15 years, I'd totally had enough. I was ready to move on to solids and try some grown-up conversations.

Jimmy Bullard's brief stint on the TV programme *I'm a Celebrity ... Get Me Out of Here!* gives us a great little window on to this changing-room mentality that others just cannot grasp. For a start, Jimmy needed a few bob having walked into the wrong deal. Poor Jimmy put £600,000 into Michael McIndoe's scheme and took his dividend in kangaroo bollocks somewhere in the Australian jungle as he tried to recover. Jimmy is a good guy, but all that his sudden hardship means is that after a lifetime in the game, the people who could afford to help Jimmy out spend a lot of time avoiding Jimmy. That's the brotherhood of football for you in a kangaroo nut.

Then there was the banter business. People looked away from their TV sets in horror when they thought that Jimmy was bullying some talent-deprived lump from Rotherham while they were stuck in the jungle. Eating crocodile anus with cockroaches was entertaining and not at all demeaning, but Jimmy was bullying the beefcake.

It wasn't bullying, it was bantering, Jimmy said in his defence.

If you thought that Jimmy Bullard was bullying people then you'd have no chance as a youth team player in a changing room. Think of that before you send your darling son to work down the football pits.

When Jimmy began telling people that he'd never heard of them I can guarantee you that every footballer watching that was laughing. The crux of changing-room banter revolves around being able to subliminally point out the pecking order to somebody who is weaker than you. 'Who are you, mate?' 'Never heard of ya, mate.' Or even, 'Have you paid your dues?' Sound familiar?

It's just the bog-standard daily banter of football. Jimmy Bullard isn't a bully; he's just struggling to understand why this sort of banter doesn't translate outside of the training ground, the only place that he has ever known.

If the first rule of banter is no talking about banter, the second rule is never lose at banter. To do that, you have to pick a topic where you can win. Then you hammer it to death and it becomes your calling card. In the dressing room money is the obvious battleground. I've got more than you, and I earn more than you. Therefore you are shit, mate.

The easiest example I can give you is when one of our players drove into training in a brand-new Audi TT. He was very pleased with himself, and when the lads came out to have a look he happily showed it off. One of our older professionals, an England player no less, asked if he could drive it around the training ground and, naturally delighted that an England player was showing such interest, he tossed him the keys. Our England man drove off like the Stig and after a couple of circuits he pulled up, back where the lads were standing, and jumped out. 'Mate, that is really nice. I like that a lot. Where did you get it?' A new Audi TT and now this. The dog's golden bollox. The player couldn't wait to tell the Stig and the assembled company the good news: 'I got it from the guy down at Audi. He's doing deals for Premier League players, and he says if any of the lads go down there he'll sort them out.'

The England player looked suitably impressed. Nodded. 'Have you got a number for the guy?' he asked.

'Yeah, yeah, on my phone. I'll send it to you when we go back in.'

'Excellent, cheers. I'll give him a call this afternoon after training and go down there. I've been looking for a couple of these for the kids.'

Brilliant. That was the last time the Audi TT ever turned up at our training ground.

I have never been able to get my head around the players who say they miss these day-to-day exchanges. In the end your knees ache, your hips are sore and the banter gives you arthritis of the brain. I couldn't wait to get away from it. I was very rude to my teammates in the process, when asked what I thought about this car or that bird, or this watch. I just couldn't have the conversation so I removed myself from it. A curious thing happened because of that decision – the players left me alone and seemed to respect me more as somebody who had bigger fish to fry.

Banter got more and more tired. I enjoyed, at the end, a guy like Nemanja Vidić at United. I once asked him to swap jerseys with me at the end of the match. I just wanted to annoy him. 'Thanks,' I said, when he handed it over. 'I have to clean the car during the week. This is perfect. I'll text you a pic.'

'Yeah, no problem,' said Vidić. 'Same here, but I'll have to send you pictures of all my cars one by one if that's OK?' He got me fair and square but those moments were rare.

In the end I was left with the banter running all round my brain and a list of people who will cross the road if they see me coming. You look back afterwards and wonder, was there something retarding us all? Did we get fined for having real conversations? Could you be arrested on suspicion of having an IQ? Would they burn your house down if they thought you had books in there? The answer was no. Banter was just easier – it's just the way people talk to each other during a life in football. Nobody wants to stand out.

For instance, we beat Birmingham at St Andrews one day. I was walking off the pitch with a huge African player beside me. We looked like different species. We'd taken our tops off prior to swapping along with our peers in the tunnel. As we trudged off the pitch at fulltime, Steve Bruce was waiting in the tunnel, presumably to have a word with the referee, which is what managers tend to do when their team has been tonked in a game. I, and my African friend, were first off the pitch and as we funnelled down the tunnel I received the first snide comment.

Steve Bruce: 'Don't take your top off, pal, unless you look like your mate there.'

TSF: 'Mate, did you make that nose out of Play-Doh?'

Brucey is fine. With others the banter just expresses your dislike of them. Take Craig Bellamy. Please. We were partaking in the sporting pre-match handshakes before a Premier League game when Bellamy suddenly stopped me and as he shook my hand he looked at me and spoke: 'Are you gonna shut the fuck up today?'

TSF: 'Are you gonna grow a neck?'

To this day, I have no idea why he stopped and decided to come for me. I can only assume that he had me mixed up with somebody else or that he was trying to unsettle me as one of our better players. One day I might get round to asking him about it, but I actually hope I never see him again.

In football the cure for hardcore banter is generally just to pretend that you haven't heard and keep moving.

Here's a story. A coach puts four cones out. You know the drill. A player in the middle, four players around. Keep it away from the lad in the middle. Eventually the player in the middle will be a black player and the ball will hit a cone. Somebody will ask how hard is it from five yards to keep it away from the cone. And the coach will say, 'Hey, don't be racist!' The coach is pretending he's heard the word 'coon'. The black players are pretending that they've heard nothing at all. Every morning that little hilarity plays out somewhere. You either laugh or you ignore it.

Michael Ballack should have ignored me. John Terry has played for one club all his life. That covers up a lot of short-comings. He looks at the Stamford Bridge crowd, they look at him. They see themselves staring back at each other. He is an extension of them. I don't like either John Terry or the crowd he resembles. Yet when I have played against Chelsea I always hated Ballack the most. He was the most arrogant footballer ever – and exceptional, which made it worse. So let's paint a scenario involving Terry and Ballack together. Not going to be pretty, is it?

John Terry put an elbow in on me once. It almost disintegrated my face. His elbow and my face met like two particles in the Hadron Collider. His elbow was harder and uglier than my face, though. I could have turned the other cheek, but by then that other cheek was actually the last cheek I owned. So I said, 'Fuck that.' I told our free-kick taker where I wanted the ball floated, just so I would have a run-up to kill John Terry. I hit Terry. He went down like a sack of shit dropped from a high wall. I bent over him and gave him a little kiss. All the Chelsea fans behind the goal went crazy. Next thing, Ballack started following me around for the rest of the game. Having a go all the time. A ball goes up between us and he chucks his elbow at me. First Terry, and now his German minder chucking elbows at my face. (My face is a thing of extraordinary beauty if you believe my mum, and if I weren't a wonderful footballer it would probably be my meal ticket, my mum has said so. So not the face, boys, OK?) Ballack is snarling in German. Banter doesn't translate that way. I thought about this and how to bridge the cultural gap. Then I turned to Ballack and I called him a Nazi.

I can only say that if you are going to get into a bit of sledging out on the pitch it has to get inside the other guy's head. Otherwise, don't bother. You have to fuck with him. You have to cross the line. It's better that he leaves in tears calling you a wanker than he should smile to himself and urge you to try a bit harder with the abuse. Look at Italy's Marco Materazzi: whatever he said to Zinedine Zidane it played a part in winning (and losing) the World Cup.

So I called Ballack a Nazi and he got all angry on me. He started shouting even louder in German, and for a moment I thought he was actually going to annex me. Then I asked him if he knew how many men had died so that a German could come over here and earn £120,000 a week?

It was all going well until Didier Drogba smashed one in the top corner. Ended that awkwardness. I really do like Drogba but ...

For the sake of comparison I should say that I have also called Dietmar Hamann a Nazi. He laughed to himself and at the end we swapped jerseys. Either he is actually a very cunning Nazi or he's just a decent guy who knows how to handle himself and appreciates that I'm a twat sometimes. I got no enjoyment out of calling Dietmar a Nazi but I still chuckle to myself about Ballack.

REAL WORLD

I'll be honest, when news of my retirement flashed across the ticker bar of Sky Sports News, I thought that I'd be inundated with media requests. I didn't expect a nationwide strike as the people begged me to come back to football, although I am a player who has played at every level of the game, scored in every division, and played against almost every professional team. Just saying.

I've played at pretty much every ground. I've played in games that are in the record books. I've created history. I know everyone and everyone knows me. At the very least I'd be an asset for any company. We'd never lose at banter. And let's not kid ourselves, I've paid my dues. And then there's the media types within football who've waxed lyrical about the Secret Footballer – the press, the outrage and the infamy have been off the scale. Indulge me, I'm building up to something.

And yet, the phone didn't ring with media requests. I worried if Lineker and Lawro actually had my number. And if they had, were they running scared? My phone didn't ring to the point that I felt I might have to take it to the nearest Vodafone outlet.

Be careful what you wish for. Thirty minutes later, having confirmed that the phone was in fact in perfect working order, I received a call from Manish Bhasin, who asked if I'd 'do' *The Football League Show*. I entered careful consultation with the nearest and dearest, namely my agent, and took his answerphone message as a clear-cut sign to do the show. It would be money and it would be fun.

One day in the life.

Have you ever been waterboarded? Detained against your will for long periods?

I retired in part to spend more time with my kids (OK, not really, but hear me out) and as such I had decided that anything that would take up my Saturdays had better be worthwhile financially and nourishing in terms of food for the soul.

The Football League Show was neither ...

I arrive at midday, in plenty of time to walk to wherever I need to walk to and talk to whomever needs to be talked to. What I find on the outskirts of Heathrow is an Indian receptionist who deftly calls a woman who I determine to be somebody not quite attractive enough to sleep her way to the top but full of enough beans to ensure her survival at IMG Ltd, the company that holds the rights to the highlights package for the leagues outside of the Premier League, hence the name, *The Football League Show*.

I know she speaks highly of me too.

She shows me to a broom cupboard and asks me if I'd like a tea. (Maybe it was a tea chest and she asked if I would like a broom. It is hazy already.) I decline on the grounds that if I'm too much trouble then they'll never invite me back. An hour later, Manish walks in followed by a few producers who have clearly missed the boat to success and have wound up putting together TV shows that none of them give a fuck about. Still, Manish has an entourage. It's 1 p.m. and one of the six screens showing live matches that afternoon is spitting out coverage of the early kick-off. I make notes furiously as my co-pundit, who we'll call 'Lloyd', does his best to ignore the fact that there is a game going on. Lloyd orders a tea while complaining that his knees hurt. I conclude that he last played football at least 10 years ago. I refrain from telling him to shut up, as his top half looks in decent nick even if everything below the waist screams paraplegic.

The game finishes and I'm drowning in notes and sheets of A4 paper with diagrams pointing to God knows where; sheets and sheets of the stuff that I've had to condense after I drew the scale of the pitch incorrectly at the start of the game, and then things got out of hand. As I begin to lay the sheets out across the tile-carpeted floor Manish looks at me like I'm some kind of backward has-been.

Before I know it, the clock hits 3 p.m. Business time. The screens fill up with the Championship's top teams, but nobody cares. Manish is more concerned with his Twitter feed, and Lloyd is texting God knows who. The producer is nowhere to be seen. I'm frantically pointing to the screens as goals go in left, right and centre, but nobody seems that interested. I should at least be with Jeff Stelling and the Sky Saturday afternoon boys, so good am I at pointing to a screen whenever a goal is scored. At *The Football League Show* this talent remains under-appreciated, and at halftime I order a tea from a very pleasant young girl who seems to know only too well that she will either remain here being smashed all over the shop by yesterday's pundits-turned-players, or she *will* find her way to the bright neon lights of post-production Soho where that sort of thing comes under 1.1 on any would-be employee's CV. Wherever she ends up, she can add 'decent tea-making skills' to her curriculum vitae.

The second half comes and goes and for some reason I've been left alone in the green room. Personally, I don't see what's so fucking green about it. For the last three hours I've been sat on a sofa that only an interior designer would order and yet the window that has been concentrating the light inward has somehow managed to sunburn my ear.

The games come to an end and I conclude in my notepad that Pritchard is a decent player for Brentford and that Bournemouth look like the type of team that play my kind of football, though I question the squad strength in depth and the pitches cutting up in the winter. I write that Millwall are Millwall, without the horrible blood and guts that generally makes the Den a tough place to go to, and that Wigan and Fulham had better get used to having to 'mix it', as the sort of pretty football that both want to play won't wash in the Championship, especially if they get off to a bad start at this level, which both do. The green room also decides that football does not exist outside of the Championship – not that it exists outside of the Premier League, of course, but I point out that we could do something about that.

Alas, my ideas fall on deaf ears. We have a situation. Two floors up the chef is serving Thai chow mein. The green room empties quickly. Not wanting to cause a meltdown yet being equally curious to see what Thai chow mein looks like, I follow Manish and Lloyd. If Lloyd has been tweeting God about his knees it has worked. Despite that career-ending knee replacement he blazes a trail ahead towards the Thai chow mein.

Thai chow mein is suitably disappointing, as it turns out, and I return downstairs to the green room, unsure of the next steps. Nobody comes in, so I make more notes. I text, I Instagram. In desperation I call my mum, who tells me she's busy; it's Saturday, after all, did I forget? She has a life.

An hour later, Manish walks in and tells me that we should work out what we want to talk about in tonight's show. Who impressed me, who should we look out for, what was that Thai chow mein all about? Having made notes purely out of boredom earlier on, I can fill in his blanks, of which he seems to have many.

I know this, but I play ball. We should talk about 1, 2 and 3, I say, because of X, Y and Z.

'Good idea,' he says. 'I'll lead, and you jump in with your thoughts. See you in the studio.'

Fantastic.

The make-up girl comments that someone must have been talking about me as my ear is unashamedly red – did I sit in the chair that the interior designer insisted upon, she asks? I flirt with her unashamedly before confessing that yes, I did. She takes mercy on me, going to work on my ear until all I see in the mirror is one giant, beautifully manicured ear and nothing else. I am a former footballer with one big, beautiful manicured ear. I tell myself that it's no bad thing as I head towards the studio.

The studio is fucking freezing, and I make a point of telling that to the girl who seems to be in control of proceedings. Her excuse is that the colder the room, the less likely we are as pundits to sweat, thus giving the impression that we know what we're talking about. I point out that while that may be scientifically correct, I will not be held responsible for the unintentional etching on to the lens of the £100,000 crane camera should it come too close to my twin peak nipples. It remains cold.

I'm nervous, of course, but also determined to revolutionise the future of *The Football League Show*. This, despite the fact that the producer tells me it is highly likely that IMG will lose its contract at the end of the season, and all my work may be in vain. Even better, this now has 'saviour' potential.

I refer to my notes. Lloyd tells me that he prefers live production, like *Match of the Day* – not that I can recall ever seeing him on *Match of the Day* – because apparently, 'You can fuck up, and it's over, it's gone, whereas here you have to re-record it again.' Determined not to fuck up even a pre-recording, I do the honourable thing by forgetting the point that I'd wanted to make about Nottingham Forest after their highlights open the show, and duly fuck up.

It's not a problem immediately. 'Resetting,' cries the girl destined to be at IMG for life in one capacity or other, and the crane camera is reset. Manish and Lloyd don't appear to be too bothered. I tell myself that they are pros. Then, in the next intro, Manish fucks up. I cheer inside and joke that he's put me out enormously and that I'll have to call the taxi firm to put the car back.

The make-up girl steps forward but it turns out that 'touch up' doesn't have the same meaning as it does inside a football changing room. I flirt, nonetheless, by pretending to bite her brush when it comes too near to my mouth. I've done it before, why wouldn't it work again? It doesn't. Well, what about my red ear?

Lloyd ventures an opinion that *The Football League Show* would be far better served if it were broadcast live. By that he means that we could have been out of here two hours ago. We rattle through the rest of the professional football pyramid with myself and Manish each messing up only once more before the producers in the technical room opposite our studio call our performance a wrap. It's just as well because the girl destined to spend her life at IMG points out that we've finished with only 15 minutes to spare before the end of *Match of the Day*'s live broadcast.

Even so, it turns out that I'm not finished.

According to those who know about these things, should the master tape have an epileptic fit halfway through its transmission then we'll have to cut back to live in the studio, which means we can't go home right now – instead, we'll have to watch the show back in real time on the off chance that something goes wrong. The show finishes and it's a race for those of us who don't have to stay behind because they've nowhere else to go to jump in a pre-booked cab. I've been out since midday. My take for the day is £600. I get home and rest my head next to my wife, who is keen to know how things have gone despite the hour hand fast approaching the number three. She gets an answer, bless her. 'Fuck that,' I say.

Now, £600 a day is a lot of money for most people, but not when you have two boys who wanted you to take them to their first football match on a Saturday, and you don't need the money. I'm sorry, but that's just how it is, I'm afraid.

I got a little stick when I told my friends, family and agent that I wanted to retire from football two years early, but that was nothing compared to the shit I took from the same people when I said that punditry just wasn't for me.

But I know I'm right. And now when I look at *Match of the Day* and I see some of the guys on there that I've no respect for, I think that at least that isn't me. I didn't have to resort to that. I made it out alive, barely. But here I am.

And then I see those who have lost everything, players who have put a shift in and been hammered off the back of one bad deal brought about by retrospective government legislation. I was told that Danny Murphy owes £2.5 million to the taxman. Been there, got Danny's T-shirt. I don't want to be that guy any more. After *The Football League Show* I decided that, while I could do punditry, it wasn't going to be the enthralling post-football career that I was after.

As a pundit you have to be prepared to be despised in every changing room up and down the country unless, of course, you're Gary Neville. Players who go into punditry do so for any number of selfish reasons (listed below), which make them appear to us as players left behind, or as less than authentic.

1. The pundit doesn't know what to do with himself post-football and is scared of mixing it in the real world so says things that are overtly safe so as not to upset anybody (Jermaine Jenas, Martin Keown, in fact, you can take your pick)

2. The pundit doesn't know what to do with himself post-football and is scared of mixing it in the real world so says things that are likely to cause social-media storms which are good for ratings (Robbie Savage)

3. The pundit has financial problems and needs the job badly (Danny Murphy)

4. The pundit is after a managerial job. Punditry is, after all, the managers' shop window (Neil Lennon)

5. The pundit is just too big a name not to have on the TV, regardless of the fact that he isn't very good at the job (Thierry Henry)

6. The pundit has played for Liverpool, which is important in the media world after the *Sun*'s atrocious lies in respect to the Hillsborough disaster (Jamie Redknapp, Jamie Carragher, Danny Murphy, Mark Lawrenson, Alan Hansen)

The rest of the playing fraternity sort of hover around the edges looking for an opening, or aren't overly fussed and dip their toe in when they can be bothered. That said, punditry – good punditry – is an art form. You need to be succinct, fresh, and remember your media training that says in big bold capital letters which are underlined and in italic: *TRY TO START A SENTENCE WITH 'I REMEMBER WHEN'*. Seriously. Roy Keane is a master, Souness is brilliant and, to be fair, Jamie Redknapp has worked out how to fill in around the anchor and the co-pundits with surprising dexterity.

Back to me. I had other offers, offers that all seemed to want me to lace my boots again and enter the arena one last time.

Having been a Premier League player means that, even if you are falling back down the leagues, the other players will hold you in awe for having made the holy land. They will hang on to your every story. If you have played in the Premier League then you always have some currency in the game.

And it isn't just the players. My neighbour – a rich businessman with Indian connections, who arrived in our little corner of the countryside a few years ago with his wife, children and about £250 million in his pocket – is equally in awe of my Premier League link.

The association with the Premier League is something that stays with players their whole life, and that continually leads to new opportunities. Recently, I was offered the chance to play in the newly formed Indian Super League. I trundled over to my neighbour's country pile to discuss the pros and cons of playing football for 12 weeks in the subcontinent. 'My friend,' he began, 'you must go. India is a joy; in fact, I will come with you! We will go together and you will see what an incredible place it is.'

At first glance the concept of the Indian Super League looked impressive. The marquee players plying their trade that year included the legendary Alessandro Del Piero, Luis García, the former Liverpool player, Frenchmen Robert Pires, David Trezeguet and Nicolas Anelka, and the one-time Manchester City midfielder, Elano.

The list of men tasked with managing these former stars was equally impressive. Legends such as World Cup winner Marco Materazzi, and the mercurial Brazilian forward, Zico, to name but two. Peter Reid is also there. And then there is the player/manager of my would-be club, the Kerala Blasters, David James.

A critical factor in my decision over an Indian journey came when I was told that David James would be my manager.

Most people who knew him from the game here told me the former England keeper was notoriously difficult to get on with – that's putting it politely, anyway. I preferred to work on the basis that he must, in fact, have a brain, because that is generally the reason why other players write off somebody who pronounces their 't's.

Two years ago I went to visit a couple of investors in Iceland and happened to bump into James. At the time I was told that he was in Iceland to fast-track his coaching badges while playing for Hermann Hreidarsson's team, ÍBV. After the game, we all got incredibly drunk with the rest of the ÍBV team, and the two of us began talking about a range of subjects, where neither of us could find any common ground whatsoever. I suggested to him that he always took the opposite view to mine just to be difficult and, in fairness to him, he stuck out his bottom lip in a way that suggested Sigmund Freud had just defined him perfectly. The truth of the matter is that David James has got a brain and he is incredibly difficult to get on with. When I returned to the UK, the Icelanders invested, James did not. If he was about to go bankrupt, he did an unbelievable job of hiding it.

But there were other factors to consider. I'm not on the level that the players just mentioned are at; there are rumours of payments in the region of half a million pounds. My payment was to be £60,000. I deducted the tax, took into account the 12 weeks away from the family, factored in a bout of inevitable Delhi belly and chewed over the advice given to me by security, that it would be best for me not to stray too far from the hotel after training.

The conduit for the deal was an agent who gently nudged me towards the decision that he clearly wanted me to take. 'Don't forget,' he said, 'you're their first choice.' That only means something if it comes from, say, Alex Ferguson as the manager of Manchester United. Any player would sign immediately, but not in this case. More thought was needed. 'That £60,000,' I said. 'Is that tax free?'

It was a fair question. 'Well, no it isn't,' came the reply. 'But, you know, you can ask to be paid in cash, and then just make a few trips back and forth to India taking a bit home with you at a time in a suitcase.'

Decision made. For those of you who have read my previous books, you will know that the taxman and I get on about as well as bare feet stumbling around in the dark on smashed glass. The last thing I need is a knock at the door from those arseholes. So, I politely declined, as did the next player on the list, Chris Iwelumo, before eventually the club that I was due to sign with turned to the former Newcastle and Ipswich striker, Michael Chopra, who himself has an Indian father.

So when I told my rich Indian friend that I'd declined the Kerala Blasters offer and wouldn't be travelling to work in his native India, he looked at me slightly saddened and certainly offended. Putting his hand on my shoulder in the kind of patronising way that only mega-wealthy people can, he said to me, 'My friend, you have made a bad choice. India is a wonderful, wonderful country, and you ought to see its beauty with your own eyes.'

All of which left a very large and awkward-looking Indian elephant in the room. If it's so great over there, why are you living over here, mate?

In retirement it turns out that nearly every room has an elephant in it. You are a former professional footballer. Not a professional footballer. You might have a lot of money, but it is the same money that everybody else has. In fact, you are the same as everybody else. That is fucking crushing news.

6. HOW TO BUILD A FOOTBALL CLUB

Not long into retirement and I am exhausting the possibilities one by one. I've been burning up and shredding good ideas until there is almost nothing left. Some of the ideas were OK, provided that you liked the lifestyle that went with them. Living in the US on $60,000 a year in some place like Kansas and playing MLS? Well, only if somebody would pay for a lobotomy beforehand.

Most of the ideas were not what you would risk uprooting your wife and kids for. Eventually, I made the decision to at least stay put and concentrate on building up a few businesses, including the one that brokered deals to buy football clubs. I also had the small agency business, with a few decent players and the one really good player, who I liked and cared about. Time to be getting on with that work.

It's funny. Like all footballers I spent a good part of my playing days complaining. In fact, I like to think I spent more time than most complaining. I was a very good complainer, versatile and quick and imaginative. I could have complained for England, but I never got picked. Bastards. And yet now that it's over I'm going to hang around in football for at least some of my time – at least as long as the business of owning or running a football club interests me and remains a realistic possibility.

The Secret Footballer hereby announces his campaign to become the Secret Chairman. Financial backers, please form an orderly queue. Right now, the idea of running a football club interests me for all sorts of reasons. There are practices in football that I have complained about for years and I want to see if my ideas work. There are ways of running a football club which can make the club a vital and enjoyable part of the lives of the people who work for the club, and who support and live close to it.

So, am I a fit and proper person to run a football club? The bar hasn't been set too high, but that's the first test. The fit and proper persons test. There are key issues here, a bit of box-ticking required. You have to provide 'proof of funds'. That's obviously an easy one. If you haven't been struck off at Companies House, or whatever the Russian equivalent is, if you're still a friend of Putin and have the Christmas cards to prove it, you're in. And from there it takes off. Questions about this and that. One long exercise in official arse-covering. There is one thing we know: 90 per cent of the time in football, when clubs are being bought, it's a case of, 'Well, you either sell to me or you've got an administration on your hands. You know what will look worse. Do you want an administration?'

Bring it down to this level for a second. Stewards don't do enough at football matches. They are just a bunch of high-visibility jackets placed around a stadium like scarecrows in a field. I've been on the bench when someone's been called 'black cunt' from just behind us. That was at West Ham. It came from a West Ham fan and it was directed at Carlton Cole. Everyone heard it. No steward moved a muscle. Stewards won't ever do anything about it. Nothing whatsoever.

Why? When you've got a brand like the Premier League, what looks worse? A racial insult that you can't hear on TV and which the people around you are happy to ignore? Or a load of men in high-vis jackets, seen by millions around the world, wading into the stands? The steward turns; he sees a big ugly skinhead. He knows he should do something. Even worse, he might see a man with a shirt and tie and glasses and a foul, racist mouth, and a lawyer who will sue anybody who lays a finger on him. Again he should do something. But 99 times out of 100 the steward will say, 'OK, I didn't hear that, so nothing has happened.'

Not at my club. Not a chance.

It is almost the same when a football club is going to go into administration. They'll find the best of a bad bunch of interested parties and do the deal with them. Anybody with enough money and decent lawyers will pass the fit and proper persons test. The selling club may know that they are selling the club to a group of chain-smoking sharks who will asset-strip the club and leave it for dead, but there is a brand to be thought of. The fit and proper persons test is all that stops both sides from shaking hands on the deal and appearing on the front page of the local newspaper. It is the only calming mechanism.

It doesn't look good for the FA or the Premier League to throw spanners into the works. The FA or the Premier League are reluctant to become that steward in the high-vis jacket. Interference just creates more problems at emotive times. We've all seen what happens when clubs go into administration. It hurts. And the result is that a lot of big-footed clowns end up running football clubs. It's always Red Nose Day somewhere in English football. Blame gets tossed around for this, but the blame stops at the top.

As it happens, despite this pessimistic view of the world, there is the Championship club we have taken a look at. A good club. I like the club. (Looks bashful.) But ...

As a rule of thumb the more debt a club has, the harder it is to sell. This particular club has been loaded like a pack mule with debt.

But then what if the club has assets which will be realised in a year's time, maybe two years. Well, you can always load it up with debt to ward others off, and if you sell you leave the debt to somebody else and treat it as pre-payment to yourself for the assets.

With this club the projections for developing the land around it are £60–80 million net profit after spending between £25 and £30 million. The club haven't got £25 million. Which is why they're having to bring in a third party to help pay for the development before splitting the proceeds with them – most likely a developer. They've already got planning for a small town on the land around the stadium. They've not got the money to build it, though, and the planning permission only lasts for five years.

So the club is being saddled with loans in order for the existing owners to take their profit without laying a brick. Which means that any would-be owner who comes in and wants to rescue the football side of the club has to pay off the debts that have nothing to do with football. It also ensures that nobody will buy the football club purely to develop the land, because there is so much debt in the club side of the business. 'But?,' I hear you ask, 'how are they going to pay the debt back, then?' They're not. That's the point. They're going to develop the land with borrowed money, take the profit and piss off back to the other side of the world and leave the club in administration. I know it, everyone knows it. I feel like a white knight riding to the rescue. Except, when I get to the gates, the princess herself won't let me in. It's a bizarre place to be in. Maybe if I had £25 million ...

So a football club is being killed by people who breezed through the fit and proper persons test with no regard at all for the actual club itself. I would love nothing more than to take that club into the Premier League, to sit in the various boxes and wage war against everything that is bluff and phoney in the big league. I'd love to watch the club win every week, and for the club to have the balls to plan to win the Premier League in my lifetime. I want a football club for the purposes of football.

You can't quantify that in the fit and proper persons test, though. We all like to sit around and pretend that what is happening in football is not really happening, but you know we're not going to settle it with names and ticks in boxes.

Do you think 'clowns' is a harsh characterisation? Probably not if you follow a club closely. Put it this way. Of the 92 league clubs, how many would have coherent five- or 10-year plans? Of the 92, how many of those plans include trying to win the Premier League within 10 years? Six maybe? Liverpool want to win it – Arsenal, Man United, Chelsea, Man City. One other maybe? I don't think that Tottenham want it. And I love Tottenham. I think their sole purpose is to stay up there, qualify for the Champions League, and get into a new stadium – so that's them out of the title race for at least five years. Everton don't want to win it either, but the reason I respect Bill Kenwright so much is that he's not going to sell the club to just anybody.

The rest of the Premier League comprises just a different set of business plans, really. Some good, some bad. None of the clubs are overly ambitious or imaginative. No business plan relates to becoming a top team at the pinnacle of the Premier League. And no matter how astute some of these plans are, for the most part everything revolves around a series of lucky coin tosses. Look at Swansea. They have done well. If you ask the owners about it, they are going to say, 'Well, the reason that we actually flipped 10 heads in a row is because we've got this special system for coin tossing. We are good at it.'

Bullshit. You have so many people out there trying to flip the 10 in a row that somebody is going to do it. It happens, and you say, 'Yeah, we have a strategy; we want to play football on the floor, we're going to try to get a manager who plays that way. We have a club ethos.'

That's not fucking business, guys. It's luck. You brought in a manager who chose to play a certain way and when it worked and he left you thought, 'Well, that worked – let's get another one like that.' Three coin tosses right there, and you're looking for that manager at a time when Brendan Rodgers is available. Another toss right there. If one of those guys becomes available at the wrong time, and the players don't respond to what you view as a reasonable alternative, you could be on the way down.

That might be the Swansea thing at the end of the day. Close but no cigar. Swansea do things right. I admire that. But luck is part of the deal too.

The thing is, I know how to 'make' a football club, as the Americans might say. I have a clear conviction of what makes a successful football club. Of course, I have to start with the raw ingredients. The Premier League is coveted by some of the richest financial vehicles and highest net-worth individuals in the world and, as such, that largely rules my consortium out – but even so, there are no bargains in the Premier League. Whenever a new TV deal is announced, owners come out of the woodwork. In February 2015, the Premier League announced that it had agreed a new three-year deal worth £5,136 billion, a jump of 71 per cent from the last deal in 2012. Sky alone will pay £11.7 million per match for 126 live games. The numbers are fucking outrageous, to be honest, and if these were companies in the FTSE 100 that didn't have 'FC' after the name, all of them would be snapped up by the biggest companies in the world. The proof is in the pudding. Less than a week after the announcement, West Bromwich Albion chairman, Jeremy Peace, reported a pre-tax profit of £14.7 million while claiming, 'I said then that I was open to proposals regarding investment in the club and would not stand in the way of a new owner, providing they convinced me their intentions for the club were in keeping with its traditions and values and their ability to deliver on them was realistic.'

Shameless, isn't it? That's probably why Jeremy Peace brought in Tony Pulis. Regardless, Peace is a businessman and he has a point. The numbers in the Premier League largely outstrip anything that any bear market can achieve anywhere in the world. And for that reason, it is not the place to be for me on day one. Because to stay in it, you have to bet big, and failure doesn't just mean that you lose your stake, it means that you lose your shirt. I was always told that in business it is far better to use somebody else's money to achieve success. That's what I plan to do, and in football the easiest way of doing that is to go for TV money. But in order to do so you need to have your house in order first.

West Brom achieved their success by stockpiling cash against a solid Championship team that were forever being promoted and relegated to and from the Premier League.

And that's something like what I want to do. What I want to achieve with my chosen Championship club is a cross-pollination of West Brom and Stoke City. The truth is that you never know quite how well (or badly) things are going to go once you reach the Premier League. Sometimes a manager will put a team together that punches well above its weight, but sometimes they just about cling on to survival. Somewhere in between? Well, there lies the happy hunting ground. And after that, there lies the chance of glory, real glory.

In the Championship we struggle with that most subjective and most difficult of terms to quantify: value. I confess here and now that I am a fan of the principle of 'moneyball'. That is to say, I believe – no, I know for a fact – that players who have been overlooked, undervalued or underappreciated by the biggest teams in the land can be found every year in the lower leagues, and that with the right management, board structure and philosophy, it is possible to assemble a team that is capable of winning promotion to the Premier League. Easily. It all depends on putting the right people in the right places. So let me tell you how I will structure my football club based on what I know about this thing of ours, and depending on whether I can pull this off.

7. A-Z: THE MAGICAL MYSTERY TOUR HITS BURNLEY

BURNLEY

Listen, this seemed like a good idea when I made up the draft structure of this book. I'd stroll down memory lane, as they say on *Football Focus* when it is FA Cup third-round day. I'd cough up a few memories and anecdotes from every club in the Premier League (Burnley were still in there when I embarked on this), then tie each of them to the main themes that run through professional football. Twenty hairballs. Each would be a little insight into what it is like to play against the great and the good and the damned. I thought these might be pages that a young player could browse through, pages that give an impression of the country ahead. A kind of *Lonely Planet Guide to Professional Football*. They would contain the things I tell the kids in my agency so that their eyes will be open, in either wonder or fear. Then I got to Burnley.

I don't think I'd sense there was anything missing from football if Burnley weren't around any more. If I went away for five years and came back and Burnley had disappeared, it would take me quite a while to notice. And unless there was a funny story attached to the disappearance of an entire town and its football club, it would take even longer for me to care. That said, if I return 20 years from now and discover that Turf Moor is still there, I can guarantee that nothing will have changed.

It's not personal, Burnley. Some clubs are like that. If you woke me in the morning and told me that Coventry City had vanished I'd be back to sleep in seconds, smiling to myself about never having to hear another word about the time they won the FA Cup.

I'm not sure if Burnley have ever won the FA Cup. I could Google it right now but really I don't want to know. I don't care. I don't dislike Burnley. The club just means nothing to me. I get a deep sense of depression when I go there (Blackburn, too). We go through the moors looking at these little stone houses, and I gaze out the window wondering who exactly would live there. I know that when I have played at Turf Moor it has always been cold. Burnley is the town that global warming forgot. If it's always a rainy night in Georgia, well, it's generally a cold Tuesday night in Burnley. And one of our players always picks up an injury. There are no great injuries, but at Turf Moor we always get the injuries you hate to get on a freezing cold Tuesday. Always.

When I imagine the place I imagine fog, but maybe that's just the name. Turf Moor is hardly inviting, is it? You have your moor and … it's got turf. I have bad dreams about a movie called *Werewolves of Turf Moor*. I get ligament damage while being chased by werewolves. The werewolves are from Ukip, and I'm shivering like a shitting dog.

I know when we ran out there it was always cold and the blunt racism rolled down over us from the stands like it was an expression of local culture. Once, during local elections there, the parties of reason flooded the place with a leaflet showing the local townhall decorated with a huge swastika. They asked, 'Is this what you want?' A few days later the population elected six British National Party candidates. That's not the club's fault, of course, but you get the sense of a place where it is still 1973 in diversity terms. It's a strange kind of ignorance. It's not the racism that you might expect from, say, Millwall fans; it's more like your nan's. 'How's the new helper, Nan?' 'She's very good, thank you, dear. For a darkie anyway.'

They play hard in Burnley, and I imagine the words 'southern' and 'softie' are never far from their minds. They don't do flash.

They hit the Premier League by establishing a settled side in the Championship. Having slid back out of the Premier League I reckon they'll still stick with the management of Sean Dyche. They ain't pretty, either of them, but they seem good for each other. Dyche, in particular, is a guy who will carve out a career managing clubs like your Watfords and your Burnleys. Even though he appears to know the game, you get the sense that he will never be afforded a top job – it's almost as if Burnley have that effect on a manager. I should imagine that he'll end up in Cardiff one day, or maybe Blackburn or Leeds.

But Burnley have continued to do what they know how to do, even in the big league. I think they have enough self-belief to stick to that formula if they go down again.

One of the clubs I played for is always described as 'friendly' and 'welcoming' whenever they crop up in conversation. I hate that. It's about winning. Not being 'friendly' and 'welcoming'. No such problem for Burnley: they are hard and hostile and nobody likes going there. Turf Moor isn't very friendly or welcoming. The pitch slopes alarmingly and the changing rooms are shocking, with a couple of bloody awful, pathetic, dripping showers next to one of the old fashioned-style deep baths that now serves as a physio area to massage players before the match. If you wanted to fill that bath it would take you a thousand years. I didn't like going there and, when I come to think of it, that's a good thing. For Burnley, that is a huge 'win'.

CHELSEA

Given the choice, I'm with Elvis Costello. I don't wanna go to Chelsea.

To be precise, I don't want to go to Stamford Bridge. The bus can drive in and leave you by the dressing-room door. Fine. But the tunnel is so narrow that even when you lubricate the outside of the bus and drive down the track, when you come to get out the wall is just ... there, in your face. And you've got that big fucking mirror hanging off the bus, so you have to sort of squeeze yourself underneath and walk down to the changing room. There are also fans wandering around the buses, and there is a stairwell bringing people up to the stand. Basically, you are going to get spat on. I always expect the worse with fans, always. And I expect the very worst with Chelsea fans. They never disappoint.

I dislike Chelsea. I dislike the way they play. I dislike their owner. I dislike their fat layer of celebrity fans and, most of all, I dislike John Terry. I hated playing against Chelsea. I think they are bullies in almost everything they do.

Other than that? I don't mind them. Didier Drogba makes up for a lot. Didier Drogba is one of the greatest players I've ever played against.

Success has to be instant at Chelsea. Just add hot water. When I look at Chelsea players I wonder how they would fare in other sides. What would Eden Hazard be like at Barca? But he's not at Barca, he's at Chelsea, playing in this Mourinho-devised chess game. Chelsea buy players and make them into the players Mourinho wants them to be. That's fine, but I just find it a little soul crushing, because lurking in nine-tenths of them is a great player.

A few years ago, hopscotching around the Continent like the great *boulevardier* that I am, I touched down in Denmark. I was accompanying a friend, the chief scout of a Premier League side, who was taking a look at a kid playing football. Andreas Christensen was turning out for Brøndby. Every big club in Europe was giving him come hither looks and sticking large denomination notes into the waistband of his shorts while finding out how to pronounce Brøndby. He was young, maybe 15, and he had played for the Danish under-17 side already. He was six feet tall and elegant and he looked like a footballer. He played well. We were impressed. We kept an eye on him as all the big boys gathered around him like he was a bitch in heat.

I noticed the other day that it's now over three years (February 2012) since Christensen signed with Chelsea on a free transfer. The word in football then, and now, is that he signed for £20,000 a week, but I've never seen his wage slip. The kid moved from Denmark to London. Not long afterwards André Villas-Boas moved out of the manager's office in Stamford Bridge. Three years later and Chelsea have told Andreas Christensen that he is needed for the senior side just twice. A League Cup game against mighty Shrewsbury and an FA Cup game against Bradford. He was played out of position, at right-back, on both occasions. The FA Cup game is the more celebrated of his appearances. Bradford won 4–2 at the Bridge. Chelsea coughed up a two-goal lead. Mourinho called the whole evening a disgrace. You had to laugh – unless you were Andreas Christensen.

Christensen looks at John Terry, the splintery old warhorse, and sees not just a centre-half who won't go away but also the last player to come through Chelsea's youth system and become an established player in the first team. It was 1998 when Terry made his breakthrough. Christensen looks around and sees brave old John Terry and his sidekick Gary Cahill, plus Branislav Ivanović and Kurt Zouma, then Nathan Aké – all of them hanging around every morning looking for a start in a central defensive position that he is last on the list for. When Terry finally has to be humanely destroyed they won't be chanting Christensen's name at the Bridge, demanding that he be allowed time to settle into the team. They'll be telling José to get his hand into Roman's arse pocket and keep it there till he has a wad big enough to buy a world-famous centre-back. And then maybe Christensen will go on loan to Bolton or Wigan or somewhere and start his career for real with a big payoff from Chelsea to supplement the inevitable wage drop. 'Sorry about that one, old boy. No hard feelings, eh?'

It's a football career, but not as most of us know it.

For every player like Kurt Zouma, who Chelsea are bringing through now, there are hundreds of kids beneath that whom they've shafted. Christensen may go on to become the new John Terry – they haven't cut him adrift yet – but how difficult has it been for this kid to come from Denmark on £20k a week with a couple of European Cup winners in front of him in the team? The kid took most of the risk. He would have been better off at Dortmund or Hamburg or Schalke for a few seasons and playing games. Then move. Kids are becoming almost willing to forego four years of playing for a chance at the long shot. It's become a business decision. Not football as we understand it.

For Chelsea, getting their way is an institutional reflex. Of all the teams that I've played against, Chelsea were the team who could influence the referee the most. They are an intimidating bunch, and at the time they had players like Terry, Lampard, Ballack and Alex – big, big guys with a very intimidating manager behind them who backed them unequivocally.

What I will say, begrudgingly, is that the recruitment at Chelsea is some of the best I've ever witnessed. The players who come into the club seem to hit the ground running – from Michael Essien and Ballack, to Cahill, César Azpilicueta and Hazard. There are notable exceptions, of course, Torres being the most obvious, but that is what happens when an owner gets involved in transfers beyond paying the fee. It is rare for somebody to get to the first team and then lose his place, and that is down to the fact that José Mourinho prefers the same 11 every week where possible.

So well done on that. Otherwise I don't have even a modicum of admiration for Chelsea. John Terry slipping over and missing what would have been the winning penalty in a Champions League final remains a highlight of my career and I wasn't even playing – though I guess that does kind of put my career into perspective somewhat.

CRYSTAL PALACE

I once had a chat with Steve Parish and Neil Warnock, who had for some reason both turned up to the launch of an outpost of a company that I'd invested in. I had met Neil's son in Sheffield on a night out and he'd scared me to death. He was, in all honesty, a total walking, talking bomb scare – and he was trying to latch on to anyone who had an interest in the fact that his dad was Neil Warnock.

At this particular shindig, a friend of mine – the founder of the company – and myself had sought them out. Having started our football agency I had bent Neil's ear on the player I wanted him to sign (our skilful prodigy).

'Sounds interesting,' said Neil. 'How old?'

'Eighteen,' I replied, without blinking.

Cue fits of laughter from Warnock. 'He's no good for me then, is he?!'

The truth is that he wasn't. Neil was 65 years old and was at Palace to keep them in the Premier League, and no talented 18-year-old from the leagues below was going to do that. I knew that but, with his chairman standing next to us, it was the perfect time to test his mettle. Parish was interested. I could tell just by looking at his facial expressions. Warnock, obviously, was not.

It is interesting to me that a kid, particularly one as good as this kid, has his career dictated, to a certain extent, by the age of managers and the reason that they are at a particular club. I can recall Bobby Robson, who at 68, when he was the manager of Newcastle United, signed Jermaine Jenas for £5 million and said, 'We have 14 players here who are 22 or under, like Hughes, Bellamy, Ameobi, Cort and Dyer. I might not see the best of Jermaine; I bought him for the next manager, in a way.' When was the last time you heard a manager say something like that? Right now, I could do with a legend like Bobby to talk to.

What did come out of that fleeting meeting was an interesting sideshow, and proof that in some cases the longevity of a manager can be a good thing and the short-lived tenure of some managers can be a curse. For the second time in a year, Parish went on to sack a manager who was not going to back the budget that Palace were committed to, which involved bringing in kids coming through the ranks to subsidise the first team. In fairness to Warnock, his was a bad appointment by Parish in the first place – but Warnock was hardly about to turn down the chance of a Premier League job at 65, and I couldn't blame him for that.

At least that's how I read the situation, but with Palace you never know. Palace are an odd club and they like being that way. Everybody hates going there. The tunnel under the Thames is awful and ominous. Everything about the place is awful. You come in on a coach and have to park in the stadium; the fans are buzzing around, abusing you. The tunnel narrows on to the pitch and is only big enough for one at a time – suddenly you're jostling to get in front of the player you were standing next to a moment ago. And then you get out on to the grass and there is immediate abuse from the right-hand side, soon heard in stereo from all sides. Kids are giving you the wanker sign. Or sticking their hands out to shake or high-five you before pulling their hands away at the last second. No thanks. You engage with it, you're a wanker. You don't do it, you're a wanker. You call them a wanker, you're a wanker.

Palace always produce really good young talented individuals. They never seem able to hang on to them, though. But that's OK because it's all part of the plan. If they lose those players, the players themselves never seem to do so well else-where. It's like Palace have a spell on them. The Palace fans are great to their own. They love their own. A lively bunch of fans if you play for them. If not, well, it's not a surprise that the place where Eric Cantona chose to deliver his kung-fu kick was Selhurst Park.

Palace have always smacked of the difference that exists between winning football matches at home and winning away. I've been to Selhurst Park as a young player, think-ing the experience would be like the image they give off – a slightly groovy, progressive and friendly club. I've gone there and been abused for 90 minutes and come away wonder-ing just what goes on there. How had I ever offended them? In the years that Palace achieve something their home form plays a key role – as the fans get louder and more excitable, the place doesn't exactly become a fortress but it's certainly harder to leave with three points. But, in most years, if you take them a mile or two up the road then the fight dribbles out of them. The fixture list comes out and you look at it and bank on beating them three or four nil when they come to you, and hope you'll get a draw when you go there.

That's Crystal Palace – more a state of mind than a football club.

8. UNDERSTANDING TSF ROVERS

Let's deal with something that cuts to the heart of the relationship between fans and the people working for a club. As an owner it can sometimes be prudent not to tell the fans and those people on the outside, such as the media, why you have taken certain decisions. And that is tough because fan engagement is crucial – the fans, if they're on your side, really can be the 12th man. But, trust me, there are times when you are better off not knowing ...

Sometimes, things work in football in the way that they do because ... they just do. No one said it had to make any sense. To that end, it's like any job – if I walked on to the building site where my father works and tried to help him put a roof on a house, I'm sure I'd be asking something along the lines of, 'Wouldn't this be twice as fast and so much easier, and less dangerous, if the whole thing was assembled on the ground and then lifted on to the brickwork in one piece?' And, in the heat of a busy day, he wouldn't take the time to say, 'Well, we do it like this because of X, Y and Z.'

No. He'd say, 'Stop asking stupid fucking questions. We've been doing it like this for a hundred years. Are you going to walk in here and tell us we're doing it all wrong? What do you know about it?'

We know that football doesn't work like any other business, but that doesn't mean it doesn't evolve like a business. After all, a good idea is a good idea, no matter who has it. But there are some things that are the way they are because experience tells us that it is the thing to do. We have examples of it, but we palm the fans off with, 'I've played and you haven't.' So here goes, and I fully expect a wrath of shit from the people on the outside for what I'm about to tell you.

There's a lot of criticism right now of the Southampton academy for going after players who are predominantly young, white centre-midfield players who can control a game of football.

Dirty little secret: there is a fundamental mistrust among managers and white players over the ability of black players to dictate the tempo of football matches. Now, you might be sitting there reading this book, thinking, 'Well, black players can do anything that white players can do.' That is a perfectly natural reaction, but, at least as we sit here today, it's hard to find the evidence to support that.

We debate why there are so few black managers and so few black owners or chairmen. Look at the pitch. Look at the dynamics of team selection and how teams are put together and why they are the way they are. All the answers are right in front of you.

The black players you see on the pitch are either quick, strong or athletic, or they don't feature. They are certainly not trusted to have the key attributes needed to dictate the tempo of a game. Now, think about all the teams in the world and look at their midfield? Who are the tempo players? Oh yeah, they're not black, are they? Even Manchester United let Paul Pogba go because they preferred white players who knew how to dictate the tempo of a game. Pogba doesn't know how to control a game like Roy Keane and Paul Scholes once did; like Juan Mata, Ander Herrera or Michael Carrick do now – he just does his own thing, and is brilliant at doing it. But with Juventus, where Pogba is currently pulling up trees, it's the 35-year-old Andrea Pirlo next to him who's been tugging the strings.

There aren't many black players who dictate the tempo of a game. Name one. Now. Quick. You see? Possibly Yaya Touré, but then there are always exceptional exceptions, and his job is profoundly easier with David Silva and Samir Nasri around him. Touré being at his best in a 4–4–2 formation? Never happening in a million years.

Managers in the modern game just do not trust black players in certain roles – and the tempo-controlling midfielder, the most important position in the game relative to how the team plays, is the role in which black players are trusted the least. There is a line in the cult movie, *White Men Can't Jump*: 'A white player wants to win first and look good second; a black player wants to look good first and win second.' In modern football, there is a sort of managers' illuminati that believes the saying to be truer today than it ever was.

Dictating the tempo of the game requires absolute concentration, 100 per cent of the time. There's nothing to say black players can't do this, but there's no question that today – and this has been the case since time immemorial – black players are not recognised in football for that skill. It requires the ability to recognise when to speed the game up and when to slow the game down which, in turn, requires the individual to spot all the warning signs on the pitch. Things like, if a bad tackle has gone in, who might be looking for revenge; do I need to keep the ball away from that side of the pitch? Or recognising when the game plan of the opposition has changed and what needs to be done to counter it. Maybe it is recognising when your team is on top and the opposition back four can't get their breath, so ball recycling becomes key in trying to capitalise on that. All these things come down to a player who can speed up or slow down the game as required. In football, managers look at black players as having one gear: breakneck speed.

Still don't believe me? Let's look at the clubs on the world stage, starting at home in the Premier League. At Chelsea you have Cesc Fàbregas, Nemanja Matić and Oscar, any one of whom can dictate the tempo of a game, though it is important to remember that holding midfielders aren't always the players dictating the tempo. Occasionally Mourinho will play Kurt Zouma or John Obi Mikel in the holding role, but only because he fears the opposition. A good example of that occurred in the Capital One Cup final recently, where Chelsea could not dictate the tempo against a passing, flowing Spurs team, so they played Zouma in a holding role and shut up shop from the start, scoring the first goal from a set piece. Ramires' energy and athleticism just in front of Zouma eventually allowed Fàbregas the room to dictate the game as Spurs began to wilt, and the Spaniard went on to find the pass that picked out Diego Costa, who scored the second. The wings at Chelsea now have the look I'd expect of a top club: Juan Cuadrado has come in from Fiorentina and can play opposite Willian.

It's the same at Manchester United, where big money has been spent over the years on Carrick, Herrera, Mata and Rooney, all of whom can dictate the tempo of the game, with black players such as Ashley Young and Antonio Valencia using their athleticism on the wings. Ditto Arsenal. Aaron Ramsey, Jack Wilshere, Santi Cazorla and Mikel Arteta are the players tasked with setting the tempo, while Alex Oxlade-Chamberlain and Theo Walcott provide the fire on the wings. At Liverpool, Jordan Henderson and Philippe Coutinho will pick up dictating from Steven Gerrard, with Raheem Sterling and now Jordon Ibe, who will become a winger, offering speed and width. Mark my words, Ibe will work the wings.

Tottenham are doing the same, hastened by chairman Daniel Levy's shrewdness in keeping Spurs on the cusp of success and the arrival of Mauricio Pochettino. Gone are Jake Livermore and Tom Huddlestone, and in come players who directly influence the speed of the game in Christian Eriksen and Ryan Mason, while Andros Townsend, Danny Rose and Kyle Walker give pace to the wings. You might argue there's Mousa Dembélé and Paulinho but, again, those players, although employed in central midfield, do not dictate the ball – they are retrievers, ball winners; they add legs and strength.

None of this is a coincidence. It is true that the athleticism of black players is part of the equation, but the real reason this occurs time and again is down to an overwhelming distrust of black players when it comes to letting them use their brain to play football. One of my managers once told an entire changing room full of players, after an African player had kicked off, that he'd always thought of African players as 'a ticket-back-to-Africa short of putting a machete through someone's head'. And that mistrust is in place on the pitch too. Look across Europe: Xabi Alonso swapping places with the younger Toni Kroos, but essentially the same player; Paris Saint-Germain splashing money on Yohan Cabaye; Barcelona are gradually replacing Xavi, Iniesta and Sergio Busquets with Ivan Rakitić and Sergi Roberto. Atlético Madrid? Tiago and Gabi. Borussia Dortmund have one black midfielder out of 12 registered midfielders. I'd go to Italy, but with Roma and Lazio lying in second and third in Serie A respectively, I feel the decision is probably one of trust and blatant racism.

The position of centre-half is another place where that mistrust surfaces, arguably to an even greater extent given we're talking about the last line of defence. A manager still working in the game told me that he would never play two black centre-halves together as they had 'tunnel vision' and that 'you always need a white one to make sure the other one doesn't go wandering off'. I can promise you that he is by no means alone in that thought process – most managers, providing you can get an honest answer, would agree with that.

If you're looking for more evidence then look no further than the captains of Premier League clubs. A captain is a player who needs to be able to lead on the pitch, simultaneously looking after himself and sorting everybody else out. At the start of the 2014–15 season, 10 Premier League captains were centre-halves, six from midfield. There were four black captains, all playing at centre-half, and all of them playing alongside a white centre-half. These are just the bare facts of it. It's no coincidence to me.

People use this sort of statistic to hit football over the head with the racist card from time to time. I'm not naive enough to think that there is no racism in football. There is. But this attitude hasn't been consciously thought through; it just gets passed down the generations. And the positions of centre-half and ball-playing, tempo-dictating centre-midfielders go to white players because they are the ones trusted by managers to do those jobs; they are the ones with the best attributes for the job. Flip it on its head and which players have the best attributes for great wing play? It's generally black players in the Premier League, because the game is so fast and it is felt by managers that the black players have the best physical attributes for the job, and the least responsibility in terms of managing the game.

White players are used to dictating the game because, as managers see it, they are the brains, whereas black players provide the fire. If you don't believe me, you need look no further than one of the most commonly heard phrases in football, one universally used to describe young black players: 'Speedboat, no driver.' You'll hear that at one training ground or another, every single day of the week. That throwaway line refers to the fact that the young black players coming through are generally seen as being quick, with fast feet, but seemingly clueless about where to run or what their position should be at any given moment. They need a player who can tell them those things. So the black player goes to the wing where the white player in the middle can manage that part of his game for him.

Look at the kids being produced by Southampton: fast black wingers; ball-playing, tempo-dictating white central midfielders. Southampton's academy knows what it can sell and what the big-hitting clubs like Arsenal, Manchester United, Tottenham and Chelsea want to buy from them. It knows which kids need to be produced in which positions.

In the most successful teams that I have played for there has been a very obvious mix of white and black players, and nine times out of 10 it has been the white players who've taken the responsible roles in the team, while the black players have provided the fire, the brawn, the pace, the athleticism. Honestly it has. I remember back to all my teams, and that's just the way it was. Today, at the top level, it's exactly the same. There are diminutive forward players from South America, and lots of tempo-dictating midfielders from southern Europe. In between there are strong, pacey, direct and sometimes aggressive black players who make up the 11.

Now I've pointed that out, take a look at your own team. What do you see? Is there a reason they're doing well or not doing so well? Is there a reason why your manager never makes it to the top of the game? The managers at the top are those who look at the game in this level of detail and then execute that detail on the pitch, ruthlessly, in the squads they build and the teams they field. They don't get to the top by accident; they aren't lucky. They know what works, but you have to have the balls and the courage of your convictions to deploy it.

I like to think that the players who play are those who are the best for the job, but the players who are the best for the job are being bred right now specifically to do that job, because everyone in football knows who they want for the various positions.

We would all like to change the world, but in football there is always a game next Saturday; there is always a relegation or a promotion next May. You don't redesign the circle; you accept that, as circles go, it's a vicious one and you make the most of it.

So that's what the criticism of Southampton, behind the scenes in the game right now, is all about – but it is coming from people who don't understand the game in these terms.

Are Southampton doing anything wrong? You could argue that they know exactly what they are doing and that they have proved it time and again. They are producing great players whom the big clubs are buying, ready to go, perfectly suited to the role that they are trained for. In that regard, you might think that a lot of talent goes to waste, but you'd be wrong. Southampton are the top of the Christmas tree. They are the finishing school for an industry and a country that sees things the same way, often without even thinking about it. We're not racist but ... Asians fit here and blacks fit there and Eastern Europeans are just fine over there. You'll have an Asian accountant but you won't ask an Asian to tarmac your drive; black footballers and athletes but not in the boardroom or, say, on horseback; hard-working Eastern Europeans can get most places, but you can't trust them and the habits they learned in war-torn wherever. Aren't most of them gypsies anyway? It's the same in football – it's a painful evolution, and sometimes it doesn't make sense, but sometimes things are the way they are ... because that's just the way they are. Remember – and most footballers will say this – I've played and you haven't. I know things that you don't know, because I've been a footballer. That doesn't make me a better person, but because of books like this, you now know about it too.

SCOUTING

Here is what I'd like. In the brave new world at the club we will call TSF Rovers, I, TSF, am the chairman. But we'll start with the bottom of the pyramid, the broad foundation of the club.

The truth is that the youth team scouts, and those below them, simply sign the players who show above 'average' talent. From that moment on it is the job of the coaches to nurture that talent until such time as it is ideally suited to the first team. But regardless of whether or not the player ever makes a first-team appearance, it is imperative to remember that these players almost always have a monetary value. I learned that from one of the most respected scouts in the game.

In fact, sometimes players aren't even signed to play in the first team at all; they are signed to a Premier League club with the sole intention of being loaned out to the leagues below. The hope is that they do well and a transfer fee can be commanded. It is business. It is a side of football that exists because Premier League clubs can afford to scout way beyond the remit of the clubs they will eventually sell those same players to. They can bring players in who will never be good enough to play for them but will come for the prestige, and possibly on a free transfer.

I asked the very well-respected community manager of a well-known club if it was simply a free-for-all out there, in terms of attracting talent. I had assumed it was like the Wild West these days.

'No,' he replied, 'we have a gentlemen's agreement that works in a predetermined area. So we might consider our area to be 50 square miles, and our programmes work in that area. The programmes get the kids off the street and into roles within the club. Obviously we want them to be first-team players, but only so many can do that, so we show them what the football club can offer them behind the scenes too.'

'And does everybody respect the boundaries and keep to the gentlemen's agreement?' I asked

'Most of them,' he said, with a smirk.

At my club, the scouting network would be pivotal, integral to the entire club. And one thing about scouts who go out to watch the youngest of kids play is that they are cheap. They do a job that doesn't pay well because they love it – they love the buzz of finding an exceptional youngster and seeing how he progresses. Many of them are part-time and report to somebody in a full-time role at the club's academy, who then filters on to the chief scout, who, again, is paid way below what he ought to be.

I would like to elevate and develop the role of scouts. Players are property. They can bask in the glow of a brand. Former Arsenal youth, former Manchester United youth, and so on. The best scouts carry encyclopaedic knowledge in their heads. Information worth millions of pounds in any given year. Their loyalty and expertise is worth rewarding.

Unless you own a Chelsea or a United, in which case you sit down and say we need a midfielder and here's the best three in the world, which do we choose? Everywhere else, the most critical person in the whole show is the scout. The most underpaid and unappreciated, undervalued role in a football club is that of the really good scout. And the fact I've realised that at such a young age is something which gives me a huge amount of encouragement because, ultimately, it is the convictions of a few people in the box seats that make or break a football club. I may get a few things wrong as I go, but on the issue of scouting importance, I know I'm right.

It stands to reason that scouting networks work best once the philosophy of the club is put in place. At my club we will play football to win. Not like Barcelona or Arsenal, or even Swansea, where we never deviate even if we're losing, or if we're playing somebody we know can cause us problems given the way we play. We will play attractive football but we will evolve when and where we need to. To do that we need the right manager. We need somebody in the mould of José Mourinho.

MANAGER

Get yourself a manager like Sir Alex Ferguson. That's the key. That's all a club has to do. Actually, it's not as difficult as you might think. Essentially, a club has to lay down its ethos from day one. Once it does that, it becomes easier to find a manager who can work within that ethos. For example, there is no point employing David Moyes at Manchester United because he has played a brand of football with Everton that is the total antithesis of the style employed by Sir Alex Ferguson at Manchester United over a period of 25 years. What you want is someone who simply carries that style on with better players.

The truth is that we get bogged down with this word 'experience'. What good is rocking up to play at Chelsea for 10 years with the sole aim of drawing the match 0–0 if, as with Manchester United, you're expected to go there and win? You have no experience of the situation that is facing you. The point is that Ferguson built United from the ground up, and now the club is at a level where it demands a manager who is an expert in handling top-level football clubs. Any director in the United boardroom with an ounce of common sense should have seen that. It is no different to a business. You don't promote the bloke who has run a successful corner shop in the Isle of Wight to the position of CEO with Sainsbury's. Businesses should evolve, football clubs should evolve – they only regress with bad decision-making.

As I type these sentences today I remain incredulous at the notion that a top-level corporate board could have bestowed such a responsibility upon the shoulders of an utter novice – a man who had never won a title, had never won a cup, had no experience of what is needed to win a Champions League, had never managed world-class players, and was never expected to do any of the above at his former club anyway. It is just mind-boggling.

Ferguson was a ruthless genius, there is no doubt about it.

When I was a kid there was a TV show called *Fantasy Football League* hosted by the comedians David Baddiel and Frank Skinner. On that show they'd perform skits, sketches and songs, albeit on a budget, about the state of modern football. One of their songs featured a line – 'Old football, old football was rubbish, but not as bad as Andy Cole' – before showing footage of an Andy Cole miss. As kids, we thought

Andy Cole was shit, mainly because we were being fed this song and shown the misses. It was true that he'd miss a chance in almost every game, but that was the way he played – he was in it to win it, on the front line. As every coach I have ever played under would say to our strikers, good or bad, 'Make sure you're there to miss.' Which is another way of saying, 'You'll learn, you'll get better, we'll teach you, we'll worry when you stop appearing in goalscoring positions, because then we've all got a problem.'

We were wrong about Andy Cole. He went on to score 93 goals in 195 games for Manchester United, winning five Premier League titles, two FA Cups, and a Champions League winner's medal in the process. What I admire so much about Ferguson is that he didn't mess around when there was a deal to be done, especially if that deal took Manchester United forward in terms of the way that he wanted to play. He absolutely had the courage of his convictions when signing players that he felt, or was told, would push the barriers of English football: 'What we'd noticed at the time in English football was that defences were retreating back into their box, so we needed a striker who could play in the box, preferably two-footed, and Andy Cole was the perfect man,' proclaimed Ferguson. So fucking simple. Too simple for a lot of managers.

Andy Cole was a goalscorer for Newcastle United, a player who nobody on Tyneside ever believed would be sold, let alone to Manchester United. Kevin Keegan would later blow up in front of the Sky cameras, in part because he felt that Ferguson had pulled his trousers down over the sale of Cole, but it is also worth remembering that United paid a British transfer record of £7 million for Cole's services. And that was when £7 million was a joke figure in football, monopoly money.

What is great about that story is that it demonstrates not only Ferguson's absolute belief in his assessment of where English football was at tactically but, subsequently, his balls in breaking the British transfer record for a player he felt was best equipped to capitalise on the situation he'd identified. With great riches comes great responsibility, and as if to emphasise the point of complete confidence in one's own judgement, it is particularly telling that six years later, after Ferguson had taken Cole's best performances, he was able to sell him to Blackburn Rovers for £8 million.

Thus, Ferguson created a phenomenon that came to be known as 'the United effect'. It's very simple: bring a player in, take his best years, make him successful by winning trophies and, in doing so, put him on the map as a name. Thereafter, other clubs will want to drain all of the residual benefits of signing a player who has become a legend in the game. And it went on for years: Lee Sharpe to Leeds United, Dwight Yorke to Blackburn Rovers; Ruud van Nistelrooy and David Beckham to Real Madrid, Jaap Stam to Lazio (albeit a mistake) – loyalty lasts for as long as you can do the business on the pitch in the way that the manager wants.

David Beckham often calls Alex Ferguson his second dad. If you could get an honest answer out of Ferguson today regarding his feelings towards Beckham – and it is telling that many journalists have tried and failed – then you would probably hear a man tell you that Beckham was one of the best commodities that Manchester United ever had.

But even the greats lose it. I was the first writer in the game to level the accusation at Sir Alex Ferguson that he had deliberately allowed Manchester United to stagnate in his final season in order to highlight his greatness once things went wrong for the new manager. In his autobiography Ferguson tries to skirt the blame for the appointment of David Moyes by saying, '... it was a democratic process following a thorough assessment of the candidates.' What would you give to know who came second?

And Ferguson remains resilient until the end. At one point he tried to tell us that David Moyes 'hadn't realised just how big United [are] as a club'. Are you fucking winding me up? David Moyes? Close mate of Sir Alex Ferguson and manager of Everton Football Club for 10 years doesn't realise 'how big' Manchester United are? Come on.

When I first tentatively alluded to the fact that I felt Ferguson had undermined United through years of underspending, thus leading to a squad that, by the time Moyes turned up, was on its knees, I was roundly criticised. Without wishing to slap myself on the back and proclaim myself as the born again king, when certain journalists from certain tabloid newspapers call to offer an apology, one can be forgiven for saying, 'How dare you ever question me again?' In that respect, Fergie and myself aren't dissimilar.

But that aside, there are shrewd lessons to be learned from Ferguson's tenure at United, not least for the Scot's closest colleagues. As a manager, you wouldn't want to surround yourself with coaches who have aspirations of becoming managers – not necessarily because they will perform a *coup d'état* but because it makes things easy for any chairman contemplating a decision should there be a downward turn in the results department.

It's a little different for Ryan Giggs at Manchester United because of Louis van Gaal's age. United will more than likely be the Dutchman's last job, so the relationship becomes more about the fact that Giggs can learn the trade from one of the greats, and Van Gaal can retire with dignity when the time comes.

My friend, who is currently off the managerial merry-go-round but keen to get back on it, told me about a chat he'd had with Alan Pardew after bumping into him at a dinner. What Pardew said to him was brilliant in its simplicity and highlights how smoothly football works, in particular the way clubs choose managers. 'You'll never get a job from doing an interview,' said Pardew.

And Pardew would know. He is rumoured to have got the job at Newcastle by hanging out with Mike Ashley at the Ritz casino on Piccadilly. Remember what I said earlier about making it easy for a chairman to choose you when the time comes? It's the same thing. The moment Chris Hughton's job at Newcastle became the subject of uncertainty, Mike Ashley would have asked himself what the easiest option for all concerned was. Within days Hughton was gone and Pardew was in before the media even had time to speculate. Ashley knew that Pardew was desperate to get back in and that he'd work on the cheap while fighting tooth and nail to prove himself. Shortly after he had proved himself by finishing eighth in the Premier League, Pardew signed an eight-year deal.

That's how you do it. Once you've understood the game and how it works, you simply apply logic and common sense. Football, like business, is about schmoozing and who you know. And wasn't it ever thus?

DIRECTOR OF FOOTBALL

Following on from the ruthlessness of the manager. If I was the director of football at Sunderland, I'd kick almost every single one of the players out of the club the moment I got in there. Let me tell you something about Sunderland. Nobody in football has any respect for the club. Don't get me wrong, they did once, but they don't now.

Today, Sunderland is a pigmy club – a club that could easily be in the Championship given its aspirations, a club that many feel is making up the numbers and has no intention of doing anything other than that. And, to be honest, that annoys people in the game. We can't all win the Champions League but, fuck me, we can do a lot better than throw huge sums of money at shit players in order to preserve our Premier League status. Players look at Sunderland and think, 'It could always be worse, I guess.'

Sunderland is the club where, for a serious footballer, earning the most money possible goes out of the window the moment you mention the Stadium of Light. Players carry around in their head a couple of clubs that they'll never play for no matter how much money is thrown at them. For most, Sunderland is one of those clubs.

Sunderland know this too – hence the reason why the wages on offer are so high for playing in a team essentially packed with an average collection of players.

But I digress. A great and effective director of football will never give a player what he wants – while at the same time making the player feel like he has bent over and taken one in the arse, whether that was over wages, the length of a contract or a squad number. There are exceptions, of course. Sometimes a director will be offering numbers that are a little top-heavy to the best players, but he earns his corn by making that up at the back end. Remember the players the scout brings in with no chance of playing football for the first team? Sell a few of those each year for a top-heavy transfer fee and everything works out perfectly.

A director of football is in constant communication with his counterparts around the country, if not Europe and the world. He needs to know exactly what others are paying, and the lengths of the contracts being handed out, so that when he sits in contract negotiations with agents, he knows that a player can't leave for anything significantly more than what is already on the table. Sure, a player might leave for geographical reasons, but, ultimately, pound for pound, there has to be no better contract on the table, when you take into account that the player will have to up sticks and move house.

And this is where being a director of football crosses over into something of a humanitarian role, because when he offers that deal to the agent he needs to have factored in the following: what will it cost for the player to move clubs? What will the upheaval, both financial and emotional, be like? Maybe the player's wife has a job in the area? Maybe his children go to school there? Has his house price gone down? Or up? Perhaps he has business interests in the area? Maybe his parents live nearby? Maybe his brother or sister is in the area, and perhaps they are in financial trouble? Maybe he has a lease on a car? Could it be that he is renting? Or has a mortgage on a house that he can't get out of? Maybe he's in negative equity and, if he is, what is the rental market like?

You would not believe what goes into a contract proposal. All of these permutations go into offering the player a figure that he can't say no to – not because he can't earn more elsewhere, but because he doesn't want the upheaval that comes from moving. And all the time his quality needs to be taken into consideration. Remember, contracts are only offered if the club wants to retain a player, never the other way around.

Being a great director of football means you shouldn't expect to see your kids. If I were employing one, I would choose a ruthless bastard who had no family and who was desperate to prove himself. And he would have to work well with the man or woman above him. Which brings us to the door of the ...

CHIEF EXECUTIVE

'You know what the difference is between me and a director of football?' asked my chief executive.

'No,' I said, naturally enough.

'I can read a balance sheet,' said the chief executive.

And, to be honest, that is it. The chief executive exists to distribute the budget to all corners of the football club. However, his one big standoff in the financial year is with the director of football, because that is where the bulk of his budget goes.

If a chairman can find a chief executive who works well with a director of football then his is the earth and however that line finishes too. At most of the clubs I've been at the chief executives are the lesser-spotted creatures of the boardroom, outside of the chief finance officer, of course. The one time the players see their chief executive is at the team photoshoot at the start of the season, where it is tradition to use the three new Premier League balls (which the kit man protects with his life) to try to hit the chief executive on the back of the head with a 'misplaced pass'. I never felt that the players doing the kicking were ever actually trying their hardest. It was more a shot across the bow sort of thing, flybys.

Rest assured that these men are serious. Hit one and it would be held against you forever. Chief executives don't tend to fuck about, and they are served well by a fundamental lack of football knowledge pertaining to the way the game is actually played on the pitch. They don't care about that. Did the books balance? Great, we're OK for another year then.

I've played under some real hardnosed bastards too. While some have their hand firmly in the cookie jar, most just love getting the best deal, regardless of who they upset. A chief exec deals with all the facets of the football club, but his role is increasingly about the commercial performance of the club, about bringing in cash to subsidise player sales. And it's tough. We all know that the Premier League is paved with gold but there are some big clubs knocking around in the Championship these days, so let me use one of those to give you an idea of where the numbers are at in terms of commercial revenue in that league.

How much would you pay to be a shirt sponsor at a big Championship club? £3 million a year? Maybe £5 million? It's actually more like £500,000. What about the stadium naming rights? Take Fulham, for example, who painted 'PIPEX' and later 'FX Pro' on the roof of their stadium directly under the Heathrow flight path. Millions of air passengers see that every year – £1 million? Maybe £2.5 million? These days you could paint your logo across the roof of any top Championship club for about £400,000. What about if you wanted to rent out your 30,000 seat stadium to, say, a concert promoter? £500,000? £750,000? You'd be lucky to get £50,000 regardless of whether the Stones, Pink Floyd or Ed Sheeran were playing. 'Our biggest problem in that regard,' said the chief executive, 'is that there is always a club down the road in League One, or maybe even League Two, where £50,000 to rent the stadium out for a night is a lot of money, and ultimately concert promoters don't care if you're in the Premier League or League Two, they only care that you have enough seats that they can fill.'

You could always sublet the stadium to another club – £100,000 a year, tops. What about a huge catering deal to supply all the food and beverages in the stadium? £80,000 a year. Are you starting to get a picture of why great scouting is so important? Outside of the Premier League things are tough in the corporate world.

On my board is my chief executive, the guy who knows the balance sheet and the value and the price of everything. He is my main man. He knows every number, and the history and family background of every number. Nothing escapes him. I am the Godfather. He is my *consigliere*.

CHAIRMAN

Every club needs a chairman, and that is ultimately where I want to be. My skills are far better employed nudging people into a position where, almost without realising it, they are doing what I want them to do – that, and installing my vision of how the overall structure of the club should look. A chairman should never interfere with the running of the playing side of things – how his manager wants to set the team up, or how his chief executive and director of football divvy up the budget that he sets for the year. The style of play at a football club is largely dictated by the ethos, budget and DNA (wanky phrase, but very 'in' at the moment, thanks to England) that the board set out from day one. At my club, it will be my ethos.

Unfortunately, there are always a few people who try to undermine the entire thing, either from inside or outside the club. The easiest way for negative influencers to undermine the entire ethos of a club is in the transfer policy because, obviously, that's where the money is. So how do you keep it honest? How do you keep it open? How do you make it work?

The transfer system is a swamp at the best of times. You think because you haven't heard the word 'bung' in a long time that they must have cleaned it all up. Do not believe a fucking word of it. If you want to understand it all you have to have the information that nobody else sees.

On an industry level take a look at all the clubs. By law they have to report what they paid out in agency fees and transfers, and list the names of the agents. If a club is using the same agency in an extraordinary number of their deals, there is a reason for that. Usually not a very good one.

Until such time as all transfer info is available at the touch of a button, isolating the deal-making function makes things easier within a club. All that info is provided by the director of football to my chief executive, who then asks why we are using this particular agent so much. Or not. The chief exec doesn't need to be friends with the agents; he needs to make sure that the director of football isn't too friendly with the agents.

Here's how it should be.

The director of football shields my chief executive from all the phone calls from all the agents. The chief exec gets his budget from the chairman and gives it to the director of football, who works with the manager to determine how they are going to spread it across a squad that always needs more and never needs less. (A mate of mine is the chairman of a big club in the north: 'I've yet to meet a manager who says he doesn't need money. And when we tell him the budget, he always says he needs more. Those managers who sit in interviews saying that they don't need money are talking bollocks. They need money. I don't care if I have Jesus Christ sitting in front of me. He still needs money to improve the squad.') The director of football and the chief scout are close meanwhile. The director says to the scout that the budget this year is £10 million. Then the manager comes back and says he wants a left-back, a midfielder and a striker.

Part of the DNA of my Championship club is that our strikers are always purchased from the English lower leagues. We'll pay £5,000 a week initially. Three-year deal. The striker has to be a good size and very quick. The scout goes out and comes back with three, maybe four possibilities. 'This one is quick and left-footed but he costs the most,' he'll say. 'If I were you I would go with this guy. He has goals if you put him with our wingers. And he has character.' Part of what our scout does is a fit and proper persons test on players. We don't pay money to knobheads, in other words – or players who don't want to be the best that they can possibly be. You can tell the type of players that you want very easily. They're the ones who chase nothing balls, tackle, head and kick anything that moves if it means getting the ball an inch closer to the opposition goal – they are desperate to be involved in the game. Desperate to win. Sound familiar?

Once the correct target is identified, the director of football makes contact with the chosen striker, his agent or his club, whichever comes first, and he does the deal. The manager is then responsible for the player. The director of football is responsible for explaining the entire transaction to the chief executive. The chief exec is responsible for justifying it to me. I explain it all to the board.

That all probably sounds obvious. Well, you would be amazed at how often an agent lifts the phone to a manager and just says, 'Do us a solid, mate. I've got X and he needs a move out of club Y. Like yesterday. Make them an offer they can't refuse and come the next window I'll look after you ... Yeah, I know he was five million last summer. Bump the money up to eight and a half and he's yours. See yourself and the missus down at the villa this summer? Drinks? Good!'

In a properly functioning club the people on the different rungs impose checks and balances on each other. We explain and justify everything right up through the line because, at some point, somebody will spot what's going on.

I won't overspend with money that the club doesn't have. I won't borrow money that the club can't pay back. The club must be a self-perpetuating business – that is to say, the club finds players and sells them on, until such a time that the tipping point is found, when the club either goes up or it is forced to sell a player to break even for the next attempt at promotion in the following season. The club must never gamble. It must never think that if it just holds on to this player or that player, and pulls in one or two extra players, then it will certainly win promotion.

Football doesn't work like that. All that happens then is that the wage bill increases. It's like gambling, isn't it, Mr Ridsdale? You win three hands but then you lose four in a row – but that's OK, right? Your luck will turn? No. You're gambling and you're losing. A chairman picks an ethos and he sticks to it.

All of the chairmen I have played under have had an ethos. There are mitigating circumstances, of course. Most of them were swayed by how old they were, how much money they had and how long they had left to live. But they all had an ethos. And, once my club is in the Premier League, it will spend every single available penny on as many quality players as possible. Not one here, or one there, but several players who buy into the club's mission statement. Hard work, determination and skill.

I can hear them now, 'But ... he hasn't paid his dues!'

I'VE PLAYED AND YOU HAVEN'T

There was a guy – we'll call him Freddie – who turned up at our training ground some time around 2005. To this day I don't know where he came from or who brought him to the club, but I do know that my car has never looked cleaner before or since. In fact, right up until the day I left the club, my car looked a million dollars – and not just mine, but every car in the car park. The lads were only too happy to fork out £100 a week for an in-and-out detail service, and, for however many years, he carried on. Freddie made a small fortune.

During that time he also made friends with one player to such an extent that, before long, he was putting up curtain rails for him in his new house, hosing down the driveway after training or mowing his lawn. As time went by, more and more players began to ask Freddie if he would mow their lawns too, and while he was at it, perhaps paint the lounge and pick up the new sofa that had just been ordered. Soon, Freddie had become as integral to the lads' daily needs as the player liaison officer himself – except Freddie wasn't an official and that made him preferable. If you needed something picking up or dropping off, Freddie was your man. Need new boots sorting out? Freddie would handle it. You want a busload of girls picking up from the airport and dropped into central London and bailed out again at six in the morning? All you had to do was call Freddie. He made himself indispensable.

A couple of years after that, he began appearing in the tunnel before games, handing out drinks and energy bars as the lads were getting ready to walk on to the pitch. Then, after matches, Freddie could be seen helping the kit man to clear away the lads' boots or picking the used towels up off the floor. It was only a matter of time before Freddie started appearing on the pitch, wearing spare kit he'd found lying around, and collecting up the balls after the warm-up, picking up spent drinks bottles and generally making himself useful. Nobody ever said a word.

About three years after that, well after I'd left the club, I was at a local non-league game. I'd been asked to attend by a friend, who was making his managerial debut with one of the teams. It turns out that I wasn't the only one. Freddie was there too, sitting in the stand, feet up on the chair in front of him, mobile phone glued to his ear while wearing a club jacket with his initials heat-pressed on to the shoulder opposite the badge that I'd fought tooth and nail for during the best part of my career.

We saw each other at the same time, and he raised his hand in the air as if he was appealing for an offside, two of his fingers were splayed with the intention of informing me that he'd be two minutes – he just needed to finish the call he was on. I totally blanked him. Then he whistled in my direction and I decided to check my own phone as a defence mechanism.

People like Freddie, who are living their own little dream, simply don't understand the nuances of football, the structure, the hierarchy, the 'when to shut the fuck up' moments in professional football.

Freddie leapt over the rows of chairs in front of him and grabbed my shoulder just as I was making another run at my voicemail messages. 'Hello, mate,' he said, without a hint of shame. 'What are you doing here?' In such situations it is imperative to say as little as possible, because you never know exactly how deep somebody has burrowed into a club, so always answer with a question. 'I'm good, mate. How are you? What's this jacket all about?' I asked.

'Mate, I'm a scout, aren't I? Just having a look to see what's about.' There was nothing about; the standard at that level is so bad that it is a complete waste of time to go anywhere near it, unless you're the sort of person who enjoys molten slabs of faux beef in insanely white baps on a freezing Tuesday night.

The truth was that he lived round the corner and could claim £100 worth of expenses for sitting in the stand for five minutes before going home.

'So I haven't seen you down the club much lately,' he said. 'The club' is a Premier League club that I helped to put on the map. I feel like I own it in some way, such is my contribution to its history.

'You should come down to see a game. I'll sort tickets out for you, if you want,' offered Freddie.

I could have taken his fucking head clean off his shoulders. Given that a crowd had gathered I opted not to resort to violence, but decided instead to set the record straight.

'Freddie,' I said, 'do you know what the difference is between you and me? You'll turn up on Saturday to watch us [I still say "us"] play against Chelsea, with your little jacket there with your initials on, and the girls in the ticket office will still ask you for ID. Whereas I can turn up 10 years later and kiss the girls in the ticket office on both cheeks before they ask security to take me through to my seat. Do you know what I'm saying, mate?'

Somebody, probably me, should have said that to him years ago. Once I'd calmed down, I thought about the reality of the situation. Here was a guy who, through sheer hard work and general busyness, it has to be said, has worked his way into a position where he feels he can talk to me like that. Now he feels he's one of us. But he isn't one of us; he's a chancer. I'm not out to belittle a man's work – it makes no difference to me what a man does for a living, as the Godfather once said – but it's about respect.

I can think of one or two players who would have knocked Freddie's head into the opposite stand if he'd approached them in the same way. Imagine asking Roy Keane if he wants a couple of tickets to Manchester United's next match? Or if Frank Lampard fancies taking his missus down to Chelsea's next home game?

So, the point is, when you next get fobbed off with the answer, 'I've played and you haven't', it's generally because any other response would take a fair amount of explanation. Not that I'm saying I've made a brilliant job of it here, but hopefully this gives you a little window into why some things in football are the way they are. No, they don't make sense when you first look at them, but it's important to remember that these things didn't come about overnight; they have evolved this way, over a number of years.

The examples above, particularly the way that managers pick their teams, is an example not of institutional racism – though I'm always willing to be proved wrong on that count – but of managers who know what types of players work best in certain roles and positions. I sometimes think that the real reason that fans get fobbed off with the 'I've played and you haven't' line is because very often what you're asking has never occurred to us before, and the answer cannot be explained with a single catch-all sentence. If you'd played then you'd get it, and you wouldn't ask. After all, it's been that way for a hundred years, not that I'd swap it for a building site.

9. A-Z: STOPPING AT MOST STOPS TO W

EVERTON

Everybody has moved on but Goodison Park is still essentially the House of Moyesie. It will be that way for a long time. David Moyes liked a bit of hardship, his favourite aftershave was Burning Martyr. From nothing he made Everton into something that was a little bit better than nothing. It was solid and dependable. And going nowhere.

Circumstances hold Everton hostage in a way that no other big club need worry about. When 20 more years have passed it will be plain that Moyes was probably best suited to life at a hostage club. He thrived within that mentality, moving his club up and down that patch of real estate that begins just north of the relegation zone and finishes just south of European qualification.

Everton are broke. Also, they live just a couple of hundred yards down the road from one of the most revered clubs in the world. Not only are Everton broke, they have an owner, Bill Kenwright, who will never sell the club to somebody who doesn't pass the Everton FC fit and proper persons test. In other words, he won't sell to somebody who doesn't love the club as much as he does. Kenwright will divorce from Everton so long as Everton doesn't make out like a good-time girl as soon as Bill's back is turned.

It's not just money and geography which hem Everton into their place. The entire current of history runs against them. Everton existed before Liverpool FC did. And they played at Anfield before Liverpool were even founded. When they got into a sulk over rent at Anfield and moved up to Goodison Park a new club was formed to fill Anfield. They are still there, and Liverpool FC fills the sightline every time Everton look up.

Everton have spent only four years out of top-flight football since they were founded. That would be wonderful if all the other years had been exciting and memorable. They haven't been. Three championships and three FA Cups in the last 50 years. Down the road at Liverpool in the last half-century they took 12 championships and seven FA Cups and ruled Europe. How many times did Everton folk sit at home listening to the sounds of great European nights spill out of Anfield and into the dark of Stanley Park? Liverpool fitted a famine and a couple of genuine disasters into the same timeframe.

And Everton bowed their heads and prayed with their beads. Does all their good housekeeping buy them any comfort when the raucous Reds up the road are tilting at windmills? No.

Worst of all and forever unsayable was the timing of the disasters at Heysel and Hillsborough. Heysel denied Everton access to Europe for their best ever team – their greatest team were kept in England because of Liverpool, who had enjoyed all those nights of European glory. Everton, as one of their players from that time has since told me, allowed themselves a little hate to drive themselves on. Then Hillsborough happened. Resentment and hate suddenly seemed unseemly and un-Evertonian. The Blues must grieve when the Reds grieve. Them's the rules if you are the People's Club. The Blues must always be the hand proffering help in bad times at Anfield. Everton plod on in their heroically dull and decent way, trying to do things in the Everton tradition, while Liverpool breathe and flirt with the bad boys like Stan Collymore, Luis Suárez and Mario Balotelli. And you think that until Liverpool are free Everton will always be in their shadow.

I love the city of Liverpool and I love talking to football people there. They like to stop you and ask you what you think of this and that. I would hate to be a born and bred Everton fan, though. Liverpool have succeeded over the years and suffered too, but Everton have suffered through no fault of their own. A former coach of mine, who played in those great Everton sides of the eighties, said to me, 'It just seemed that whenever we'd get it together and try to take Liverpool on, something would happen beyond our control – a European ban, the Hillsborough tragedy – it was just unfortunate timing, and tragic at the same time. We could do nothing except offer our support, which we did.' I won't lie, at the time he spoke those words, he moved me a little, and I didn't overly like him either.

Everton is a stadium going nowhere, boxed in and disproportionate; the club needs to move but Kenwright won't budge. I actually look at Bill and, although I admire his principles, you do get the feeling, overwhelmingly so, that the 'I won't sell to just anyone' mantra is another way of saying, 'I'm doing rather well here, thank you.' I would love to see Everton fulfil whatever potential is there, and I do believe that the club comprises more than just a run-down stadium with shit changing rooms.

Those days in the late eighties and early nineties must have been a terribly confusing time for my old coach. Here was a great Everton side, but the world wanted Liverpool to be victorious because of the terrible tragedies that had befallen the club. Everybody was rooting for Liverpool at that time (I remember it well because I was one of those people). Everton have had to play the bridesmaid forever it seems, and there is little that they've ever been able to do about it.

Football comes in phases. Fads come in and out of the game all the time. Some of them actually become more than fads; they stick and become useful. Sports science is one such example; analytics another. Depending on the manager, these trends are seized upon or discarded. At Everton, Roberto Martínez took analytics to a new level when he first arrived. After a match he would send the players home and watch the playback with the analytics department across six televisions, all with cameras pointing at different players or parts of the pitch. It seemed to work, but let's not kid ourselves: ultimately Everton's success was built on having the right players in the right places doing the right things.

In Martínez's second season there was a shift in the rigid predictability of Everton, and it wasn't for the better. Somewhere along the way the Everton players began chipping in with their own thoughts, and that sounds a massive alarm bell for any manager. In an innocuous interview England prodigy Ross Barkley dared to suggest that it would be better for everyone connected with Everton – but no one more so than himself – if he was played just off the front man. Instead of adopting a Ferguson tone that pushed Barkley back into his box Martínez inexplicably obliged. The results have been a disaster for both Everton and Barkley.

Seeing that Barkley had got his way, other players waded in. Leighton Baines used to take the penalties for Everton and generally Leighton Baines would score. Over the 2014–15 season Everton were awarded five spot-kicks and Leighton Baines didn't take a single one. Instead, Romelu Lukaku scored three out of three, but Kevin Mirallas and Ross Barkley both missed one apiece.

The danger signs for managers are all around them, but sometimes they dig their own grave. If Martínez continues on down the path of devolution it will only end in the sacking of the Spaniard. Those who want respect give respect, and some of the players at Goodison do not deserve it.

HULL CITY

Tuncay, the Turkish midfielder, once came on as a sub for Stoke City when they were playing away to Hull City. Maybe he was surprised that two such modest places could call themselves 'City', but when he was taken off again after six minutes of play, he jogged down the tunnel to the dressing room, picked up his effects, got into a taxi and asked if he could be driven straight back to Stoke.

When I tell that story to friends, they always say the same thing: 'Hull to Stoke? How far is that? Where the fuck is Hull?'

The answer, of course, is that it doesn't matter where Hull is when you are getting £60,000 a week. You can afford to ask the taxi driver to dismantle his car and walk it piece by piece from Hull to Stoke if you so wish. You don't need to know where Hull is.

Until you play for them, of course.

When we went to Hull we stayed where most teams stay – a little hotel that looks out on to a little marina. I think it's a Holiday Inn. The marina is small and twee and in the morning you had a little walk around it as part of the ritual 11.15 a.m. stroll before the pre-match meal.

This has nothing to do with the city, but when I think of Hull it is the only thing that I think of. Martin Allen, who is an absolute bomb scare no matter where he goes or where he manages, was walking his team around the marina one morning. He detected a lack of enthusiasm among the lads. If you've seen the marina at Hull you could be forgiven for thinking it lacks in certain detail – there's no Sydney Opera

House or Golden Gate Bridge, for example. The Holiday Inn is probably the great architectural statement that the marina makes.

So when the team was getting close to finishing their walk around the marina, Allen stopped the captain and said, 'I bet ya I could swim across the marina. Get the lads to all throw in a fiver … I'm going to do it.'

Rolling his eyes and talking softly, the captain went among the players: 'Here, give us a fiver, lads. The gaffer wants you all to bet that he can't swim across the marina. He's going to jump in and swim from here to … er … just over there.'

By now Martin Allen was standing at the edge of the marina in nothing but his red jockey briefs.

'OK, gaffer. The lads are all in,' shouted the captain.

Martin Allen dived into the marina. The players reached the door of the Holiday Inn as their gaffer pulled himself out of the water, roaring his own commentary – 'They said it couldn't be done but he has done it' – before running after his players to get his clothes back in order to walk across the lobby of the Holiday Inn.

That's not really a story about Hull but it is a story a lot of footballers tell when they speak about Hull. That, in itself, tends to reveal the lethargy and indifference players exhibit towards Hull. If a large shark had emerged in the marina and swallowed Martin Allen they wouldn't have been impressed.

'Where's the gaffer?'

'Still in the water, I think.'

'Oh, OK.'

I like the club, though. Getting to the Premier League and staying there was the definition of punching above their weight. When the club was relegated in 2010, I expected them to disappear completely, never to be heard from again. The fact that they bounced back and also reached an FA Cup final in 2014 – which arguably they'd have won if they'd made the right substitutions at the right moments – means that they've stumbled upon a formula.

OK, they're back in the Championship, but Hull have faced the same conundrum as a lot of Premier League strugglers. Could they spend enough money on the right players without getting relegated or breaking the bank?

And that's a bigger problem for Hull than most other clubs because of their geographical problem. No player wants to live in Hull. Hull are the classic example of a team, along with Sunderland, that has to spend big numbers in order to attract average players. When you list the players and their transfer fees, few of them make economic sense. Jake Livermore, a bit-part player at Spurs who cost the club £8 million. Abel Hernández was the man tasked with scoring goals for Hull, but his goalscoring record in six consecutive seasons with Italian side Palermo reads as follows: 0, 7, 3, 6, 1, 14. The game that did it for Hernández was Uruguay's last group stage match of the 2013 Confederations Cup when he scored four goals in an 8–0 win against the national team of that footballing hotbed Tahiti (population: 183,000). His fee for these less than remarkable goalscoring exploits was £10 million.

Consider this. From the beginning of the 2014 calendar year Hull picked up just 0.87 points per game despite spending more than any of the clubs around them – £40 million. Hull were almost damned if they did and damned if they didn't.

Ultimately everybody knows why Hull are having to spend money this way – a friend of mine went there for wages of £35,000 a week when he was worth, at most, £20,000 a week – but Steve Bruce will always be the man who will carry this round of questionable spending as a blight on his CV.

I imagine Steve Bruce and the club are getting a little bit tired of each other by now, and that may be a danger, because sometimes owners change managers for the sake of it. But you get the feeling that Bruce is probably the right man, even if he just pays lip service to management. I always feel that Bruce became a manager because he was the captain of Manchester United, who at the time were in the first throes of their incredible success – he's a manager because of association in the same way that John O'Shea and Wes Brown continue to play Premier League football. So far, in what is now a fairly lengthy managerial career, Bruce's achievements are sort of ... OK.

Hull's next move into the managerial cattle mart will be a big one – but I do know a man who can swim the marina if needed.

LEICESTER CITY

If you get promoted to the Premier League the best thing to do is to aim to finish 10th every year. If you chase some station high above that 10th place with everything you've got, then you will probably get relegated, bringing an overpaid panel of mercenary vultures back down to the Championship with you. They will pick every scrap of flesh from the bones of your club, and there'll be nothing you can do about it.

If you don't chase the safety ledge of 10th place you could very well get relegated anyway. And you can't not spend, because that way you'll only get sucked down in that swirling vortex of mediocrity you thought you'd escaped when you won the play-off at Wembley with a fortuitous penalty hoofed in by your legendary centre-half.

You definitely shouldn't overspend. Those fucking vultures will block the sun. Five years of chasing 10th place is the thing to do. There'll be security, and enough excitement for those season ticket holders who never darkened your turnstile before you made it into the big leagues.

Leicester have owners who don't get that. They made Nigel Pearson look like a complete meathead. I mean, more so than normal.

There are other things that I wonder about when I look at Leicester. For a start, the crowd inside the stadium are a different colour to the people outside.

When I was at school we'd have big football matches, 16- or 17-a-side. It was always Asians v Whites, and despite the fact that all of us were in mixed classes the teams never changed. All of the Asian kids supported either Liverpool or Manchester United, and I always thought that was because they had no geographical ties to a club so they supported the teams that were successful – the older kids were Liverpool fans, the younger kids were all Manchester United fans.

By the time we reached 16 and 17 years of age, my friends and I were discovering the pub, girls and trouble. Some of the Asian students were moving into higher education, but most were leaving to join the family business – more often than not selling alcohol to me and my friends from their shops. It always seemed odd to me that the Asian families were forbidden to drink alcohol yet were allowed to sell it.

The Asian kids in our school were never out on a Saturday night, never. As far as we could tell, they had no social lives to speak of, and were discouraged by their parents from mixing with anybody outside of their own faith. I remember knocking on the door of an Asian friend when I was about 12 years old, and his father telling me that my mate was out, but I knew he was upstairs in his bedroom.

By the time I was 17 or 18, all of the Asian students I knew had moved into business or, in a few cases, gone to university; and some had moved to India or Pakistan to learn a family trade. There was no sense of loss on either side; it was accepted. That's what the Asian community did, while the white community had two or three years of drinking heavily before falling into crappy jobs in the local area.

It came as no surprise to me that the Asian students who played in those matches at school did not follow up on their talent – and, believe me, some of them were talented. They simply never dared to believe that they could do something outside of what their families had planned for them. They accepted their working fate with what seemed to me to be a repressed fear: they never had girlfriends at school, they tried not to mix with the white kids, and they set about their school work in a way that was alien to the white kids. Everything they did was leading up to the working life that was waiting for them when they finished their schooling.

For me, historically, the lack of Asian players in the professional game has had little to do with scouting or racism. I'm sure that scouts in football would love to scout a huge pool of Asian kids but, for the most part, certainly where I grew up, there was simply nothing to scout.

Today, there is no talk within football about a lack of players from the subcontinent, but every now and again somebody wants to ask the question, even though I suspect they already know the answer. On a recent Saturday morning trip to QPR's academy, the pitches were full of Asian kids playing football. I may be wrong, given the rewards on offer, but I would be surprised to see any come through professionally in the next five years.

Imagine how big Leicester could be if it could persuade every creed within its catchment area to get involved with the club, or at least to come through the turnstile. The stadium holds over 32,000 people, and you have to take the view that with a bit of 'work in the community' the club could easily have a solid fan base of 40,000 to 50,000. Those are real numbers – then, and only then, do you think about taking the next step. In football these days, 30,000 fans is nothing; 50,000 or 60,000 through the gate and you're pissing with the big boys. It's not about how much money you can spend, necessarily; it's whether or not you have the assets worth backing up with cash.

I look at Leicester and I see the raw components. I see a decent stadium plonked on a bit of land where expansion would be easy. I see a huge catchment area and, above all, for the time being at least, I see Premier League football.

And they also have a celebrity fan base. When I played at Leicester, I'd been introduced to the band Kasabian and, in particular, Serge Pizzorno, by a mutual friend. We were up in some corporate box and I had just finished the game. When you play a game of football, depending on how hot and humid it is, and how hard you've worked, a player can lose anything up to a stone in weight. As a result, it's easy to get pissed with the mere smell of an open bottle of Budweiser, and when one was thrust into my hand that is exactly what happened. I vaguely remember asking Serge about drugs and music and what he'd been on when he wrote the first album, an album that had had a massive impact on me. He indulged me, but also formed the opinion that I was an utter knob talking about this stuff in these surroundings. They do say that you should never meet your heroes, but I'm glad that I did. Serge, if you're reading this, I'm not a knob; I was just pissed. Oh, and while we're at it, write another album like the first one, for fuck sake.

10. SEEN AND NOT HEARD, LIKE GOOD FOOTBALLERS

An old player once said to me that he joined a football club at the age of 15. He had a good career and then retired 18 years later. At the age of 15.

First day at a new club. I walk in the main door. Look around. No welcoming party. Nothing. Next thing, a voice.

'Oh my God, what is this?'

I see a head down the corridor. He may know me, but I don't know him.

'Look at his jeans,' says the head, approaching. 'What have we signed here. Oh, Jesus, what a wanker. 'Ere, come with me a minute.'

I follow. The head leads me into the dressing room. 'Lads, look at the state of this. Look at his jeans, for fuck sake.' He's laughing so hard that he's now gasping for air. (There was nothing wrong with my jeans, by the way.) He introduced me to my new colleagues, some of whom I knew, most of whom I'd seen on *Match of the Day*. That's how you introduce a

player to the lads. Everyone equal. Human resources gradu-
ates, take a deep breath.

I roomed with the head for a year. I like him a lot. He's as
genuine as they come. I know he is as mad as a box of frogs,
but there are worse to room with. Believe me.

We didn't live near the club, so the night before games we
would have to check into a local hotel and, out of habit, we
always roomed together on those nights too. It would have
cost nothing to get single rooms, but sharing is just the done
thing if you are a footballer. You need a roommate who is
normal. Insist on being on your own and you are either old,
a weirdo or worth turning into the cops.

We used to get a little pistachio ice cream on room service
before turning in. This was the routine: I'd call down and,
after a few minutes, there would be a knock at the door. I
would get up off my twin bed, put my tracksuit bottoms on
and go to answer the door to let the waitress in. In that time
my roommate would have stripped naked, lain face down on
the bed with the pillow over the back of his head and my
mobile phone sticking out of his arse.

I would always forget, and walk back into the room with
that excruciating feeling of wanting to burst out laughing
while trying desperately to give the impression that I'm not
part of the fraternity – I don't stick mobile phones up my
arse, not even if they're on vibrate. The waitress, and sadly it
was always a waitress, would do the decent thing and pretend
she was blind. Nothing would be said until she asked me to
'sign here'. The words would trigger my man.

'Hello? Hello? Is somebody there?' he'd say in a frightened voice. 'It's all gone wrong. Can you call the police? A supervisor. Please help. Please don't ignore me.'

'He's just being an idiot,' I'd say. 'I'm so sorry.'

The waitress would never take her eyes off me and not because she found me incredibly attractive, but because she was petrified of what she might see if she shifted her gaze.

I'd take the ice cream from her as quickly as possible and show her out. My roommate would be on the floor in the foetal position, laughing so hard that there was no noise coming from his mouth, tears streaming down his cheeks.

I tell this story because of all the ones flashing through my mind at this point it is among the most mild and most printable, and best explains the mental state of somebody coming out of a professional dressing room after a decade and a half.

At the same club a little dressing-room game developed where we'd throw our socks at each other's heads after training had finished. I don't know why, but it was pretty funny and seemingly innocent. Then it escalated in the blink of an eye. I threw my socks at the head of a foreign player who, for some reason, took offence. He picked up his very large Nike runner and walked towards me before cocking his hand above his shoulder. There was a second when I thought he was joking. Another second when I knew I was fucked. A third second when I just dived and turned my head. The runner caught the back of my head. Just a glance, enough to make me look stupid in front of everyone, enough not to fuck with him again. If I hadn't moved it would have smashed my face from point-blank range.

There's plenty of ego and testosterone sloshing around a changing room and, while it's no excuse, such stories perhaps illustrate why later, when you leave all that behind for the world of grown-ups and big decisions, life can be a little difficult to take seriously at first.

It doesn't help that professional footballers are kept in an almost infantile state.

For instance, clubs today will still insist that all minibars in players' hotel rooms are emptied. First World problem, I know. I understand that minibars are going to contain Jack Daniel's miniatures, Toblerones and Pringles, but I will guarantee you that any player preparing to play a match the following day won't touch that crap anyway. And if you do have to empty the minibar, at least leave the fucking juice and the water. Why take that out too? Idiots. It happens at every single club, and nobody has cottoned on to the fact that players might actually want an orange juice or a bottle of water while they're watching crap Friday night TV. Now you may not think that sounds like a big deal, and it isn't, really, but I'm telling you that every footballer reading this paragraph is now nodding enthusiastically in agreement. Revolution, brothers.

Players often act like kids because they are treated that way. One of my old managers, who is a control freak and many other things besides, once went one step further and banned room service. We were playing Chelsea at Stamford

Bridge, staying in a lovely glass-fronted hotel on the Thames, and I rang down asking for spaghetti bolognese. The order was taken, but 10 minutes later the phone rang and a gentleman from the subcontinent informed me with great regret that my manager had forbidden room service. His hands were tied. Metaphorically, I assumed back then, but knowing now what I know about the manager it could have been literally. (If so, I'm sorry for not getting help for you, mate.)

'It's pasta,' I told him, 'not McDonald's.'

This edict was from the same lunatic manager who banned the chef at our training ground from using salt.

If you'd rocked up to our training ground for lunch a few years ago you'd have sat down to boiled brown rice, rock-hard broccoli (allegedly steamed) and either plain white fish or plain chicken breast. A cup of sand would have done wonders for moistening that plate of food. Then when players began drifting off in groups of threes and fours to a local Italian restaurant in town, the manager introduced a £100 fine for those failing to have lunch at the training ground.

Now, when you have players on £30,000 or £50,000 a week, that isn't a lot of money, and so some players, particularly the foreign lads who treated eating with an almost religious reverence, simply paid the fine every day to escape the food on offer. That's over £2,000 a month from just one player who did not want to eat at the training ground, all in cash – and we had maybe five or six players who did that, all foreign. I always did wonder what happened to that money, but the players throwing it away never gave it a thought – it was a case of money just making their world move easier again.

The same manager tried to control every single facet of the club, pretty much to everybody's detriment. The local journalist had to have his articles on the club scrutinised by the manager every day over lunch (unpunctuated prose over unseasoned food) before he could go to print. That is not unheard of, but it was sufficiently shallow and insecure to turn the manager into a joke.

Our manager also brought in a great coach who had coached some of the game's biggest stars. Whenever the coach tried to talk to me and pass on some advice about how these global icons had gone about their business, the manager would step in and stop him. It was like supervised dating. It reached the point where that coach phoned me one afternoon while I was at home and said, 'Look, I shouldn't be saying this, but you've got some great ability. I would have loved to have got hold of you a few years ago. Where you are now is completely the wrong team for you, and my advice would be to move as soon as you can and play for a manager who will get the best out of you.'

He didn't have to do that, and I appreciated it – the fact that this man was one of my heroes also meant that I listened to his advice far more closely than I would have anybody else's, because he really knew his stuff. It was tough and I made a few enemies after I'd pulled it off, but four months after that phone call I managed to get the fuck out of there, sacrificing over £1 million in the process – that's how desperate I was to leave. When I look back now I can't believe I waived that money, but I was so unhappy I just wanted to get out of there. I'd have given a kidney too, if need be, but they don't let kids donate kidneys now.

Our fitness coach also suffered at the hands of the manager's kindergarten cop approach. He would plan out the week way in advance, because he knew the run of games and which players would be playing. The ones who played would do a pool session the next day to stretch off and cool down while the other players would train as normal. We'd be given an itinerary at the end of the previous week, only to come in on Monday to find the manager now wanted everyone to train, or had changed it in some way. Now that too doesn't sound like a big deal, but when players are trying to plan their own day and they have to do things like pick up the kids or arrange appearances and commercial events in the afternoon, it is a total ball ache. It was made worse by the fact that phones were banned at the training ground. As a result you'd simply not turn up for something, and the advertisers and sponsors who had booked you, or the school you were supposed to be giving a talk at, would be let down and you'd look like the bad guy. Above all, it was incredibly narrow-minded and selfish. Eventually, our fitness coach told him where to go and he was promptly 'let go'. He is now the fitness coach of a very big team doing very well in the Premier League and he couldn't be happier. It was a risk, because nobody who left that club ever got a good reference from the manager.

Our manager is still the same miserable controlling fool he ever was, and footballers are still being treated like highly paid babies off the pitch while being expected to show leadership and decision-making qualities under pressure on the pitch.

When the merry-go-round finally stops and we step off, is it any wonder that we hardly know how to cope with marriages and bills and debts and responsibilities? Just recall those stats again. We're all speeding headlong towards divorce, addiction, depression or bankruptcy.

On the other hand, the great big structure all around us is full of high-flying, high-operating grown-ups who wheel and deal and make up the rules as they go along. They know that at the end of the day whatever they come up with we will go along with because we love the money, we love the fun, and we need to be on that merry-go-round for as long as we can. We know virtually nothing. So we don't hang up our boots and become club chairmen. Hardly ever. We don't know enough. We aren't encouraged to know enough. Most people wouldn't let us drive a milk float. And we are the next generation who will run this multibillion-pound business.

Question: how much is one point in the Premier League worth?

How much are three points worth? How can we buy them? Legally. Nobody knows. Well, nobody in a dressing room does. We're all babies. In a way we are waiting to be told what the club thinks those points are worth before we throw our toys out of the pram, and then realise that we have run out of time to negotiate. Usually after that we get a slight concession, maybe an extra £100,000 a season to split among the squad, and we sign our lives away on a shit bonus sheet. We think times have changed. But in relation to the staggering rise in TV monies, we remain fucking clueless as to what those points are truly worth.

The rest of this chapter is about what I've learned from the people who do know. Football is like *The Truman Show*. Sometimes you bump against the edge of the world and realise there is something much bigger and manipulative out there.

So. Three points? How much? Our education starts here.

It is fair to say that if Sky Sports are happy to pay over £11 million to cover one match then the three points available to the competing teams for winning that match must be worth considerably more than, say, £25,000. Indeed, if the match is between two of the top five or six teams then the value of the points on offer are tough to estimate. I am sure, though, that somebody somewhere has run the metrics and algorithms and knows what those three points are worth.

Put it another way, it amazes me that when you win three points or sometimes even a point, you have a very real sense of just how big it was. It's like a scaled down version of the original 'six-pointer'. Sometimes you might be scratching around for a win and the ball will 'come off somebody's cock' as we say, land in the net in the last minute and, hey presto, you've nabbed a draw away to Spurs. Big point. You walk into the changing room and switch on the TV and see

that everyone around you has lost. Big, big point. You watch
your manager on *Match of the Day* later that evening saying,
'Come the end of the season that could be a massive point
for us.' And at the end of the season it turns out to be a £100
million point. How much is it worth to a player? The same as
all the others if you're at a club at that end of the table fighting for that point. About £3,000. Seems a little out of sync
with the club's value of that point, doesn't it? And yet, with
the next season on the horizon and the next set of bonuses
up for negotiation – which they are immediately after the
last game of last season, up until 1 August – everybody has
fucked off on holiday and negotiating the bonuses for the
players is something that, until the end of training on 31
July, nobody wants to think about. At that point, there is no
negotiation, just a very happy chief executive and a load of
pissed-off players.

The truth is, lots of people know the value of those points.
Let's backtrack a little.

A few years ago I was summoned by the FA to defend
myself against comments I'd made about the performance
of the match officials during a league game. No player that
I know has an intimate knowledge of the rules of the game
which pertain specifically to the dos and don'ts away from
the pitch. That said, everybody knows when they're sailing
close to the wind, even if they haven't actually realised the
exact moment that they've blown past a legal roadblock.

And that was the case when I cited the officials and, in
particular, the referee for what were, quite frankly, a series

of bizarre decisions that baffled not only our players but also the opposition. As a player, you are acutely aware that you're up against it the moment a player on the opposite team, despite his side being the beneficiary of every decision up to that point, says to you, 'This guy hasn't got a fucking clue.'

My 'rant' referred to several decisions that had all gone against us and, as is usually the case, had a direct hand in the outcome of the match, which we lost. There was an extremely dodgy penalty decision, and fouls that went unpunished, including a blatant bodycheck that took out one of my teammates when he was running towards goal. Then there was the penalty that we should have had in the second half and which after three minutes' consultation with his assistant referee somehow ended with the award of a throw-in.

But the worst incident came when one of our players was completely taken out by a shocking tackle that left him with a broken leg. Initially, the referee gave another throw-in, then five or six seconds later, which is a long time between a tackle and the whistle if you stop and think about it, he awarded us a free-kick. The rest of our team were frantically waving to the bench for the leg brace, stretcher and oxygen as our teammate held back the tears. Once the player is being attended to, your attention, as an enraged player, immediately switches to the referee: 'What kind of tackle is that? You weren't even gonna give it! It's a fucking red card! Send him off! You've given us nothing all game! Speak to the linesman! ...' And so on.

That kind of pressure and genuine outrage is usually enough to secure a yellow card, no matter how bad the referee's performance has been up to that point, and so it proved. It should have been a red card for their player; our teammate ended up having surgery the next day – he'd ruptured all the ligaments in his ankle and broken his foot. The referee made a case for the defence: 'He won the ball!' That only made things worse. 'He won the ball?' said our captain. 'So why have you given a throw-in to them if their player won the ball, you idiot?'

As soon as you have a person bang to rights that's when the arrogance kicks in: 'Everyone go away or I'll book all of you. Captain, get your players away or I'll start sending people off.' 'You should be sending him off,' said our captain pointing to the opposition defender. 'A fucking yellow card is a joke – you'd have sent ours off.' That sort of accusation is unquantifiable, of course, and as such is treated with utter disdain by all officials, and probably rightly so.

Just then, our injured teammate uttered his first words: 'Ref, what sort of tackle is that, for fuck sake? It's a joke, you fucking idiot.' That's when the referee shot himself in the foot. 'Swear at me one more time and I'll fucking send you off,' he said, then he turned to shout at our striker as he was retaking his position. 'That's right, walk away before I fucking send you off too.' That's when I knew we had him.

Rightly or wrongly, once the game was over, I absolutely destroyed him in the post-match interviews. All I knew was that I couldn't have gone home after that match with all that anger pent up inside me. I wanted people to know what had happened; I wanted to draw attention to it. Two days later, the FA charged me with misconduct and bringing the game into disrepute. Perfect.

That same afternoon, our chairman rang: 'We're going to back you on this. We think we can fight this and draw attention to it – that referee was a disgrace and we can't tolerate it any more because it's going to end up costing us. You are being singled out because you are a high-profile player, and now that's knocking on to the other players, who aren't getting any decisions because of the association. Whatever you need, let us know. We're right behind you.'

Within the confines of our club there was a sense that I was being singled out by certain officials, and now we had the perfect chance to nip it in the bud. We had a DVD of one of the most calamitous refereeing performances anybody could ever wish to see; we had a case of a referee swearing at our players; and, most importantly, we had witnesses who were all prepared to put their names to individual statements that tallied with one another. We had to shit or get off the pot. So I pleaded guilty, which meant that I had the right to request a personal hearing and explain the mitigating circumstances at the heart of the case.

But don't be fooled into thinking that this was a noble cause, even if it started out very loosely that way. Our goal was to place every official in a very awkward situation whenever they refereed our games, particularly the home matches. We had done some growing up, because I had seen in the

Premier League what the big boys do week in and week out. They had sussed the value of three points.

Why do you think Sir Alex Ferguson sounded off at the drop of a hat every time the slightest decision went against Manchester United? Do you have any idea how hard it was as an opposition player to get a decision at Old Trafford under Sir Alex Ferguson's reign? I have, and let me tell you, it was fucking impossible. Imagine being a referee taking charge of a game at Old Trafford, with 75,000 fans, a clutch of the world's biggest egos, and the most famous manager in the world scrutinising his watch on the touchline. You know the slightest contentious decision will almost certainly see your name on the back page of every newspaper come Monday morning, as well as on *Match of the Day* and all over Sky Sports News for the rest of the week. And if for any reason there was a dodgy decision against United, Ferguson would shoot his mouth off, go down to the FA, pay the fine and, in doing so, almost guarantee that United won their next home match.

And that, in a nutshell, was the plan. We had a great opportunity to turn our stadium into a really uncomfortable place for an official to give the opposition a 50–50 decision. As I've said, we weren't the pioneers of this strategy but we certainly saw that the benefits of it were huge. But we needed a fall guy.

The FA hearings are like a very informal court, and in such an environment cases are decided on legal technicalities, not mitigating circumstances – but even so, the latter can help to reduce the punishment meted out.

As this was technically a dispute between a player (me) and the FA (the referee), the case was held by an independent sports tribunal in London, whose only real involvement, it seemed, was to provide a meeting room and a pitcher of orange juice. In the meeting room there was a long grey table with three gentlemen seated down the left-hand side. The first suit belonged to an ageing gentleman from the football panel, the second had the task of chairing the meeting, while the third scared the hell out of me.

The last man was clearly very proud to work for the FA. He had to have been working for them for at least the last 120 years; he had the stay-pressed FA tie, no doubt removed from its clear plastic case and tied up to the sound of the London Symphony Orchestra playing the national anthem in front of a Wembley backdrop. On his lapel was the ubiquitous England pin badge. I couldn't read what it said underneath, but I guessed that it was something like 'celebrating the 25th anniversary of the FA'. All the above was accessorised with a liberal sprinkling of dandruff that made you question the logic behind a jet black suit while feeling compelled to break the ice with something like, 'Is it snowing out?'

On the other side of the table I was flanked by two men in slightly less severe attire. To my right was a man from the FA, who seemed to be there only as part of the legal formalities and hadn't been brought to these proceedings by me. To my left was a gentleman from the PFA, the Professional Footballers' Association, who had helped to put my case together and advised me on the best way to present it. The first time that we spoke on the phone to get our story straight was an eye-opener. 'OK, what are the main mitigating circumstances that you're going to put across?' he asked. 'I'm going to tell them the referee is unstable and needs help,' I said. There was silence at the other end of the phone before I broke it with an uncontrollable snort. 'You bloody idiot,' he said. 'I can never tell if you're being serious or not.'

I told him that I wasn't going to concentrate on the refereeing decisions because anybody can have a bad day at the office, and there was absolutely no evidence that the referee was in any way biased – he had just had a shocker that particular day. Instead, I'd focus on his swearing at our player while he was lying on the floor with a broken foot. That, I reasoned, was enough to call the referee's performance into question. 'Good,' said the PFA rep. 'I'll write a statement to that effect, then.' He did, and it was superb.

The chairman of the committee introduced everybody and asked my FA man to make the opening comments. He said, 'I can confirm that this hearing is in respect to comments made by [player A] after the match against [insert opposition]. He plays for [club X] and has requested this hearing himself as part of the mitigation ... that's it, really.'

'That's. It. Really?' I said, leaning over to him. 'Was it worth you coming?'

'Thank you,' said the chairman. 'Mr Secretary, can you confirm whether the player has any previous offences, please?'

'The player has no previous offences to his name,' said the secretary.

At this point, the 200-year-old from the FA shut his right eye.

The chairman straightened up and looked at my PFA representative. 'I gather you'd like to read a statement on behalf of the player and other statements from the players involved in this case? Please do so now.'

The statement was very good, concise and factually damning of the referee. But it was the statements from the players that turned the hearing in my favour. Nobody ever asks the other players to contribute statements, but ours were so incensed that I simply had to grasp the opportunity and take full advantage. With all the players singing from the same hymn sheet, the FA simply could not brush under the carpet an accusation of a referee swearing at an injured player while he lay on the floor with a broken foot.

The awkwardness in the room swirled around the fact that I had pleaded guilty to making the statement to the media and so I had to be punished. However, the fresh, swearing allegations completely undermined the charge. The punishment was going to be a token gesture. There had been talk of being fined two weeks' wages and a suspension for calling the referee's integrity into question and implying that he might be biased – something I argued away as simply a turn of phrase while pointing out that what we had here was nothing more than a case of 'my word, your word'.

Just then the 200-year-old's elbow slipped off the table and startled him awake. 'Uhh ... can you very quickly tell us why you said the referee was arrogant?' he said. What he really meant was, 'I haven't been listening and I'm aware that I need to make a contribution for the record but can we hurry this up because it's getting on for lunch.' I was as brief as I could be: 'Sir, if I approach you to ask why a tackle that has broken the foot of my teammate has not been met with a red card, and then you tell me to "shut the fuck up", then I am going to form the opinion that you are an arrogant person.' 'Mmmm ...' said the 200-year-old, slinking back into his chair, 'perhaps so, yes.'

'OK', said the chairman, 'can we have some time to discuss the finer details of this case amongst the three of us and we will reconvene once we've agreed on the outcome?' The FA and PFA representatives followed me out into the corridor where, two minutes into a discussion about possible punishments, the door swung open behind us and 'Mr Secretary' said, 'OK, gentlemen, if you could please return to the room now.' I hadn't even managed to get the wrapper off an emergency flapjack that I'd purchased and stashed in the inside pocket of my suit jacket.

We took our seats once more and the chairman leaned forward: 'You have pleaded guilty and brought to our attention something which, I think I am right in saying, has deeply disturbed all three of us on this side of the table, and as such that has been recognised in your favour. However, I think that everybody here today is aware that the media is not the place for the comments that you have made even if, again, we take your point that you did not mean to bring the integrity of the referee's performance into question. On this occasion we have come to the decision that you should be warned as to your future conduct [I honestly thought that that was going to be it because in the newspapers you always read about the offence last and the amount the player has been fined first] and impose a fine.'

For the record the fine was in the hundreds – an utterly token gesture that had to be implemented because I had pleaded guilty. But at least it was not the many thousands that the PFA had been expecting. It was a very good outcome, made even better by his next comments. Turning to my FA representative, he said, 'We are deeply disturbed to hear about a referee who is swearing at players, injured or otherwise. The FA is at pains to get across to the players that they must respect the referee but clearly, on this occasion, that respect was not reciprocated. We cannot have match officials swearing at players and we would implore the FA to investigate this matter further.'

'Noted,' said the FA official. 'Once again,' I said, turning to him, 'thanks for coming.'

Outside there was a mini-celebration between the PFA representative and myself. 'I'll tell you what,' he said, 'that is as good as you could have hoped for.' Initially, he had been very sceptical of my approach to these proceedings, arguing that they didn't want to hear any excuses; they were just there to mete out the punishment. 'I think we all learned something today, didn't we?' he continued. 'Some things are worth taking the trouble to explain to these people.' Still high from his 'success' he later emailed me: 'Thought you'd be interested to learn, that must be one of the lowest fines ever handed out to a player for criticising a referee.'

'Brilliant,' I replied. 'So I suppose an appeal is out of the question, then?'

He didn't email back, but I don't blame him. What I will say is that his efforts in representing me were fantastic – he could easily have put his foot down and told me not to bother – but I had swayed him. Even so, he didn't have to back me, but he did so, and that is to his credit. (There, happy now, Gordon?)

In the following game we walloped the opposition. They had a man sent off very early on for what was a fairly innocuous-looking tackle on one of our players. The referee later said that the offender had both feet off the floor. When we looked at the DVD of the incident both his feet were on the floor. Don't let anybody tell you that officials cannot be influenced – it's just that football has now worked out far more ingenious ways of doing it than by simply squaring up to the ref on the pitch and calling him every name under the sun. What was a dull day out at the disciplinary hearing had surprising consequences for us. We had learned the truth.

Picture this: a few times a season the same disciplinary meeting room will be box office. An Alex Ferguson or a José Mourinho will rock up, completely unrepentant. The referee was wrong, they'll say, and furthermore he is a cheat and all you people are trying to cheat our little club out of the rewards that it works so hard for.

Everybody will shake their heads and a £25,000 fine will be imposed.

Guess what? Best bargain ever. Nobody is going to jail. Nobody is getting points on their licence. You have just bought three points for £25k. On Saturday night sitting at home with his Prosecco and his Marks and Spencer's biscuit selection, no referee wants to be looking at a 10-foot hologram of himself floating around the *Match of the Day* studio as the boys surgically dissect his performance. Having a Sunday morning pint, dropping the kids to school on Monday, having a coffee with the papers ... no referee wants to be interrupted by anybody who isn't slightly starstruck.

They don't want pity or controversy, or to have to answer questions. They want big matches and to run around having banter with players who they call by their nicknames. And they are fully aware – and this is a massive, massive point to remember – that they have absolutely no recourse whatsoever in the media to counter any player or manager who comments about their performance. I wish I'd worked that out sooner. They are human.

11. A-Z: HERE WE GO AGAIN, SPEED FANS

LIVERPOOL

Every football stadium has its own unique place in the history of English football. I've played at famous stadiums which have since been demolished or turned into 'luxury apartments', like Highbury, and I've also played at their 'follow-ups'. But of all the stadiums that I've ever played in, Anfield is like no other.

The first time I heard 'Walk On' after I emerged from the tunnel, I had a little wobble, the hairs on the neck stood up, and even an old cynic like me had a lump in the throat. It's just an incredible atmosphere – an atmosphere that most big clubs don't afford a club smaller than themselves. With Liverpool it's different: you feel as if they are paying you the same respect as they would for, say, United, or Arsenal.

I only wish I could have played there at the club's peak, when the Kop was swaying with fans holding up banners telling the rest of us how successful they were – maybe on a big European night, with Barcelona, while we're dreaming.

I never saw any of that during the United heyday, no banners or massive flags – just a couple of shitty bedsheets that proclaimed 'Manchester United "the religion"' etc. As much as Fergie and 70,000 United fans liked to tell the outside world that they had surpassed their rivals, the truth is they'll never get anywhere near Liverpool. But for Heysel and Hillsborough, Liverpool would still be the reigning league champions and probably 10 times European champions. Liverpool and Real Madrid would be *the* game in European football. I feel Liverpool Football Club is a victim of circumstance, and it upsets me greatly. To my mind Liverpool are our Real Madrid, our Bayern Munich, our AC Milan. They are England's premier club. But no matter who you vote for, the government always get in.

And these days, the very things that should be daunting at Anfield – like the sign in the tunnel, like the flags, the 'Walk On' homage – tend to just galvanise players instead.

But I played against some great players at Liverpool: Torres, Alonso, Gerrard, Carragher – some team. Steven Gerrard, in particular, was on a different planet. Together with Paul Scholes he is someone I've always admired, the type of player who seems able to get hold of a game at any point and make something happen from nothing. I do enjoy being able to tell people that I've played against Gerrard.

Paul Scholes was a hero of mine, a great player, a man of such talent that it almost seemed unfair. But he did what he was supposed to do – he didn't deviate; he left some things to the players around him. Whenever I played against Gerrard he assumed those things as if they were his own personal responsibility. I have never seen a player take on as many roles in a team as Steven Gerrard without making a hash of it or getting in the way. Gerrard could cross, tackle, score, defend, track back, get forward, head the ball, take free-kicks, score long-range goals, short-range headers, diving headers and powerful headers. People laud Xabi Alonso for his passing ability and little else. But, having witnessed it up close several times, Steven Gerrard's range of passing is twice that of Xabi Alonso's – the passes are accurate, and delivered with authority. He made other players come to the table in a way that they simply wouldn't have at any other club; he made them see what it meant to somebody to play for their boyhood team. And that is why Liverpool won the trophies they did when he was at the club. He was quite simply an astonishing player.

With Jamie Carragher you could never quite work out how he was doing what he did. And I'm not necessarily talking about the level of his performances, his positioning or his technique. I'm talking about the fact that I have never seen any other player in my life get away with so many offences on a football pitch – holding, tripping, bad tackles and especially handballs. He used to get away with fucking murder. Players would just be looking at each other and saying, 'Did I just see that?' It was incredible how he'd get away with so many things on the pitch.

But we're not all saints. I used to kick Adam Lallana to pieces, and he'd snap back and make a bad tackle. Then

I'd hammer him to the ref – as a player who makes tackles regularly you can get away with five or six strong tackles and influence the referee if you get one wrong, because you're known for that side of the game. Lallana isn't known for that side of the game. When a player like Lallana makes a bad tackle it is amplified, and you can really draw the referee's attention to it.

On one occasion I did just that, and Lallana came running up to me. 'What are you trying to do, you fucking idiot?' he asked. 'Why are you asking the referee for a yellow card?' At this point he'd already been booked, but at the time it had just become illegal for a player to ask the referee for a yellow card for an opposition player – although it was one of those rules that referees were never going to adhere to, because we'd have no players left on the pitch.

So I told Adam exactly what I was doing. 'You're on a yellow card, mate. I'm trying to get you sent off. What the fuck do you think I'm trying to do, you little twat?' And he is little. Very easy to pick on. 'It's not a yellow,' said the referee, 'but stay on your feet from now on, OK, Adam?' And that's how easy it is to plant the seed in the referee's head – even if I had made five challenges before that, all of which were worse than his. (When you see players crowding around the referee, it is usually because they all know what's happening in this regard and, in the haste to defuse the situation, it becomes a mêlée that leads to a few pushes, a few grabs and maybe the butting of heads, at worst a punch. The simplest of things escalates into a battle of the mightiest, based purely on the fact that we know the cameras are watching and it will never really spiral into all-out war.)

In Brendan Rodgers, Liverpool have a very good manager. I know Brendan; he used to suffer terribly from telling everyone that he knew José Mourinho although, thankfully, he's knocked that off now. But the ego is still there. I asked a mutual friend who also works in the game what he thought of the TV show, *Being: Liverpool*, when it was aired. 'Not bad,' he said. 'The fans probably found it interesting. Should have been called *Being: Brendan* though, shouldn't it?'

And he has had his skills tested at Liverpool, just as every manager has. The club managed to snatch what looked as if it would be a pretty popular championship away from itself by conceding a three-goal lead away to Crystal Palace in May 2014. Shortly after that, their talismanic captain, Steven Gerrard, slipped on home soil, allowing Chelsea's Demba Ba to score Chelsea's first in a 2–0 win. And that was that. I felt for Brendan.

And in the 2014–15 season Raheem Sterling, the club's 20-year-old flying forward, made Rodgers look ridiculous by saying in an interview that he would have signed a new contract with the club a season earlier for less money if they'd offered him a new deal back then, but, right now, he wouldn't be signing a rumoured £100,000-a-week deal.

A tough spot for Brendan: no manager likes being told in public by a 20-year-old upstart that he's fucked up. But at that time Brendan has to be careful, he can't hammer Sterling too much because ultimately he needs to have him onside and feeling loved by all at Anfield if the club is to have any chance of signing Sterling on a long-term deal (though we all know how that worked out: in July 2015 Sterling transferred to Man City for £44 million, with a further £5 million in potential add-ons, making him the seventh most expensive transfer of all time). Rodgers needed him to be successful for Liverpool because that would make Brendan successful, and Brendan needs to be successful with Liverpool because it is his dream to manage Barcelona. There aren't too many places that I'd ever leave Liverpool for, but Barcelona might just be one.

MANCHESTER CITY

I have some friends who are Mancs, all typical Mancs. You hear so much shit from Manchester City fans. They used to say things like, 'We know we're shit, but there is only one club in Manchester and it is us – we are the club of the people. Real Manchester.' So, now, you'd expect them to say that they really miss the old Maine Road days, when City were a proper football club, the laughs they had with their big bananas and crooning 'Blue Moon' and being useless and stylish and fun.

But no. I never get any hint of nostalgia from any of them, not a scrap. They don't give a shit because they're winning, competing, beating United. They have their own huge impersonal stadium and they don't, for one second, want to go back to being loveable and fun. They don't give a shit where the money has come from or that most of the players are foreign. It is as if United have had such a hold over the city that all the usual questions are swept under the carpet for another day. And why not? If I know Manchester City fans, and I know at least three, it is because they think that somebody is going to come along and tell them that it was all a big joke, there never was a sheikh. A £200 million training ground? Are you pissed? You can see that in the famous old banner that hangs from the Etihad Stadium – 'We're not really here' – except they very much are these days.

The first time I played against what I'll call 'modern Man City', they weren't up to much. They had guys like Vedran Ćorluka, Richard Dunne, Elano – one of the most disappointing players I've ever played against – Hamann (not a Nazi) and Martin Petrov ... they weren't great.

When the real money came in and City put together a squad capable of winning titles, I played against some truly world-class players. Pablo Zabaleta turned up, so did Robinho, although when we played against him he generally couldn't be arsed. And Vincent Kompany appeared, without doubt the hardest, dirtiest player in the Premier League upon his arrival. It was as if he'd spoken to a fellow countryman who'd just finished a career in the Premier League and said to him, 'Whatever you do make sure you protect yourself if you're headed to England. They're animals over there.' Kompany was the first player I saw on a football pitch who actually tried to elbow players from goalkicks and didn't bother trying to hide the fact. In one of his first games for City against us, the referee took the time to tell him that we don't really do that here, rather than send him off; it was as if he could see that somebody had played a joke on Kompany, it was quite bizarre. But it can be good to have that edge. Marouane Fellaini was the same when he turned up at Everton – it must be a defence mechanism that the Belgians have.

City as a whole, however, despite winning the league and a couple of cups since the new-found wealth flooded in from the United Arab Emirates, are still trying to find themselves as a team. As a collection of individuals they have some truly world-class talent but, tactically, it is hard to pinpoint where the team is and what they represent. Every top club has an identity, a philosophy, if you like. Chelsea play their football against the weaker opposition and are generally too strong for them; but against stronger opposition they will sit back and counter. Arsenal play their own game against anyone who crosses their path, as do Liverpool. Whereas other teams lose their identity, lose their pecking order – Manchester United, Tottenham and Manchester City have, to my mind, hit the rocks in recent seasons while trying to find their true identity.

It's all very well setting up the training academies and having the big stadium and the fans to fill it, but without an identity you don't create the dynasty you need to maintain success – instead, you lurch from the odd success to failure and back again. City need to work out what they are, because when they're bad, they're very bad. Yaya Touré and Vincent Kompany, players who should be the men in the changing room rallying the troops, were both awful in 2014–15, with Touré, in particular, crying off to his agent and in the media that he didn't feel loved enough at City. Big man, small heart. As we say in the trade.

And that leads on to the fundamental question about City. Are they a big club? Or do they just have lots of money? Yaya Touré and his agent are at the centre of that argument. 'Some people at City are trying to blame Yaya for what has happened this [2014–15] season. But those people aren't taking responsibility for their own mistakes,' said Dimitri Seluk. 'I am talking about executives who have bought players for a lot of money – and then put those players on the bench. Executives who spend a lot of money on Stevan Jovetić and then drop him from the Champions League squad. I feel sorry for Pellegrini. He's a good coach, but a weak manager.'

During Touré's time with City, neither the Ivorian nor his agent have ever talked about what they are going to do to help the club out of the situation. Ever. They never talk about giving more, or stepping up. They only talk about what they can take away.

I think that at his best Yaya Touré is a fantastic footballer, but there is a caveat to that. Success during Touré's City career has, to my mind, come on his own terms. Surround the 32-year-old with world-class talent and Touré finds it easy to stand out, covering blade after blade of grass and scoring goals from nothing. But if one or two players around him should suffer a loss of form, and the form of the team dips as a result, then Touré struggles to step up to the plate, preferring instead to turn to his agent who, in turn, goes to the press to point fingers at others. That is not the mark of a true champion.

As if to prove the point, Touré offered the following comment when quizzed by a journalist about his options in the summer of 2015: 'For the future, I don't know more than you do, because I will always go where I am offered new challenges. That is in my nature. When things are not necessarily going well in a club, the key players take the fall.'

You might be tempted to say, 'Suck it up, you big baby.' But you'd be missing the point. At the time City had all but lost the league title to Chelsea, and so the challenges for the following season didn't really come any bigger. The club needs to find a way to wrest the Premier League title back from Chelsea, while trying to improve on an unremarkable history in the Champions League. I'd call that a pretty big challenge. So it wasn't about that, not really, anyway.

The Manchester City executives that Seluk has openly mocked know that if the club asks Touré to leave then City will have to pay the Ivorian every penny remaining on his contract. With two years left on a contract worth around £240,000 a week, that's the best part of £25,000,000. And those same executives know that if Seluk requests that his player be allowed to leave City, then Touré will by law forfeit every penny remaining on his contract. Seluk has been trying to get one of the City executives to say something publicly that could cost the club millions of pounds, yet not one of them took the bait – because they're not stupid.

So it's about the money, but for whom? Where is the pay day should Touré switch clubs? It will be for the agent who moves him – one last big transfer could be worth £10 million in agency fees. But for Touré, just a change of badge on the shirt and a possible stain on his character back in Manchester. Is it worth it?

Clearly for one man it is. The worst outcome for Seluk is that his client signs a new deal at City – after ruffling all those feathers he only gets £5 million; if, that is, City even want him.

The shadow across Manchester in the 2014–15 season wasn't that of another raincloud floating inevitably towards the Etihad Stadium, it was just Dimitri Seluk opening up his wallet to see if there was any room left. Big clubs, truly big clubs, don't have these sorts of problems. You don't see big players demanding to leave Chelsea, because Chelsea have established themselves. City are in the realm of attracting players to install instant success while they work on the dynasty, and that creates a type of mercenary atmosphere. City will work through that, but only after they deliver success after success, including the Champions League.

But, believe it or not, there was some fun to be had at the Etihad once upon a time. I remember having a bet with Micah Richards that he couldn't reach our goalkeeper from inside his own half, after City had opted to kick a drop ball back to us. I baited him to the ref: 'Ref, should I just dribble this back to our keeper? He's never gonna reach, and it'll be embarrassing.' Richards was laughing when he hit it, but I lost the bet. Nice guy, Richards, always laughing and playing the game in the right way. His mate Joe Hart was the same when I bet him that I'd score from a corner. I got my head on it, and the ball stuck between his legs perfectly as he collapsed on it. He looked up from the floor with the biggest grin on his face. That's how football should be played. There's a time and a place to throw your elbows about and be a knob, or indeed, throw your toys out of the pram.

MANCHESTER UNITED

After 26 years under the guidance of Sir Alex Ferguson, Manchester United seemed to have a patent on winning trophies. As such, a whole generation (outside of the red half of Manchester) has come to loathe them. I grew up watching the start of that success – the Cantonas and Keanes, then later the Yorke and Cole show – before eventually I, too, would have my chance to step out into the theatre of dreams (a name that is so contrived it's easy to despise) against a team that included Rooney, Scholes, Ronaldo, Tevez, Ferdinand and Vidić. It really was one of *the* great Premier League teams.

I only played in one match where Manchester United totally blew us off the pitch. They played Edwin van der Sar as a sweeper and totally dominated the ball. We couldn't get out of our half, and it turned into a very long afternoon. But I also played in matches against United where we ran them very close, employing a whole range of tactics in the process to dig out a draw.

At Old Trafford we once played three at the back and used the spare man to man-mark Cristiano Ronaldo, following the Portuguese all over the pitch. Our manager really did feel that if we stopped Ronaldo then we'd stop United.

I completely disagreed, especially when they had playmakers such as Rooney and Scholes, but ultimately our manager was right and I think we caught United in a moment in time when even their own players had been wrapped up in giving the ball to Ronaldo. As the saying goes, you can have all the playmakers in the world but if they don't have anyone to play with, then what's the point?

Ronaldo did not get a kick; he didn't even look threatening accidentally. We drew that game and, as with all great moments of triumph in the face of Goliath, nobody on United's team wanted to shake hands. This was something that used to give me enormous personal satisfaction – I'd make sure I ran up behind most of them and slap them on the back and say, 'Well played, mate. All the best for the future.' It was a time when you could really patronise the top players; it's a delicious drug, that little bit at the end of the game.

Not all the games went so well, of course. In one match against United at Old Trafford in front of a full house of 75,000 fans, I received a red card, and that was a fucking long walk to the tunnel. You don't often hear the fans at United, but you could hear every single one of them as I made my way, deliberately slowly, towards the tunnel, observing the 10,000 iPhones filming me. That must have made for great viewing, a player walking off the pitch down the tunnel.

As you walk up that tunnel, you take a little left along a narrow, Astroturf-covered walkway. The home changing rooms are on the left, the away ones to the right. You walk in and the first thing that hits you is that these changing rooms are small, very small. There are showers to the right, but the main changing rooms are not much bigger than some pavilion you'd get changed in on Sunday morning. In the top right-hand corner there's an old box-style TV looming down. I could see the pundits discussing my sending-off already.

I apologised to the players when they came in. They grafted their nuts off and drew the game – a fantastic result given there were only 10 of them against a formidable United. I was already changed, so I wandered out into the tunnel while the lads were showering, and was immediately collared by our press man. He's the guy who sits between the media and the players in terms of interviews and social media. He begged me not to say anything to the press.

No chance. I allowed the papers to pin me to the wall and ask me questions.

'Was it a sending-off?'

'No.'

'Do you think he was play-acting?'

'Absolutely.'

'Will you appeal?'

'I'd like to, but I don't think the FA will overturn a red card against Manchester United.'

'What do you mean by that?'

At which point our press man jumped in shouting, 'OK, that's enough, that's enough.' Then the photographers moved in, more microphones came piling in, more questions: 'Are you saying the FA are biased towards Manchester United?'

'NO COMMENT,' shouted our press man as the scrum continued.

After I left that club I joined another Premier League club, and as the FA so often do when looking to spend money, they turned to Sky and appointed one of their on-the-road journalists to come and present a media-based training day at our stadium. The idea was that the FA didn't want any players getting into trouble for saying things to the media that they perhaps shouldn't be saying, particularly after a match, when emotions are typically on edge. This was their way of educating the players in newly promoted teams who had never played in the Premier League before.

The Sky journalist showed us some of his interviews and asked us questions about what we'd have said. Then he showed us some managers ranting and raving, and then he asked each of us in turn to come up on to the stage and pretend to be interviewed, with the Sky man asking some really dangerous questions. He gave each of us a subject – 'you've just been caught having an affair'; 'you've been accused of calling a black player the N word'. In that last scenario, he asked, 'I've noticed you haven't swapped your shirt with any black players this season. Do you think you're inherently racist?' It was really awful stuff, and some of the players became tongue-tied. I thought it was utter bullshit. No reporter would ever dream of asking something like that, so why ask the bloody question?

And then it was my turn. I took to the stage, and he put it to me: 'So, you've never really got on with any of your managers, have you? Would you say that you are a difficult person to deal with?' I told myself this was just a training exercise, but I couldn't help visualise him in some poxy office, coming up with questions he knew would really piss off a specific player. I told myself not to see red, but I couldn't help it. 'You know what?' I said. 'You can train us to answer all these questions, or you can just stop asking stupid fucking questions.'

I think he saw it coming. 'I'm just doing my job,' he said.

'Ah, that's all right, then,' I said. 'They heard a lot of that at Nuremberg too.'

'You really are difficult to deal with,' he said.

'Maybe I am,' I said. 'Or maybe you just ask shit questions.'

After that, the tables turned. The players were on my side – they respected the fact that I had already played in the Premier League and that all of this was a total waste of everyone's time. The players started chipping in and the pressure got to our man from Sky.

'Let's move on to tackling,' he said. 'Now, in the Championship, you may well have got away with some tackles, but the Premier League isn't quite the same. If you continue to tackle as you did when winning promotion, then you'll have a man sent off every game. Let's run through some tackles and you tell me if they were sending-offs. And then I'll show you if they were or not.'

He played a video of some awful tackles, followed by some that most of us thought were decent challenges but had ended up in yellow and red cards. In fairness, that part of the presentation was an eye-opener for the lads, and they took note. 'Stay on your feet' became the mantra for that season, even if we did lose one or two – ironically, the worst for a foul on Ronaldo, as I recall. Ironic because, just as we were wrapping up, came the last tackle, my tackle at Old Trafford in the season before. Cue a big cheer from the lads and laughter from the Sky man. He'd planned the whole bloody thing: when to call me up for the interview and when to play the tackling video. Now that he'd had his little moment, he was happy. 'That's what we call a Man United sending-off,' said the Sky man. As you'll have worked out by now, this game is all about winning people over when the odds are overwhelmingly in your favour. The trick is to keep doing it no matter how hard it gets, and with complete disregard of what others think of you. If you do that over a sustained period, as Sir Alex Ferguson did for Manchester United, eventually all of those people get caught up in the success. They want a little part of it for themselves; they want to be able to tell people that they know Sir Alex and have spoken with him; indeed they have his number in their mobile phone. Success, celebrity, call it what you like, in football it ropes people in just as much as a teenage girl getting a tweet from One Direction. Costs nothing, means the world, hooked for life.

In his time as manager of Manchester United, Ferguson ploughed that furrow. Referees were scared to death of giving things against United because they knew that Fergie would call them out in public. Even if Man United lost the tribunal, the FA would routinely remove referees from United matches because Fergie had now put them in an impossible situation. It was a clever ploy: the referees who were left were the ones who wanted to referee at Old Trafford; it would be the pinnacle of their career, and they were hardly likely to do anything to upset the apple cart; they ended up favouring United heavily.

Ferguson did the same to the media. When he refused to give interviews to the BBC, Sky stepped in, only too happy not to rock the Ferguson gravy train. Suddenly, Fergie had the media on board. Perhaps most impressively, though, he cultivated relationships with his contemporaries. I've seen managers absolutely in awe of Ferguson. One of my old managers rang Sir Alex to ask him his thoughts on the best way to beat Chelsea. Ferguson sent him a two-inch-thick scouting report on Chelsea's main weakness which, in essence, United felt was John Terry going to ground. Our manager couldn't wait to tell us about the phone call he'd had with Fergie. We lost the game with Chelsea – of course we did.

Ferguson's influence cannot be underestimated. Back in the nineties, United had a very talented youth team midfielder by the name of Michael Appleton. Unfortunately, later, as a player at West Brom, he ruptured his cruciate ligament and the resultant surgery was bodged. Appleton took the surgeon to court, claiming negligence. Negligence was indeed found to be the case, but the insurers disputed the settlement. Ferguson showed up and gave a star turn as a character witness for Appleton, claiming that, even though

United had sold him to Preston in 1997, the boy would have become a great if it weren't for this botched operation. That sealed it. Appleton won £1.5 million in damages – at the time, the largest award of its kind ever for a professional footballer.

A phone call from Ferguson in the right ear when a new manager is looking for a job goes an awful long way. An appearance at the right race, standing next to the right horse, is just as valuable to some people. Ferguson worked them all. But for me, Fergie's legacy isn't all in the trophies that he won. It can also be seen in two of his disciples.

In the 2014–15 season, Newcastle parted company with Alan Pardew and temporarily appointed coach John Carver to the first team. Carver made no secret of the fact that he wanted the job. In his interviews he didn't miss an opportunity to drop in a name. 'Bobby Robson always said to me that if ever I got a chance to manage this great club then I should take it with both hands,' he said. Shortly after, Newcastle played Chelsea at Stamford Bridge and were duly bopped 2–0. Thanks for coming.

Carver's remarks after the match were nauseating. 'He [José Mourinho] said to me, "If you keep playing like this you'll get a five-year contract as Newcastle manager,"' Carver claimed. 'It was nice. At the end of the game [Mourinho] said, "You deserve the job, you're ready for it now ... I hope you get it." We just laughed, and he gave me another hug – he must have hugged me 10 times today.'

I sat at home thinking, 'You poor fool. Do you really think that José Mourinho gives two fucks about you?' It's all an act, an act designed to weaken the opposition before they even step foot in the building, and Carver bought it hook, line and sinker. Two more fixtures every year for Chelsea that have now been made that much easier by their manager's ability to morph his 'legendary' status into the common touch. It's clever, but it doesn't fool me. It fools suckers like John Carver. If I ever went into management, Mourinho would get a handshake and a 'hard luck' from me, the same as everybody else. But he learned from the best in Sir Alex Ferguson, there is no doubt about it.

And say what you want about Ferguson's former captain, Roy Keane – and there are many who do – but he saw through all of this bullshit with Fergie and Mourinho a long time ago, because he understands exactly what they were trying to do, and how this game works. When Chelsea were beating Villa at Villa Park early in the 2014–15 season, Mourinho walked towards the Villa dugout and began shaking hands with everyone – the physios, subs, coaches and the manager himself – as he likes to do to really put his would-be admirers in their place. All of them lapped it up, they loved it; they were in awe of him. But then the Special One got to the assistant manager. Roy Keane didn't take his eyes off the pitch. 'Sit the fuck down and show some respect. There's still two minutes to go,' said the Irishman.

And that is the difference between an actor and the real deal. There are some people who you just can't bullshit, because they can see through it from a mile away.

12. LOTTERY

I knew the kid was good. He stood out the moment I saw him. The proof is in the queue of people looking for a slice of the pudding. Other agents are ringing every day looking for a taste. I tell the kid to leave them to me. Sometimes I call them back and say, 'I understand you were trying to get hold of the young lad? Well, I'm TSF and I represent him.' Always there is a phoney apology while they tell me that they didn't know he had representation and they thank me for clearing that up. I don't mind; it's a good sign in one way.

You get a few of the flash boys running around putting the name out there among the big guns in the Premier League and it's no harm, really; it helps. You just have to watch your back and make sure your player isn't abducted along the way. It's dog eat dog.

That's all a long way off for now, though. We have a career path laid out. Step by step. Circumstances might alter, of course, but we know where we are going and what we want. From here, we will go to the Championship. Maybe half the clubs in the Championship have expressed an interest to me directly. The benefit of the Championship is that a promising young player will get games there. They don't spend good money just to stock the bench for those long campaigns, and maybe three years of Championship football will turn the potential into something more firm. Don't get me wrong, as an agent, you can make money from decent Championship players, but this kid's potential deserves more. I've told him that. From Championship then to the Premier League. Mid-table solid club. A place where he will play and where he will learn. And when the kid is 22 or 23, then he hits the top echelon.

That way he plays his way up. He doesn't disappear into a reserve team never to be heard of again, only to go back down to the Championship to start over. He could go to a top team soon, perhaps, but if he isn't hailed as the messiah after two games he'll be quietly spirited away, never to be mentioned again. Clubs with obscene amounts of money don't offer on-the-job training in the first team. Not when they can buy the finished article out of their spare change.

His dad doesn't see it, of course. The dads never do. Their naivety is terrifying, and when I try to explain how the little nuances of football work, they look at me as though I've just told the world's biggest lie. 'Well, if we don't get a bigger contract here, what is the story?' he asks. 'If he is as good as you say he is, why don't we sign for more money here for a few years?'

I take a deep breath and sit him down. I say that he needs to trust me, but I'm aware that, as an agent, that sounds like the worst thing in the world to be saying. There is nothing more frustrating than trying to sell yourself while attempting to sell somebody else at the same time – very often you need to let situations play out, which makes it seem like you aren't doing anything. Of course, the dad doesn't see the daily phone calls, the gentle nudging of people into position over a number of months, so as to get them in exactly the right place when it comes time to strike. People moan about agents and the money they make but, trust me, the time that it takes to do a deal is painful, and there are a lot of people trying to get in the way while you're doing it.

The kid is doing well. He will have off days, but he is having more good days than bad right now. He stands out in this team, and because of that the cat is out of the bag.

It's tough entrusting somebody else with your son's career, though. And the world of football is a mystery to the man. There's a generational problem too. He's of an age that was taught to take what was on offer today because who knows what tomorrow might bring. Which seems like a good policy, but it's also what football clubs and other agents prey on. On the table from the other agents trying to take him away from me is a new car for his sister, who is leaving for university, a new house for the parents – seriously, that's nothing for the big agencies. I can't compete with that and, if I'm perfectly honest, I don't want to.

When I speak with the dad I have to take a punt and say, 'Listen, this is the situation your son is in. This will happen and that will happen and then this will happen, and these are the reasons why. You will end up here but you have to back yourself, you have to back your son. You have to hold out for what is best in the long term. You have to listen to me. Trust me, I assure you that I know what is coming, just hold tight.' But dads get nervous, and the vultures know it.

We have these chats, and then I have to sit back and wait for the things that I have predicted will happen to actually happen. I have to deal with those things on the player's behalf and his family's behalf, and then I have to tell them those things have happened just as I predicted – all without being a smart arse about it, so that they can see it for themselves.

I believe that I've paid my dues but, not for the first time, those around me feel that I should be offering my bone marrow too.

It is odd, but apart from when I'm having tea in this kid's house, most people recognise the head start I have in this business, having played in the Premier League. The dad never sees that, though.

As an ex-Premier League player gets older and falls down the leagues, it is assumed that he can put bums on seats for a lower-league team. Then, when he can't do that any more, he still has a little cachet left to trade off. He might assume an 'elder statesman'-type role at a club, even though they know next to nothing about him as a man and a human being. One way or another people in football generally lift the phone when a Premier League name calls.

The dad rings me one day. I lift the phone, slightly wary. There has been an approach from Ireland for his son to

play in the under-21s. News of some Irishness in the DNA
is a shock. I'd asked him several times about his ancestry,
and Ireland never came up. In fact, Ireland has never been
mentioned in all the while I've known the kid or his family.
But if anybody is going to find out that you have a drop of
Irish in you it is the FAI.

That said, has he been wearing the green jersey from
under-15 level? No. Word has got out that he's a prospect,
and Ireland happen to be the first out of the blocks.

He shouldn't play for Ireland. He is too good. I explain
this to the kid and the dad, and tell them that my plan is to
use Ireland to flush out England, for whom the boy really
wants to play. I think that's fair to Ireland. To England. And to
the kid. Let him make his choice when he sees what choices
there are. I explain that my friend, an old coach of mine,
heads up talent for England, and it will only take one phone
call. I haven't made that call yet because the kid really needs
to have played more games for his team rather than the 10 or
so he has under his belt. However, our hand has now been
forced, so I'll make the call. In the meantime, I'll tell Ireland,
'Thanks, but no thanks.' 'But,' says the dad, 'Ireland are on
the table today.'

It's a recurrent theme. The kid has been underpaid where
he is now, but the solution isn't to grab the first slightly
improved contract they slide across the table. The solution
is to hang tough and let them shit themselves that they will
lose him for nothing. The solution is to bide his time, back
himself, and come the summer transfer window take a good

cool look at what else is on offer – which, I might add, is a fucking lot, thanks to me.

The same with an international career. It's a big step. If his heart isn't in playing for Ireland, how will he feel in a few years when people are telling him that he should be with England at a World Cup, or whatever? If the kid plays for Ireland in the upcoming qualifiers then he can never play for England. That's a massive loss on a footballing score alone.

And commercially? I called 'the suit' at Nike – you'll remember him from the last book, *The Secret Footballer's Guide to the Modern Game*. He tells it like it is. 'The truth is, mate,' began the suit, 'that Andros Townsend's 15 minutes of fame with England is worth more, commercially, to us than Robbie Keane's long, heroic stint in an Irish jersey. England are overexposed, they punch above their weight, commercially. Their hype reaches millions more ears and eyes around the world – everything they do is a hundred times bigger than Ireland; Wembley alone is a global brand. Mate, I'm telling you how it is. If he plays once for England he'll make a million quid from us as a minimum; if he plays a hundred times for Ireland, we're not interested, I'm afraid.' Contacts like that are invaluable. And I have them.

Is the Premier League the best league in the world? Probably not. Is it the richest? Oh, yeah. Are England one of the top three teams in the world? Definitely not. Are they the best commercial prospect after Brazil? By a mile. Every nation wants to play England and beat them, and every nation will pay for that opportunity. It's not fair, perhaps, but them's the breaks, I'm afraid. This kid is too good to give up on that straight away.

But his dad is adamant. '"We" are going to play for Ireland,' he tells me.

When a father starts to use the word 'we' to describe his own son, the sirens go off in your head. Even so, I advise him, as professionally as I can, that if 'we' play in competition for the Irish under-21s 'we' will never be able to play for England.

'Oh,' says the dad. 'We didn't know that.'

I can almost hear him letting the air out of his inflatable shamrock. Of course you didn't know that. That's why players have agents. Players employ agents as experts in the industry, so they can navigate their careers for them and ensure that the players don't drop a massive bollock. Like playing for Ireland in a rush of excitement when they are good enough to play for England, for whom they really want to play. Ireland and the granny rule will still be there when the kid is 27. England won't be.

Even so, it just so happens that the next two games the Irish under-21s have are qualifiers, and Dad is desperate for his kid to play because it's now, it's really happening, they can reach out and touch it. It's as if the father will be capped for fathering an international. He says that playing under-21s for Ireland will 'put his son on the map'.

What map? Can I name off the top of my head any English-bred 20-year-old kids who have played under-21 football for Ireland and were never heard of again? No, I can't, and that's the point. Never fucking heard of again. It's as poignant as a mass tomb of unknown soldiers with acne. Kids playing underage internationals believing that this is the bottom step on the ladder to the stars. I can promise you now that if you play for Ireland under-21s, nobody gives a fuck. Christ, nobody gives a fuck if you play for the full Irish team. Idiot. Naive, greedy, idiot. If we are planning a career on the premise that this kid is good enough then it's time to start acting like we all believe that to be true. If he is good enough the choice will be there. *When* England ask, not *if* they ask, he might decide that he would prefer to play for Ireland. Fine, but it was an informed choice.

I point out that the only map that matters is the one that I have in my head for the years ahead – and, believe me, the kid is already firmly on it.

And the dad just looks at me with eyes that say, 'What's your angle here?'

Throughout my career I loved the dogfight over contracts. I loved giving advice to younger players and talking them through deals. I know many who had similar careers and can hardly remember signing a contract, but the mechanics of the game have always been an interesting curiosity to me. Club managers call me and they know that they can't bullshit somebody who has just finished a long career as a professional footballer with a reputation for being able to look after himself. Everything is still so fresh. I know where the bodies are. I know where the bluffers are. Some managers call me, full of bluster and bullshit and I feel like asking them whether I shouldn't ring them back before they run out of credit. I remember the small things, little pixels that make up a clear picture of the world of football. I bring them up if necessary. There are direct experiences, and there is what comes on the grapevine. You have to know the terrain, and you can never believe the hype.

I can recall talking to a manager one day, and I remember that only a season or so ago his club was in such dire financial straits that it imposed a ban on shirt swapping among its players. So let's get real and talk about something you can afford. Six figures or more is like a holiday to the moon for them. It ain't going to happen.

I once played for a club where cash was so tight that the kit man managed to remove the name from a shirt of one player who had been moved on before replacing it with the name of a player we'd signed to take his place. In that same season, just before the last game, in fact, the manager instructed us not to give our shirts to the crowd after the game. I didn't hear him or, rather, I just wasn't paying attention, and at the end of the game I gave my shirt to a boy of around eight years old who always sat by the tunnel and had asked me for it after every single home match. I had promised him that he could have it at the end of the season. In the changing room the manager sat us down and thanked us for our efforts over the course of the season. 'Where's your shirt?' he said, turning to me. 'I gave it to that kid who sits by the tunnel,' I replied. You would have thought that I'd just shagged his wife. He went fucking nuts, shouting, 'That's ruined my fucking day, that.' We showered up and I got changed into my suit and walked to my car. Coming the other way was the manager. He had a huge beaming smile and was holding my shirt in his hand. 'Got it!' he said. 'I saw the kid leaving the ground and got it off him.' I was absolutely fucking disgusted, and I never forgave him. It turned out that the kit was going to change for the following season in any event. The manager needed my shirt because he was selling the shirts to fans on the side, and my shirt for that season was the star lot.

I'm waiting for him to ring me about a bit of business.

The kid will have a Premier League career. Further afield, if he wants it. It's nice to be handing that on. It's good to know the challenges from the footballing side as well as the business side.

The other kids, the ones I have gathered so far, will have careers too. How far or how high they will go nobody knows yet, because they are learning and developing all the time. They live in a world where a run of a few games could get them a big move and change their lives. Or they could earn a decent living from football for the next 15 years without ever becoming household names. Even so, they all have a road map. Is that what they want? My advice is that if they are bright enough it's an option they should take.

I look back now and some of my friends are lucky enough to have won League Two or been promoted from League One as the pinnacle of their careers, and I take my hat off to them. They'll say to me, 'Yeah, it's good, but can you imagine what Messi must feel like when he wins the Champions League?'

That's bullshit. The feeling that comes from winning is determined by what you can expect to achieve. The pleasure is in getting the best out of yourself and the fools around you. Lionel Messi playing for Barcelona in a team that lives and breathes big expectations is doing what he is supposed to do. Success is often a relief as much as anything else. They were bred for this. It is required of them. At Real Madrid it is the same for Ronaldo and co. They expect to win La Liga and the Champions League, and when they don't it is a failure. In that respect, and although they are great players, most top-flight footballers have more failure in their careers than anyone else.

When players tell me that they've won promotion with Crawley or Brentford, I know how happy they are because they have got as much out of themselves as Messi has. They haven't got the money, of course, but in the grand scheme of things, and relative to their talent, expectation levels and the standard they play at, they have succeeded. Apart from the money, that's a good reason to have a career in football. You might just fulfil your potential. How often in life does anybody get to do that?

On the pitch, I lost count of the number of times I hammered a player who was clearly better than me because they hadn't won the Premier League or Champions League or an international tournament. It pissed them off every time, and was a sure-fire way to get under their skin. I said it to so many Chelsea players before they actually won the Champions League. Believe me, nobody was more upset than me when Chelsea actually won the Champions League. 'Best left-back in the world?' I'd say to Ashley Cole. 'Are you sure? There are five left-backs still playing now who haven't even won the World Cup who are better than you, mate.' Throw that kind of line at them and it makes them so angry.

I'm decent; I'm getting better – but it's never easy walking away from football. It's probably the agent's life for me. That over the manager's, anyhow. Management is not for me. Watching Gary Neville confirms this.

I love to watch Gary Neville. Not so much his 'best boy in the class' routine, where he dances around the screen making arrows point at spaces. I like to watch the Gary Neville big picture. HD. As in, I sit there and point at the big screen and ask Gary out straight: 'What you gonna do next, Gaz?'

Management is a political combat course. Being a pundit is different. Even being a very good one. You don't have to be reactive; you can sit in the cold light of day, thinking logically and philosophically, which is fine. Here's what they did. Here's what they should have done. Stuck? Somebody will give you a statistic in your ear, the punditry equivalent of spinning the bow tie.

People have different attributes and different qualities which they bring to the table. The trouble is, as a manager, I wouldn't want to have too many meetings with me. Even when playing football, supposedly the happiest and best paid days of my life, I was a very angry, frustrated fucker and hard to deal with. As a manager, dealing with the likes of me 24/7, my balls would be broken. Not only that, you'd get the whole kit and caboodle coming at you with their problems. It's incessant. You get the boys to the training pitch during the week. You plan. What's best? How am I going to prepare for Saturday? I need to think about resting these players because they're coming back from international duties and they're tired. I've got this media shit storm about someone tweeting some other fucking idiot. I have an agent poking my butt about two transfers. The French players won't speak to anybody who isn't French. The goalie was drunk in a night-club last night. I have three suspensions and four injuries. There's an academy kid who'll do well, but he'll leave in the summer if he gets his name in the paper more than three times ... and that's just the stuff I know about and can vaguely control. Then you have Saturdays just to turn your high blood pressure into a great fucking gushing geyser of a coronary.

Every week is a kind of mad avalanche rolling down towards Saturday. Then maybe you are in Europe. Over the course of a few months, with two games a week for a big team, trying to plan and cope and pick the team and win the games, it can get away from you very quickly. Management, to my mind, is the fastest way to fuck your credibility, because there is so much that can't be controlled, and the bits you can't control are generally where people are trying to fuck you over.

Which brings me back to Gary Neville. He is a smart boy. I think he might be smart enough to know that he isn't smart enough. I'll never forget Gary's old boss, Alex Ferguson, saying once that after two minutes of a game at Chelsea (a game that United lost) he had known that he had to bring

Ronaldo off. After two minutes! Hats off for that alone, because at least Fergie spotted it. He knew he couldn't take Ronaldo off, though. Why? Because his management gut told him not to. United may or may not win this game, but for the rest of next week and possibly longer he was going to have one of the best players in the world dragged through the media for something negative that had happened (should he have withdrawn him early) – and United may still have lost anyway.

So he made the decision on the bench that he was just going to have to take this defeat on the chin. He decided that he would bite his lip and put the defeat down to an off day. But Fergie would ride it all out. He knew as far as the squad were concerned, it was just a defeat. They would still win the league. It took two minutes for all of that to go through Fergie's head while in the heat of battle when all around him, as they say, were losing theirs. One decision that impacted the best part of a season – he backed himself on Ronaldo for the long run – weighed up and executed in 120 seconds.

Gary Neville knows this. He has seen it – the Ronaldo part any way. Those decisions that nobody else sees. Those decisions that some might see but not have the balls to make.

Would Gary Neville have taken Ronaldo off? He might have paused, and left him on; or he might have decided that a win at Chelsea would give him a sugar rush of short-term gratification and a scalp to hang on the wall.

With my total respect it's not something that I would want to do, not a choice I ever want to have to make. And I think that's Gary Neville's trouble. He has the TV, he has the

columns, he has the football-themed hotels and the consultancy – sorry, coaching – role with England. He never has
to work again, he has all the boxes ticked, so why the fuck
would he ever want to go into management?

Well, because he won it all with Manchester United. And
no 'TV analyst of the year award' matches that rush. That's
mainlining joy, that is.

So, to everybody's surprise, Gary cropped up on television and explained how it was all done. He's been the best at
that, but he knows that there isn't 20 years in the gig. And
there just isn't the same thrill, the same buzz that he used to
know. He knows that if he keeps doing it he will be parodied
and bettered and eventually he will be bored.

So there is always management. The big jump into the
big pool. Somewhere deep down he knows he wants to make
that jump, he knows he has to. That's the obvious answer
to the mystery every footballer faces. What the fuck can I do
with the rest of my life that will give me some feeling of fulfil-
ment? But I don't think that Gary Neville is convinced that he
can do it. He's had 20 years or something to do his coaching
badges, yet still he hasn't done them. I haven't done them
either, but that's because I don't want to be a coach. People
ask me sometimes, why haven't you done them? You know
everyone else has done them. Giggs has done them, Scholes
has done them. Keano did them. That's everybody who Gary
knows and loves. They've all fucking done them. Why haven't
you done them, Gaz? They must ask Gary Neville that all the
time. Because, Gaz, you, out of all of them, were the one

who was expected to. And there is the pressure, the expectation, the impact on your decision-making that comes from knowing everybody expects you to get it right all of the time. Even after two minutes.

That's why I love watching Gary Neville. Big picture Gary. What are you going to do?

You see, here's the point. Cutting your teeth as a manager is a myth. Especially when you have played at the level Gary Neville has. Especially when you have given punditry of the quality that Gary has given. I think the whole 'cutting your teeth' learning curve, the live and learn thing, is utter bollox. Absolute, utter bollox. What good is cutting your teeth at an Oxford or a Cheltenham to Gary Neville, who has played his entire career in the Premier League and won the Champions League? It's a totally different type of football. We are talking about different beasts. The grounds are worlds apart, the purse strings couldn't be more different, the players are worse; the players' lives at the bottom bear no resemblance to those at the top, they act differently, they don't understand how it works at the top, they don't have the same decision-making skills at given moments in the game.

Furthermore, whereas Mr Gary Neville knows everything there is to know about Premier League football and European football – he's played it, done it, seen it, witnessed it, coached it (in his wet dreams probably) – he doesn't know anything about League Two football at all. So Gary isn't going to start off in League Two. If he's going to be a manager then he is going to have to be a Premier League manager. The problem with that is, which Premier League club is going to risk Neville in the box seat, knowing that he has never been in the role before? Football is nuts.

And if you mess up in the Premier League then it becomes incredibly hard to get back there, and Gary knows that too. It's like the first time you go outdoors to cycle across a tightrope you choose to cycle across a tightrope that somebody has placed over the Grand Canyon. It's different to the practice sessions in the parish hall that you did. There are no mats.

He can't mess up because everybody he has ever criticised with his arrows pointing into empty space is waiting for this. And I don't think he backs himself. I think he's scared of failing. If you fail as a manager it tarnishes you and it scars you like no other job in football. And it does that to the best, regularly.

Managers are getting smarter. More specialised. Tony Pulis has accepted that he is unlikely to win the Premier League. He's a rescue and salvage man now (see West Brom in the A–Z). Clever managers carve out their own little niches, and they are better at working those corners of the street than anybody else alive. You have to clock all that early and do something about it when you get your break at a club which fits your experience. If you don't realise the facts of life you end up just getting sucked down the drain. Once you get stuck down a few levels you are fucked and you are not coming back up. You're never going to get back to the Premier League because there is a room with about five seats in it, and those seats are for decent Premier League managers who are out of work at any given time. Every now and then the door opens and one of them is asked to leave the room and go back to work in the Premier League. Maybe his seat in that little room will be filled by the guy he is replacing. Probably not.

If I did go into management – which I won't – but if I was contemplating it, that is how I would look at it: what are my strengths? What niche can I carve out here? Is it motivating people? Not really. Maybe it is buying the right players and getting in a couple of good coaches to really get the best out of them? Probably. Spotting the right players? That's probably what I could do – so where does that fit in the grand scheme of things? I'm not sure – maybe a Villa, a West Brom, but who is going to give me a job there? Nobody. They can't take a gamble on me. I can't take that tightrope ride first time out. I haven't paid my dues.

Gary Neville is having the same conversation in his head. 'I don't want to go there or there. So who is going to give me a job in the Premier League?' Chairmen don't think like Gary Neville. It's very different working on a white board in a TV studio compared to the interpersonal skills you need when dealing with 30 pros whose collective mental age hovers around 16. Chairmen know that, and they know when they make a mistake with a manager these days there's £100 million at stake if they get relegated, and another million or two sorting out the contract of the guy who has just managed them back into the underworld.

Gary has given himself some kind of persona now which makes it even harder for chairmen; he is now known for something that others relate to, and it isn't management. I mean, if I were sat there in a dressing room as a player, I'd be looking at this gaffer who was a pundit, and I would struggle to get past it: 'You know you're not a manager, really; you've come out of a Sky Sports studio. We all know.' That would be the sort of thinking going on in a changing room – almost as if he's just having a little dabble with our club to see if it suits him.

That's a lose-lose scenario for Gary. Even if he does his badges now, this big clock will start ticking. People will say, 'Well, Gaz, you did your badges two years ago and no one's offered you a job. What's that all about?'

I don't know if Gary Neville would win trophies, but I think he would treat players well and fairly. The kids I am looking after now, with their careers spreading out in front of them, those kids could do much, much worse ...

My point is, though, that the back pages are filled every day with news of players who went into management just because they couldn't think of anything better to do with themselves. When you hear fans singing at their manager 'you don't know what you're doing' most of the time they are right, and you are too young and innocent to work out when they are wrong. And that is the world you trust your career too. You place yourself in the custody of a man, your manager, who is tiptoeing across a minefield while trying to look as if he is striding confidently.

That's why being an agent is a simple and uncomplicated life by comparison.

Oh, and by 'Gary', I mean 'me'. But you got that.

13. A-Z OF IMPOSSIBLE GLAMOUR

NEWCASTLE UNITED

Every time a footballer visits a school for a talk, or takes a coaching session with kids, somebody will put their hand up and ask what it's like to get changed in the dressing room at Old Trafford or Anfield or the Emirates. The footballer always says that it's an honour, that it's brilliant, and that he's very lucky that God has blessed him.

This is the same footballer who you might see getting off the team coach outside the dressing-room door and walking down the tunnel with a serial killer stare on his face and Beats headphones on his ears. He's got that 'don't fuck with me' look. Then the team walks out on to the pitch for a look around an hour before kick-off and the same player with the unapproachable stare is now taking selfies, with every recognisable landmark in the stadium behind him.

I've always thought it embarrassing, among your fellow players, to suddenly whip out your phone and begin snapping anything that moves. Before the advent of social ignorance,

Instagram and Snapchat, we footballers took pictures for us, nobody else. We took pictures to show off to our friends, not our 'followers'. Not for us the four or five players lined up, tops off, six packs on show, fingers making some sort of gesture that looks like cramp in the hands. Back then, taking pictures before the game was a big no-no. If you took a picture of say, the stadium, before the match, or the changing room, that meant you were in awe of the opposition, and any confidence your teammates had in you drained away.

But that said, one of the images every single player wanted a picture of was the famous sign at the top of the steps of the tunnel that leads out on to the pitch at St James' Park. It's half-white and half-black and has the words 'Howay the Lads' running across it. It's an iconic image. To my mind it's up there with 'This is Anfield' – even if it doesn't quite instil the same fear. The crowds in the north east are overly passionate but, if you're a southern team travelling up to play on Tyneside, somehow it doesn't feel threatening; it's just loud. The crowds are actually pretty friendly, good people. Some of them even hang around to talk to you after the game; when you walk out of the stadium to get on the bus they seem to have a genuine interest in discussing how the game went and don't rub it in if they won. They even wish you luck for the future. I like the people on Tyneside very much.

It wasn't a game I played in, but one of the most bizarre moments in Premier League history occurred at St James' Park in 2005 when Newcastle pair Kieron Dyer and Lee Bowyer were both sent off for fighting with each other. As recently as 2014, Dyer went on record to confirm the popular belief that the fight broke out because he hadn't passed to Bowyer, and that Bowyer had taken offence after Dyer had told him that the reason he was being continually ignored was because 'you're shit, basically'.

Dyer's later revelation – 'I didn't know you could get sent off for fighting your own teammate, so when the red card came out I thought, "What the hell?!"' – is telling of footballers' understanding of the rules of the game. I can remember scoring a goal in training from behind the goalkeeper but with a player on the line. The goal was disallowed and I went nuts. There was a man on the line when I put the ball in, how the fuck could I have been offside? It turns out that I don't understand the offside rule in its entirety, and neither did the majority of my teammates. If I could change one rule in the game it would be that pigmy law to the offside rule.

But Dyer wasn't alone in his (mis)understanding of the game. A couple of years ago, I wanted to employ a Secret Referee for our website and was introduced to Barry Knight – the very referee who sent the pair off at St James' Park. Barry wasn't interested in becoming the Secret Referee (not least because he had a very successful multimillion-pound business of which he was the owner) but he was keen to tell me all about his days as a Premier League referee: 'Everybody was shocked when the fight broke out, but as a referee you have to be calm and deal with what's in front of you. As far as I was concerned it was two people fighting on the pitch. It didn't matter that they both wore Newcastle strips. The swearing alone was enough to get them sent off, not that I would have [done that] because you have to ignore the swearing. In my report I cited the punches that Bowyer threw as the reason for his red card and Dyer defended himself so he had to go too.

'Alan Shearer had his arm around Bowyer when I produced the red card for him, and he started saying that it was against the rules for a referee to send off two players from the same team for fighting. Seriously, he was adamant that I couldn't do that; and I had to remind him that I was fully versed in the rules of football and that I was certainly able to send two players off at any time for anything that I saw fit, regardless of whether they were on the same team or not. I wouldn't have minded – I'm used to dealing with stupid things that players say during matches – but he was the England captain at the time. What chance have you got?'

To be fair to Shearer, there is an unwritten rule in football that no matter how blatant the red card is, you must always give the impression that the referee has just inflicted a grave injustice upon you and your teammates.

During the 2013–14 season Newcastle went through an awful run of form, with fans and pundits alike adamant that this was as a direct result of Yohan Cabaye's sale to Paris Saint-Germain in January 2014. Clearly the sale of their once talismanic midfielder didn't help manager Alan Pardew's cause, but Cabaye's departure offered an easy answer to a fundamental problem on Tyneside.

I had a handle on that situation because I know Alan and the problems that his player recruitment policy ultimately threw up. Newcastle's slump in fortunes came well before Cabaye cast an envious glance towards Paris – it came shortly after Pardew banished Cabaye's former teammate, Hatem Ben Arfa, from the club, on loan to Hull.

Let me tell you something about the insular nature of football. If a manager has a fairly tight-knit squad, as Newcastle's was in 2014, then any perceived ill treatment of a teammate is likely to anger the players. Cabaye's sale simply made the players scuttle the ship faster. At the time, there were nine French-speaking players in the Newcastle squad, including Papiss Cissé and Cheick Tioté, the latter of whom is currently the vice-captain, while another three Frenchmen were out on loan, including Ben Arfa.

Let me tell you another very well-known fact about footballers and their camaraderie. Certain persuasions and ethnicities feel a closer bond with one another than perhaps other cliques in the group. And if those certain groups feel hard done by or let down by those around them in any way whatsoever, then problems tend to arise. Moreover, if that group hails from the same country then, depending on which country that is, those problems can escalate rapidly.

And it is also a well-known fact that if the bulk of the group experiencing such a grievance, so to speak, just so happen to be French, then any problems that have escalated rapidly will, in all likelihood, become a managerial death sentence. Remember that scene in *Dumb and Dumber* when Lloyd tries to persuade Harry to go with him to Aspen and Harry retorts, 'I dunno, Lloyd, the French are arseholes.' Well, in football, they are. Now that may sound like a racist, sweeping gener-alisation – probably because it is – but, well, I've seen it with my own eyes on more than a few occasions, at various clubs. But don't take my word for it – even the French national team spat its collective dummy out at the 2010 World Cup in South Africa. When it comes to throwing the toys out of the pram in football, the French are the world leaders. I've seen French players hijack the goodwill and ambitions of an entire squad for reasons that most of us would simply shrug off – outrage, for example, at having to come in on a Sunday to cool down, or over being asked to play a reserve game for a little extra fitness. And they are as one; they stick together. If one feels wronged, they all feel wronged. And that was always the anxiety I felt once it became clear that Newcastle were going to pack their squad with (arguably) cheaper, but talented French players.

This transfer policy is now a proven one on Tyneside. Newcastle specialise in picking up cheaper foreign imports, mostly French, and selling them on for a profit once they've proven their worth in a team that is now asked by its owner to do nothing more than stay in the Premier League. Yohan Cabaye was bought for £4.3 million and sold on to Paris Saint-Germain for £19 million; Mathieu Debuchy was purchased for a fee of £5.5 million in January 2013 and sold to Arsenal only 18 months later for £12 million.

When the retail billionaire Mike Ashley completed his purchase of the club in 2007, Newcastle were haemorrhaging cash: a host of has-beens were commanding inflated wages based on earlier exploits at previous clubs. But in February 2014, the club announced a £9.9 million after-tax profit. This turnaround is down to the fact that Mike Ashley is a hard, single-minded and ultimately ruthless businessman. He sits in the stands at Newcastle with more than 52,000 fans baying for his blood and he doesn't hear or feel any of it. His thoughts are on the group of players on the pitch, and whether any of them look as if they can be sold on in the next window for a profit.

I spoke to a scout I know well at Chelsea, and he told me they'd watched Newcastle's Cheick Tioté for an entire season and drawn the conclusion that, for a defensive midfielder, it was alarming how often he was caught on the wrong side of the opponents' deep-lying striker or advanced midfielder and, as a result, very often ended up fouling the player in his attempt to get goal side.

In short, the transfer policy adopted by Newcastle could well become the rope that hangs the club. Predicting which players will become the next meal ticket is easy – anybody can do it. Getting the signings right in the first place is a completely different matter.

Ultimately, the success of any new signing comes down to a lot of factors that no scout sitting in a stand making notes can ever control. Will a player settle in the area? Will his family settle? Will he make mistakes off the pitch that he can't wait to get away from? Will he like all of his teammates and the coaching staff? If he has a bad run in the team, will it cost him an international place? Will he become jealous that some players are earning more money than he is? Will he have his head turned by media talk of a transfer to a larger club? And when the shit hits the fan and the team go through a rocky patch, will he fight for himself and his manager? Or will he take the easier option and stand next to his team-mates while looking down at the floor?

Alan Pardew's transfer policy ultimately did for him, and he had to move on to Crystal Palace. The silent majority in the changing room made the collective decision that it will support its own. I'm sure the French have a word for it, but based on what I've seen over the years, I reckon they proba-bly keep it to themselves.

Unfortunately for the Geordie faithful the joke goes on. John Carver made a shambolic attempt at steadying the ship at Newcastle and, in truth, should never have been anywhere near the job in the first place. He spent the best part of his tenure on some kind of demented campaign trail, knock-ing door to door to win as many votes for the top job as he could. In doing so, he highlighted the difference between a naive manager and those who are the masters of manage-ment – see the account of Carver's early game at Stamford Bridge, p. 225. Thereafter it was all downhill for John Carver. I spoke to a manager shortly after Carver had accused his defender Mike Williamson of getting sent off deliberately in a match against Leicester. 'Such a basic mistake to make,' said my friend. 'Letting your true feelings rule you. Can you imagine Wenger coming out saying that about one of his players? Who's going to take the boy Williamson now? He's just cost Newcastle a couple of million quid with that shout. Ridiculous.'

Shortly afterwards, the media discovered that Newcastle had approached Derby manager Steve McClaren to take over for the final three remaining games. Carver then made a horrible attempt to keep his hand in at Newcastle by claiming that he was the best coach in the Premier League. And so ended one of the worst managerial car crashes of recent times. Some people just weren't made for the hot seat.

NORWICH CITY

I can still remember counting the money that I made from beating Norwich. We'd bet on ourselves to beat them and we duly did; at the time we were underdogs and the odds were favourable. As I recall we were 3–1, which in a two-horse Championship race is a joke. I'm told that happens every now and again in gambling circles – a little teaser to draw you in. I wouldn't know as I'm not a big gambler. On the coach the lads were buzzing with talk of this anomaly and it wasn't long before I'd committed to a £2,000 stake that was matched, if not bettered, by most of the squad. By the time the bets were in we had actually pulled up outside Carrow Road and the player in charge was still trying to lay off the money through an England player we knew who used to provide this service for footballers and teams all over the country. Still does, I think.

The bet that we laid on us to beat Norwich was huge, many tens of thousands of pounds, and it was spread all over the country. The player co-ordinating the bet would go down the bus asking who wanted to put what amount on us to win. By the end of that brief jaunt he had such a fistful of promised pounds that it took the various bookies two months to pay us out in full.

That goes on up and down the leagues and don't ever think that it doesn't. Betting on matches is big business. It happens every week in every competition. As is typically the way when winning big money, it is customary to get rid of it as soon as possible; we did it by chartering a plane. Seriously.

Once on the Continent we spent the sort of money that would make Michael McIndoe baulk. Penthouse hotel rooms, food, craps tables, cigars, champagne ... we could have bought a fucking plane.

Anyway. None of that tells you anything about Norwich. Norwich as a place to play is fine. I mean it. Once you get past Delia ranting and raving and off her head on cheap sherry, it's a typically East Anglian place to play. Don't get me wrong, the fans think that they're hostile. But as players who have seen it all, you always get the feeling that because of their accents, the fans are only playing at being scary, they don't really mean it; they'd much rather invite you along after the game for two pork sausages and a dollop of Colman's Mustard once the forced unpleasantness of being a football fan is over at 5 p.m. I like playing at Norwich.

And I admire their business. Clearly the catchment area for Norwich is enormous but I maintain that large parts of East Anglia aren't exactly hotbeds for young players and, given that Norwich is a big club, the options for those kids are limited if they don't end up in a yellow jersey. But that doesn't mean that they splash money left, right and centre either – with one notable exception in Dean Ashton. I was talking to Dean about the club where he is now an ambassador (in fact he met his wife in Norwich and now lives there) and he was telling me that he loves the area, the people and most of all the way the club does things. Even though they sold Dean to West Ham and he would go on to have his career ended during an England training session, Norwich were the first on the phone offering him an ambassadorial role with the club. That warms your heart as a player. I have been trying to get across the importance of the ambassadorial role to my former clubs and they totally don't understand it. Yet ex-players can bring in sponsorship, turn up for corporate events and help to grow the profile of a club because they have its best interests at heart. I can't understand why some clubs don't go in for that. Maybe it's me? Maybe they know about that day at Norwich? Now there's a scary thought.

QPR

If somebody from QPR suggested they'd meet me for a drink next Saturday, I'd make other plans. Nobody at QPR plans for that far in advance. I imagine that twice a year the staff all wake up and ask each other the same question.

'What day is it?'

'It's transfer deadline day.'

'Again?'

'Yes.'

'How are we doing in the league?'

'Badly, I'm afraid.'

'Well, can we just buy another shedload of footballers?'

'OK. Any ones in particular?'

'No. Let's just see what we can get and we'll sort it all out afterwards.'

At one stage in my career, when I was at a crossroads, Neil Warnock rang me out of the blue – it's always out of the blue in football – and said, 'Don't do another thing, darling. Just come here and play.' It was tempting, but at the time my confidence was badly shaken and I knew that the QPR crowd could be a vicious bunch at times (all the time, actually). I bought some time, swallowed another couple of pills, and asked Neil to sell it to me.

But the truth was I wasn't quite as in demand as I thought. If Neil had wanted to sell his club to me he'd have jumped in his car, driven me to lunch somewhere and begged me to sign before paying the bill. Going by what Neil said next, I clearly wasn't going to be afforded that luxury: 'People are saying that you have lost your hunger for the game. You haven't lost your hunger, have you?' That meant that Neil was on the fence; he was in 'take a punt' territory, hoping (but not knowing if) it would pay off.

Phone calls like that always have the air of light-hearted 'you know me' banter, but there is a ruthless current running beneath the surface, and both parties are trying to get to the place where the other is at in reality, drawing on things they know to be true. He offered me £10,000 a week. A third of what I was earning at the time, but he knew I was desperate to leave, everybody did. Every line in this situation meant something other than how it first sounded, and there are some bloody shrewd operators out there who know how to go about this practice.

Warnock might have said, 'We're trying to put a few things together down here and we'd love you to be part of it, but we won't break our budget. We have a way of doing things here and the chairman won't bend for anybody, no matter how good they are.'

Roughly translated: 'Sign for us if you want, but we can easily find someone else. It's just because I've seen you play and know roughly what I should get, but you're getting on so I'm not 100 per cent sure, and the wages are going to reflect that.'

And I might have said, 'Sounds interesting. It's a great club and I obviously respect what you've done elsewhere. I've got a few options, to be honest, and I need to explore those first.'

Roughly translated: 'Do you think I don't know what you're paying players like Adel Taarabt down there? Do I look like a mug to you? £10,000 a week – good luck finding somebody for that.'

But the truth is that some deals are just unworkable. Neil really didn't want to pay any more than £10,000 a week. It didn't matter what Taarabt was earning. I couldn't sign for Warnock and leave £20,000 a week on the table where I was – I just couldn't, it would have been wrong. Stupid, in fact.

And in fairness to Neil, whoever he was talking to had given him top-notch information. I had totally lost my love for the game, I was struggling mentally, and I could scarcely handle another morsel of football. Football was gluten. I was coeliac.

But, of course, you don't say that. 'No, no, no,' I said. 'Of course I haven't lost my hunger. I just need to find a club that plays to my strengths, that's all. It's hard here at the moment and the competition doesn't help.'

Roughly translated: 'You're absolutely bang on the money, Neil, and I appreciate the call all the more, if that's what you've heard. We're not going to get this deal done, but thanks for thinking of me.'

I signed elsewhere and, in keeping with most of the stuff I was touching around that time turning to shit, that club went spectacularly wrong in the most public way possible, while QPR marched to the Championship title and the promised land.

Of course, these days, sitting in the garden sipping the first of several Coronas, I kid myself into thinking that it wasn't that bad a decision. I'm still here, just. I'm drinking beer at 4 p.m. on a Monday afternoon and the sun is shining. I'm justifying it to myself to this day.

I played QPR early in my career and learned a valuable lesson. Small London crowds are seldom pleasant. I thought that QPR, who don't win much and give off an air of not caring too much about it, would be about a 4 on the football Richter scale of player abuse. But they have a nasty side.

I've been insulted as viciously and as often at Loftus Road as anywhere else in the country. The pitch always felt swamped and small, with the crowd right on top of us. It was never a fair game, I thought. The tightness of the pitch was always to their advantage. Same for both sides? Fuck off – they play on it every other week and train on something that has exactly the same dimensions.

They are a funny little club. I don't believe, for instance, that Harry Redknapp, having done so much work there, suddenly had to pack it in when his knee got sore. He gets away with the excuse, though, because he is so amiable with the media. He slows down his Range Rover to have a bit of banter just when the Sky Sports troops are at their lowest on deadline day, being heckled by dildos and blow-up dolls. Who would question a man of such decency?

There at QPR is another chairman, Tony Fernandes, who came in and swung his dick about – well, his chequebook at least – until he learned his lesson the hard way and put it away again. It took a long time, though, and was very entertaining to watch while it lasted.

'We need a centre-half.'

'Who shall we get?'

'What about Chris Samba?'

'Perfect. How much shall we pay him?'

'I dunno. £100,000 a week?'

'Is anybody else interested in him?'

'Nope.'

'Excellent. Let's do it.'

QPR's need for Premier League football is so that the club can build enough of a cash pile to fund a new stadium. Until that happens they are making up the numbers like a fat kid in a game of kiss chase. Not Harry's style, really.

And Harry had style. Once, when I was moving from one club to another and putting in one of those stints where you have to live in a hotel for a while, with an empty minibar and a Corby Trouser Press for company, I ran into another player who was also staying at the same hotel. Harry was his boss.

'How's it going?' I asked.

'Good,' he said. 'Good.'

'What's Harry like?' I asked.

'Do you know,' the player said, 'I think I was signed just to give him racing tips.'

'Ha ha, fuck me, really? Sorry to hear that,' I said. 'That ain't good, mate.'

'Are you sure?' he said. 'I fucking love it.'

On his first day he'd turned up to training and Harry had said, 'All right, son. How are ya?'

'Yeah, good, gaffer,' said the player. 'The injury is good.'

'Well,' said Harry, 'any suggestions or tips on today's races?' They didn't drive to the bookies every day after that, but Harry genially asked for the tips of the day every morning at training, and then the pair of them would perform post-mortems the following morning. The player never played, but he was happy.

For now Chris Ramsey is in at QPR and he's doing the whole John Carver 'wonder of me' thing, but he is streetwise with it. He knows the ramifications of what he is saying. He didn't save QPR from the drop but, then again, nobody could have.

QPR was my club that never was, and there is no dressing it up: I fucked up, made a bum decision; I missed a mother-fucker of a gravy train there. It's 4.15 p.m. and I've finished the Corona and it looks as if the sun has settled on staying behind the clouds for the day. Think I'll switch to shorts.

SOUTHAMPTON

Welcome to Southampton FC, known to you as the Saints, and to their rivals 17 miles along the coast in Portsmouth as the Scummers. That's either because the water has a coating of scum or because Southampton scabs broke a picket line in Portsmouth once. But in Southampton they don't care much what Portsmouth call them any more. One of the most bitter rivalries in football is a non-contest now. Southampton have won the football war. They have the money, the big-name foreign coaches and the Champions League chatter.

Southampton are also primed to exploit their geograph-ical good fortune together with their biggest rival's financial plight to go on securing the best young talent for their academy. The catchment area is huge. With Portsmouth out of the way for now and Bournemouth's budget what it is, Southampton have the freedom of the south coast, it seems, as far north as London and the southern Midlands. What should have been their catchment area is actually the sea, so they were allowed to bend the rules a bit and set up a satellite academy in Bath. Further out to the west, the academies of Bristol City and Exeter provide a modicum of competition.

Lallana, Walcott, Oxlade-Chamberlain, Luke Shaw, Bale, Calum Chambers, Andrew Surman, James Ward-Prowse and Harrison Reed all came through Southampton's academy system. (There are others, but we'll leave Wayne Bridge and Chris Baird to one side because we don't want to look like we're trying too hard. We've made the point.)

Here's a theory: not only do Southampton have a nice catchment area and, as we've seen, a fruitful line in central midfielders, they also have common sense. And they know what to do with it. That's the twist. Half the people in football don't know a good thing when they see it. Southampton brought in a guy called Georges Prost from Marseille – which, as you know, Arsène Wenger, is the Southampton of France – and Prost realised that he wasn't going to get a supply of ready-made footballers coming through the gates just needing a light varnish.

So Southampton don't worry too much about footballing ability. They just go out and look for kids who are fast and who are clever enough to be willing to learn, and they add the football bits later. Get them young enough while their enthusiasm knows no bounds and that can be all you need. Southampton have pumped money into a gym, into computer technology, and into a hotel that they call 'the Lodge'. Those fast, clever kids go into the system at one end and come out the other end transformed into useful footballers.

By this method Southampton have come to rule the south coast. Alex Oxlade-Chamberlain's well-known father, Mark, was involved in the youth set-up at Pompey, but young Alex was sent up the road to Southampton when the time came. The latest graduate to come off the Southampton academy production line and establish himself as a first team regular is James Ward-Prowse. He comes from a large family of 'skates', the derogatory term used by Southampton fans to describe their south coast neighbours Portsmouth. Love and hate are fuelled by loyalty. But for a footballer, the game isn't really about loyalty at any level; it's about winning and looking after yourself. You might love Pompey and hate Southampton, but to be a great footballer you will go to Southampton.

So, just to be clear: Southampton don't have a catchment area that takes in most of Europe and chunks of Africa. They don't spend millions on blue-chip young teenagers to put them into their system like China dogs on a mantelpiece. If they are of the right physique and bright enough they are brought in. Then they spend the money on them.

Every team has its own grand plan, and if and when the time comes for me to unleash my own football vision upon the world then a bastardised version of this Southampton model will be the template for producing players for the first team and for the transfer market.

14. MUSIC TO WATCH GIRLS BY

Very little about the relationship between footballers and women is normal.

Initially, I was very rude to girls who wanted to talk to me. I wasn't good at it and I didn't want the hassle that it brings. I brought no respect to my encounters. Today, I'm far better at just going with the flow and having fun, but it's still a conundrum that throws up uncomfortable scenarios. Only last year I was in a members' club in London talking to a very pretty girl about everything and nothing. When she went to the bathroom, another girl walked up to me and said, 'When you're finished talking to her, come and talk to me, and don't drink too many of those.' When I got home I found the piece of paper that I'd got from behind the bar on which the first girl had written her name and number. On the back was another message, which said, 'This is the only number you need ... Jasmine (behind the bar).'

What chance have we really got? As a consequence, some of our behaviour over the years in this department has been nothing short of disgraceful, the sort of things where you tell yourself, 'Well, we can laugh about it now' – and yet you don't. You cringe. I remember ordering a strawberry daiquiri at a pool party in Vegas and then stealing a tampon from the handbag of a girl that my friend was talking to.

You see where this is going? I dunked the tampon into the daiquiri before flinging it high into the sky and watching it land smack bang in the middle of all these college kids in the water. If you're ever at a pool party surrounded by a load of American kids who are totally pissing you off – and they will because they can't help it, with their stupid caps on back to front, high-fiving one another every time the waiter brings them an orange juice – then I can highly recommend this. Never have I seen a swimming pool empty as fast as during the strawberry daiquiri tampon episode. My friend dived into the pool and retrieved the tampon by swimming back with it between his teeth.

What can I say? We were footballers once, and young.

At every club, wherever you look, there are a host of obliging women, hovering. Depending on what it is a player is in the market for there are always several women looking to meet his requirements. It took me a little while to see it when I first started playing football, because I was so naive and so intent on concentrating on being the best footballer I could be. Seriously, that's true. But at my first big club, and new to town, the captain introduced himself and asked me where I was staying. 'I'm in the hotel, mate. It's OK, should be able to get a house sorted fairly quickly,' I replied. 'OK, good stuff,' he said. 'Listen, if you get a bit stiff after training give the masseuse a buzz. She lives not too far from there and she'll give you a good once-over, trust me.'

'Hannah', as we'll call her, turned out to be a very buxom blonde woman in her mid-twenties who knew her way around a sportsman's body better than he knew his own. It is a mystery, to me at least, why these women feel the need to act in this way. The players are doing the same, of course, but it's the women who always surprise me – quite often they are well-educated, down-to-earth women. There is always one at every club; there turned out to be about five at ours. The higher you go, of course, the more there are – but the higher the profile of the player, the more spectacular the story. Rooney can testify to that last bit.

Later, these women took the form of club secretaries and, as the game grew and the money flooded in, PR girls. The one constant from then until now are the girls who 'work in the office'. Nobody knows exactly which office it is or what they do but, trust me, they're there and they are always happy to help. Sometimes they are discreet about it, and other times they go ahead and invite themselves to the Christmas party – but they all share one thing in common: the need to sleep with or snare a footballer. And just when you think that you may be about to buckle under the sheer pull of a woman who walks into the training ground to deliver the fan mail wearing high heels and a skirt short enough to show off the fact that she is wearing stockings and suspenders on a rainy Tuesday morning in January, you hear that one of the youth team players has 'done a bit' with her. And that always ruins it for about a month or so.

As you go higher in the game a new phenomenon takes over: celebrity. One of my former teammates is texting one of the Sky Sports girls as we speak – the things she's going to do to him! I'm very much looking forward to seeing the video. Her idea, not his.

The theory is that if the woman enjoys an equal amount of celebrity, then the less likely it is that the player will be caught out, because she has just as much to lose, potentially. I remember my mate telling me about a little rendezvous he had with the model, Jordan, some years ago: 'It was crazy, mate. When I saw her she'd have to send her friend out of the house in her car so that the paps would follow it. Then I'd have to meet her somewhere before she changed the address at the last minute, just in case I'd been followed without realising it.'

'Was it worth it?' I asked.

A huge smile came over his face. 'What do you fucking think?' Tosser.

Some years ago I booked a villa in Ibiza. Next door was Kate Moss's place and, as I recall, she had gone there to get over the break-up of her relationship with the singer, Pete Doherty. One morning I was taking a walk down the road to nowhere in particular when the gates to her villa eased open and, as the sun came up over the hills, the most stunning woman I have ever seen drove through them in a 1967 red convertible Mustang. It was a perfect scene. Twenty seconds later, two white Transit vans filled with paparazzi hurtled after her, leaving me standing in a dust cloud. Towards the end of the week, small planes were flying back and forth along the coast between the two houses, huge lenses hanging out of them snapping anything that moved. Somewhere out there are hundreds of shots of my arse pointing skyward. I hope they were using a fish-eye lens.

And this is the problem. When footballers entered this level of celebrity, sometime in the mid-nineties, it wasn't just the players who cashed in – the girls they slept with cashed in, and so did the media, even their own families sold stories on them. We used to be able to pay girls off with a grand here or a couple of grand there – Christ, sometimes a handbag or a pair of shoes would do it – but suddenly when the top players became box office we reached a tipping point in terms of what the media would pay and what the player was prepared to pay. Certain newspapers and maga-zines began to lavish six-figure sums on some of these girls, and not just for the ones who had slept with the top players either – big sums were being offered for a story on almost any Premier League player; after all, a good story is a good story. That Premier League brand isn't just good for us, it's good for the gander too.

This happened to a good friend of mine at a previous club. He had filmed all sorts of shenanigans on his phone, and it had slipped out of his pocket in the back of a taxi as he was on his way home from a night on the town. The outcome of this particular incident speaks volumes for the mindset of a large proportion of today's society. Rather than contacting the player and offering his phone back for a reward, the taxi driver, having seen what was on the phone, didn't think twice – he went straight to the *News of the World*. The following weekend my friend was on the front page in all his glory. And the fee paid to the taxi driver? £1,500. As my friend said, 'I'd have given him 20 times that amount to get the phone back.' Having seen what was on that phone, I would have asked him to double that figure.

But if the worst comes to the worst there is always the super-injunction, a court order restricting media reporting of a particular story. Super-injunctions are a desperate measure because they're expensive and, thanks to the media, they have a very good chance of being scuppered on social media sites in 140 characters or less. The red-tops need to print these stories because that is what their readers want, what sells copies; and they have devised a fiendishly clever way to get around any court order that might be preventing this.

The story starts with a headline such as PREMIER LEAGUE STAR IN 3 A.M. ROMP. The paper will plaster an 'exclusive' tag on the side, even if it isn't, along with a silhouette of the player, before giving the reader as many details as possible about his personal life. The chances are that he's married, with children; is highly successful; earns a large amount of money and is coming to the end of his career, and so on. That's when social media takes over, because there is always somebody out there who cannot hold their tongue any longer and is desperate to tell the world that they know something nobody else does. Within five minutes, the player's name surfaces; a week after that the player decides his cover is blown and removes the super-injunction because the retainer he is paying to his lawyer is crippling him.

There is a very famous case of four players at the same club whose chairman struck a deal with a national newspaper for over a million pounds to withhold a story about them being involved in a 'roasting'. That story was never published, and the club recouped the money by taking it from the salaries of the players every week until the debt was cleared.

But the super-injunction exists because it can and does work, though it's used much less these days. Right now my friend, who works for a top law firm in the City and gets chatty after a couple of bottles of Petrus, tells me that a very famous woman who sings for a living had an affair with a very famous footballer a couple of years back. If that story ever volcanically erupts out into the world we will all probably go into meltdown ...

In my quiet moments I sometimes wonder what I'd be if I wasn't a footballer (or an ex-footballer), and it's impossible to get past the answer that Peter Crouch once gave to the same question: a virgin.

It is amazing what playing football can do for a man but, for me, this game always reminds me of the film *Wedding Crashers*. Towards the end of the film, Owen Wilson stumbles into the house of legendary wedding crasher and innovator 'Chazz Reinhold' – played by Will Ferrell – only to find that he is living with his mum and crashing funerals. The epiphany that Wilson's character experiences ultimately persuades him that settling down isn't so bad.

In football, nearly every player settles down early, but nearly every player then cheats on his fiancée or wife. But one African player I knew at least came clean with his fiancée. My wife and I really liked this girl. She was smart and intelligent, and we did everything we could to persuade my teammate that she was a keeper; she was also extremely beautiful. But she wasn't '*Playboy* beautiful' – whatever that is. She just didn't have the massive fake tits and lashings of blonde hair extensions that are the rage right now – she was understated beautiful, natural; she didn't have to work at it. In the end, she couldn't compete with the sheer volume of glamour girls throwing themselves at my teammate, and that was the end of that.

And those girls are everywhere right now; they're an industry in their own right. A few years ago now, I remember a teammate, a player who has slept with almost anything with a pulse, watching *Take Me Out* in a hotel room we were sharing the night before an away match. He pointed to the TV as the camera moved down the line of 'contestants' and said, 'Yes, yes, no, no, no, yes, yes, no, [etc., etc.].' He said 'no' when the camera passed by a particularly attractive brunette, and I stopped him and said, 'What? You wouldn't sleep with her?'

He turned to me and, wearing an expression somewhere between pity and surprise, said, 'I'm talking about the ones I've banged, you prick!'

That's how naive I am. Those girls are on the circuit. Model agencies, talent agencies and wannabe celeb agencies put those girls on that show. They mix in an arena where everyone knows everyone and everyone is sleeping with each other. They're no more the girl next door than I'm a centre-forward for Barcelona.

But then, you already knew that.

Of all the areas where footballers lag behind in an understanding of the real world, female relations are perhaps the most critical. I guarantee you there is hardly a footballer in the country who didn't shudder when he saw the details of the Ched Evans case – a case that shone a light under a lid football normally keeps firmly closed.

For those looking closely, the interesting thing about the Ched Evans circus was the number of people just running around living like parasites off a scandal involving a player who had got himself into trouble. It was a microcosm of the great food chain that football in this country supports. Players are making a living, but there is an industry latched on to football whose only job is to separate footballers from their earnings or their peace of mind.

After his release from jail, following his conviction for rape, and during his first attempts to find himself a club to ply his trade, I had a call from a journalist who told me that Ched Evans was about to sign for a League One club. According to him the deal was done and would go through on Monday. That was on a Friday. I tweeted, 'Just been told that Ched Evans is going to sign for a League One club on Monday.'

And after that, things were never quite the same again in our house. The phone went mad. I want to say that I hadn't intended for it to go mad and, in hindsight, I hadn't perhaps given the story the necessary thought process that it was due. I naively thought to myself, 'Oh, that's quite interesting, I'll tweet that.'

But then it seemed that every journalist who had ever written a word about football picked up the phone and grilled me. Some of them knew that I was TSF, some of them thought they knew that, and the dregs were simply guessing. Either way, I politely but firmly denied and declined any involvement in the tweet or any comment on Ched Evans.

The Sunday papers went first, citing the Secret Footballer as the source of the story, and by Monday morning the tabloids had conducted a full investigation into my tweet and were now camped in the car park of Oldham Athletic Football Club. The intense media speculation dashed any hopes Ched Evans had of signing for Oldham, even if it appeared briefly that the club was going to stick to its guns and sign the player no matter what anybody thought. After a week of incredible pressure and a petition signed by 70,000 people – followed by an attendance at the next home game of 3,500 – Oldham pulled out of the deal.

Twelve days later, the journalist called again. Ched Evans had another offer, again from a League One club. Not wanting to be a hypocrite, I tweeted, 'Another League One club are interested in Ched Evans. I've heard he's going to do a public interview first, then the club will make its move.'

Almost every national newspaper, radio station and media outlet picked up on it instantly. The phone, again, went into meltdown. And then a curious thing happened. The phone rang, but this time the number wasn't withheld. It was a man I knew, and he wasn't happy. There were no pleasantries, no mention of Christmas or the New Year festivities that had just passed; instead he went very much on the offensive. 'You need to stop tweeting about Ched Evans,' he said.

'OK, are you involved with him?' I asked.

'I'm not his agent, I'm just helping him,' came the reply. 'And you're fucking things up.'

'Me?' I asked. 'What have I done?'

'Let me tell you what happened immediately after you tweeted that Ched was going to Oldham. [A newspaper] rang all of Oldham's sponsors directly and asked if they were backing the club in the signing of Ched. If the sponsors denounced the signing then the paper said that it would plaster their name all over its pages, painting them in the most positive light possible. They would be given free advertising and a promise that any bad news such as trading results would never appear. But if they publicly backed the club,' said the man on the phone, 'then they would have every bad word ever said about the company dragged through the paper. They would have the private lives of the board members and the staff scrutinised, with every dirty little secret published in detail. They said that they would actively pursue the company and its senior staff on the front page, until the company supporting the club backed down.'

'I see,' I said. 'They said all that off the back of one tweet, did they?'

'You have no idea of the damage that you've caused,' said the man.

I thought that was a bit rich given who we were talking about, but it was obvious that, because of me, people that I had no connection to had been threatened. Clearly, certain elements of the media had a vested interest in keeping Ched Evans out of football, but beyond some kind of feminist movement within certain sections of the media I still can't work out a definitive reason for that.

I made a mental note that the only way Ched would have a career in football was if he cleared his name first – and even then, it is by no means a given that he'll be accepted by all. The world I thought I knew was weirder at heart and more screwed in the head than even I had imagined it to be. I could feel those invisible forces pushing events around and shaping them. And I thought of the kids coming into the game, the surreal journey they had ahead of them. Here I was in my mid-thirties, and I was out of my depth regarding the Evans case. The storm breaking over a footballer's head was something I could hardly understand. What chance has a kid who leaves home at 14, with everybody wanting a piece of him, of ever understanding how the world actually works?

And yet, on it goes. There's a new batch who don't give a shit who Ched Evans is or what his crime was, and who don't get the chance to heed any of the lessons that can be learned, because nobody in the game wants to bring it up again. They come through academies every year, and every year a string of girls make it their business to bump into them.

In fairness to most of the women I've witnessed on nights out who are looking to meet a footballer, they're usually after something that footballers have which isn't necessarily a washboard stomach or the chance to bathe in reflected celebrity. It's the money and the things that money can bring. And, in that respect, they're part of a great network of organisms linked in their desire to trade off the wealth that top-level footballers have. They're no different from somebody providing watches, clothes, nightspots, holidays, cars ... You name it, there's an app for it.

My favourite story here concerns the car salesman at Sunderland. Any car you might want, this man could get it for you. The Sunderland players like their cars and before long this man was supplying Bentleys and Ferraris to the squad. Then James McClean turned up at Sunderland from Derry City, and he wanted a car. 'Go and see this guy,' the players told him. 'He's the man; he'll get whatever you want.' Off the back of their advice, McClean duly paid a visit to the car guy and placed an order for a brand-new shiny white Range Rover with all the trimmings – his for £80,000. It was delivered to McClean's house in no time at all. Once there, it sat on the driveway. And sat there. One problem: McClean had never learned to drive.

15. A-Z: LA VEGAS STOKE

STOKE CITY

This isn't America; the best players do not get drafted by the smallest teams. In the English Premier League the name of the game is survival of the richest or, at least, survival of the clubs that are willing to spend the most. People laud Tony Pulis for keeping Stoke in the Premier League by playing the percentages in the way the team played. But his real master-stroke was in having the balls to spend big when it was time to spend big. In his last five seasons at Stoke the club's net spend was just shy of £80 million. To put that figure into context, only Manchester City and Chelsea spent more.

There are always one or two exceptions but, ultimately, the club that is willing to spend more than those below them will usually survive. I am convinced that getting promoted to the Premier League, which is an incredibly hard achieve-ment, needs to be rewarded with a calculated risk once the promised land is upon them. The chairmen and owners who say they won't spend big are inviting relegation. I'm not talking about spending money the club doesn't have, but spending the money that it has earned in getting promoted, not tucking it away for a rainy day. If you do that then you can only ever expect one thing: a rainy day. And there is only one caveat to spending big: don't just sign a player because they're available.

Stoke have no delusions of grandeur. The ground doesn't hum on home days. It rocks. Visitors get a tough time from the stands and on the pitch. Stoke like nothing better than a busload of millionaires rolling in on a cold Tuesday night. The number of teams who go to Stoke and decide after 10 minutes that they just don't fancy it has sometimes been the difference between survival and relegation for Stoke. Good for them. Cuddly teams get relegated too. The Premier League needs these tests.

And let me quantify that last sentence by explaining something that pops up in conversation about football from time to time: the argument that the Premier League isn't the best league, but it is the most exciting. What people mean by that is that, although the Spanish league is perhaps technically superior, if you watch any Spanish game, between any two teams, you will see, more often than not, the same game. In the Premier League, on the other hand, you will see plenty of different types of game, featuring two completely different teams, and that usually makes for fast, exciting viewing.

Stoke's record at the Britannia Stadium isn't an accident. In the tunnel, for instance, they line up like fucking giants – giants who hate you. Teams size them up, and know that this is a house of pain that they will be playing in tonight.

I've been there; it's not a nice feeling. You look out and think, 'Fucking hell. It's February, it's fucking freezing cold and it's Tuesday night. This is going to hurt in every way and there'll be no witnesses. *Match of the Day* won't be mulling over this one. Their fans will be going fucking nuts. Someone usually gets maimed after a 50–50 tackle up here; hope it's not me this time.'

Stoke are one of those clubs that attempt to instil this thought process in any opposition player quite deliberately from the off. You rock up in your bus and the gate doesn't open. Deliberate. The fans are out there in the dark throwing abuse and God knows what else at the bus while the guy, whose only job in the world is to look after the key to the gate, goes off to find the key that he knows is in his pocket, while you sit and wait. He finds the key after a cup of tea inside: 'Sorry about that. Now, there's a car parked where your dressing-room door is. Sorry. Can you walk from here through that minefield. Sorry about the rain.' Into the dressing room. No programmes. No heat. No room. You walk out in your clothes to take a look at the pitch. Hostility everywhere. You are walking to the centre circle and the sprinklers come on. 'Oh, sorry about that,' shouts the groundsman from the safety of the home dugout as he reads tonight's match programme. Then there are the small goals for warming up the keepers. They can't warm up in the goalmouth, but the small goals are locked in the little shed and they are looking for the key. Meanwhile, use a jumper and the corner flag here. So the jumper and corner flag become a small goal and two dozen kids crowd behind to abuse the keeper. And if the ball is hit hard past the keeper one kid always gets hit in the face and files a lawsuit, so the goalkeepers perform a watered-down version of their warm-up, not actually getting warm in the process. Then the game begins and the ball boys take their time about giving you the ball back, and the hits are ferocious, and the ref is on the verge of thinking about giving everything to the home team so at least somebody gets an easy ride tonight. On it goes ... Every little thing to make you uncomfortable. You can feel your foreign players shrivelling. You can sense the softer players not wanting it. Sometimes they don't even have to make you uncomfortable. The fear of what is next does that for you.

If I had a club it wouldn't be soft and cuddly. It would be as welcoming as Stoke. There is a competitive advantage in being an ultra-rich club. There is a competitive advantage in complaining all the time about referees. In the absence of a sheikh, we'll take our advantage in being dour and fearsome, thanks.

SUNDERLAND

When I was 18 I went visit to my mate who was at university in Sunderland. On the first day, while he was at a lecture, I went into town for a cultural expedition. I walked around Sunderland, which takes about five minutes, then I walked up to the Stadium of Light, which is on a hill above the Wear. For an 18-year-old who had still only seen Premier League football from the stands, this huge stadium was a big deal.

Naturally, there was a door left open as some sort of trap. When you can see just that little bit of grass through the door and you are 18 and mad for football, it's not a fair game leaving doors open like that. I thought, 'Fuck it. Do it. Say sorry later.'

So I ran up and then ran down. I was still hung over from the night before, but as I got to the edge of the pitch I could see that, too late, there was some sort of stewards' convention going on in the stand. Either that, or in Sunderland the stewards live in the ground. Or I was hallucinating. There were loads and loads of fucking stewards, who all got up as one, thinking they'd win employee of the month if they brought me down. I was some sort of crazed animal, who couldn't be cornered. As they spilled down towards the pitch the fitter ones chased me right up the tunnel and out of the ground. Martin Allen would have leapt like a salmon into the Wear. I just kept running. I remember once saying to my dad that I must be the only footballer to be chased out of the Stadium of Light when I meant no harm only to go back five years later and score the winning goal but manage to leave quite freely.

I realise now that this wasn't the case at all. Sunderland had their pound of flesh anyway. I'm not sure if they still do it, but for a while Sunderland gave a Man of the Match award not only to their own best player but also to the best player from the opposition. After a game in which we'd lost, I won Man of the Match for the visitors and was ushered into a hall high in the stands to receive the award. Niall Quinn, the nicest man in the world, was there organising the very friendly proceedings. I think every citizen in Sunderland had been invited to speak that day, and pretty much all of them leapt at the chance. Eventually, I was given a huge bottle of champagne festooned with the Sunderland club colours. I knew it wouldn't be my last award of the day, though.

I was shown downstairs to the main exit by another very friendly Sunderland official and walked across to our bus. There was a cold, chilling breeze – not coming off the Wear but off the Gaffer's face once I boarded the bus, the engine of which had clearly been running for some time. There were death stares from the rest of the boys who had been sitting on the bus for at least half an hour. Many of them looked as if their weekend work towards researching a cure for cancer had been held up. The gaffer, the coaches, everybody on the bus, in fact, was fucking livid. If there is one thing that professional footballers despise, it is being kept on the bus unnecessarily after a game – especially when you've lost, and especially with all the home fans outside abusing you and banging on the windows.

I tried to walk down the centre of the bus to the back, where I sat – the bloody bottle of champagne with the cascade of Sunderland ribbons did nothing to temper hostilities. I had to apologise to the gaffer, but I could see he was raging with me, so I left it. As I walked past he grabbed the cuff of my tracksuit while looking dead ahead. He spoke three little words that meant so much: 'Thousand pound fine.'

They play the long game at Sunderland. I told that story to Niall Quinn a while back in the hope that he would admit to having kept me in the room far longer than was necessary, subjecting me to those photographs with the entire population of Sunderland. He laughed, but flatly refused to cough up. How rude.

Back then, there was at least some kind of stability to the club. Today, it is totally chaotic. A clutch of managers, all with different traits and ideals, has only helped to establish a hotchpotch of a squad. And, as discussed earlier, the salaries being paid to some fairly uninspiring players are eye-watering. My mantra that each player should always take what they can get and never apologise if somebody higher up is daft enough to offer such wages to you is severely tested when I think of some players at the Stadium of Light earning £75,000 a week.

This may sound harsh but I've witnessed it first-hand and heard tales of it, but in each of the last three seasons, from around August to March, the players of Sunderland Football Club have enjoyed a sort of prolonged stag party around the north east. Everybody in football knows it. Thus far, no manager has been able to do anything about it – in fact, they only seem to make it worse by signing the same type of player over and over again.

It was only a matter of time before one of those players tripped up publicly, and that happened when winger Adam Johnson was charged by police with three counts of sexual activity with an underage girl. Johnson has pleaded not guilty and at the time of going to press he has yet to face trial, but all I can say is that if somebody had rung me up and told me the story without revealing the identity of the player, I could have named half a dozen Sunderland players before getting it right.

Sunderland are crying out for a ruthless, experienced manager who has the balls to kick out half the playing squad and replace them with cheaper, hungrier players. But who the hell is going to take those players from Sunderland, given the salaries and the reputation they come with? The worry for Sunderland fans is that one year soon the end-of-season miracle will fail to materialise and the club will end up in the Championship crippled with debt. The law of averages tells us that, without intervention, it is only a matter of time.

SWANSEA CITY

When I first started playing professional football I had the misfortune to play at the Vetch Field. I have one piece of advice for you if you want to avoid social embarrassment in Swansea. The vetch is a type of legume. Many people think it is some sort of cabbage. It's not. Make sure to say 'legume' and you will pass freely among the elite of Swansea society.

Once upon a time the Vetch was the home of Swansea City. In fact, as I write, I can remember a certain Leon Britton playing in centre-midfield. He is still playing, which I find hard to believe. And he is doing well, a prize legume among the cabbages. Anyway, we turned up at the Vetch Field at 1 p.m. one Saturday, and the shadow of the main stand was covering the right-hand side of the pitch, which meant that it was completely frozen down that side. What followed was a football match played between 22 players almost exclusively on the left-hand side of the pitch. Whenever the ball broke on to the right-hand side you'd see a couple of players scampering after it on tiptoes, with their hands by their sides, fingers pointing out, giving off the impression they'd farted and followed through.

It was funny for a while, but midway through the second half we got a first-hand demonstration of why games are routinely called off when pitches are frozen. The long ice-skating strip had thawed a little. The ball was cleared by our left-sided centre-half and both our left-winger and the opposition right-back went scurrying after it as it spun down the channel. Our winger reached it first but the right-back was committed to the clearance back over his shoulder: as he went to hook it back up the pitch, his standing foot skid like an ice skate from underneath him, and his clearing foot could only make contact at breakneck speed with our winger's cheekbone.

I don't know if you've ever seen a fractured cheekbone, broken nose, missing teeth and a cut forehead all in one go but, trust me, it's fairly gruesome. As it happened, I was young and I hadn't seen any of these things before. I sauntered over as our winger rolled on the ground. Our man was foreign and a long way from home. 'Come on, don't be a fucking fanny,' I advised him. 'Get up and let's get on with it and get the fuck out of here.' Then he rolled over and showed me his face. It was concave. I was told later by a very tired physio who had followed him to hospital that the surgery took three hours. I hope that the words 'don't be a fanny' helped him through it, especially when they inserted the device that looks like a mini cocktail umbrella and opened it up inside his face to pull the shattered pieces outward before pinning them all together.

He never played for us again. In fact, after bumping into one of his fellow internationals in a bar in Spain, I was told that he never played for anyone again.

But this isn't all about me and my good works. Swansea are unusual in that they have a corporate plan. I'm a Spurs fan. At Spurs we have got rid of Bale and Aaron Lennon and don't play Townsend now that he is yesterday's news. Those are our wingers. All gone. We don't need them any more, it seems. Spurs are a club that have typically played with great wingers, from Cliff Jones and Ralph Coates to David Ginola to Bale himself. Was there a big plan or do we continue to just make it all up as we go along?

At Swansea I can see a plan. The difference between the Vetch way of life and the Liberty Stadium operation is night and day. It's friendlier for a start. So, many fans were banned from the Liberty from day one I imagine. The Vetch was old-style racist. Awful. Now the Liberty is quite a welcoming place to go to, but that may be because the more people you can fit into a bowl, the harder it is to hear individuals calling you a cunt. (Sorry, Mum.)

As noted, Swansea have worked out a template for the way they play – and each new managerial arrival develops that template further, without attempting revolution. There are two ways of playing against Swansea. The first involves setting up early on to stifle them by going on the front foot and really going after them. That is hard, because you don't play them with two strikers, but just have the one guy up front. From their goalkicks, when the centre-halves split out wide and the full-backs push right on, the centre-forward can't stand in the middle as he'd be too far away from either of them. The most advanced midfielder has to come in and stand 10 yards behind the centre-forward, to one side. You have to lay the trap that is to make them pass it out from the back. As soon as the keeper puts his head down the centre-forward starts running towards the defender. It makes it harder for them to pass their way out and eventually you'll force someone into a mistake.

At halftime there'll be a general stock take, and in the second half they'll come at you having sped up the tempo for the first 10 minutes. It's showtime and they come out to play. You just grit your teeth and bear it. You stay in your holes and trust that the men around you are concentrating as hard as you are.

The second way to beat them is to go there and focus on not getting beaten. You play on the counter but concede possession, only having the ball if Swansea give it back to you, not chasing it and losing shape. Did I say the thing about gritting your teeth and bearing it? Ditto here. Think of the game at Anfield, the one where Gerrard slipped over. It's the same thing. Chelsea turned up with the sole intention of not getting beaten that day. They offered nothing. And then, bang, bang. 2–0. Always a pleasure.

We beat Swansea at the Liberty once, against the odds. I know it was against the odds because we had a collection on the bus and gave the money to somebody to place a bet on ourselves to win. That's how good the odds were. We turned up and then we went 1–0 down. At which point the guy who had laid the money and was sitting in the stand got up and had an extra private bet on us to win. Lunatic. We would never have backed ourselves to win once we went a goal down. But we got out of there with a win. I can't remember what I did with the money.

What's the lesson of Swansea, though? It's as revolution-ary in its own way as the specialist relegation managers are. Swansea have come to realise that they don't live in a world where 92 teams are all dreaming restlessly of winning the Premier League title by hook or by crook. Maybe 86 teams are just surviving season on season. So to be up there, in the top half of the top division, is an achievement.

That achievement has been made without a Shankly, a Revie, a Fergie or an Arsène. Swansea have decided that stability is overrated, or at the very least overpaid for. Not long after the turn of the century, less than 15 years ago in other words, Swansea were twice sold for the sum of £1, and at one stage sat bottom of the 92 teams in the league.

They left the Vetch Field with a promotion, though. That was as recently as 2005; Kenny Jackett was in charge. Roberto Martínez came next. Then Brendan Rodgers. Then Michael Laudrup. Now Garry Monk. It takes a club with an extraor-dinary sense of where it is going to stick with the plan and establish proper Premier League credentials as managers come and go like that, and it means that each appointment has to be absolutely bang on.

At most clubs things get stale. People get tired of the same voice. Some clubs have enough money to keep changing the players instead of the manager, and the manager ends up becoming a demagogue, building the team around his personality and mowing down all dissidents. No matter how well the team are doing there will be casualties.

Outside of those top clubs your success is relative to who you are and where you have come from. That's why Swansea are impressive. They now have this DNA that says they play passing football in the Premier League. Year in and year out. Next challenge? Their own fans. Swansea will be happy with the status quo for far longer than their fans will be. Fans always want their club to overextend itself. Why don't we buy Messi and put Guardiola in to manage us?

Why not? Because you are Swansea. A decade away from the Vetch Field days and a real success story. Enjoy it for a few more years at least.

TOTTENHAM HOTSPUR

I have a note here. It's for the picture editor if we had a picture editor, or this book had pictures: *'Scoring at Tottenham while wife pregnant, picture of the family in the box.'*

I wish. I'd love to stick it in here. It makes it sound as though my entire family are on the pitch with me, my mum making the run from the back post and the missus, pregnant but defiant, lurking on the edge of the box looking to volley a stray clearance back into the war zone.

As a Spurs fan, is it too much to ask that we make that picture happen? The club is happy to make things happen for lots of other people, continually selling its best players.

I didn't get a choice in supporting Tottenham – blame my father. Actually, blame his father. All of us have seen our own greats at White Hart Lane, and football stirs something deep within us. Remember how I told you that I was chased out of the Stadium of Light? The same thing happened to my father when he was a kid – he'd snuck into White Hart Lane through an open side door, just so that he could get a glimpse of the pitch. (There's something about the pitch: you have to see it, you have to try to touch it.) A painter in the rafters spotted him making his way down the stand and shouted, 'Oi!' As my father turned to run he smacked his head on the metal barriers that fans used to stand against when the terraces were all standing, and knocked himself clean out. So he still saw the stars.

And it looks as if my son will have a star of his own to support, even if Harry Kane looks like he has just won some sort of competition in school. Gareth Bale definitely won a competition for best drawing. There was nothing about his first 20 or so appearances to suggest that Real Madrid would be among his natural predators.

I'm cold-eyed and unsentimental about most things in football. As noted, I'm not one for shirt swapping. But that is also partly wrapped up with the fear of rejection I experience in all areas of life. Anything that has the potential to embarrass me by putting me in a position where people will point and laugh is strictly off-limits. I have visions of asking Wayne Rooney for his shirt only for him to turn around and say, 'Well, who the fuck are you? Hey, everyone, this nobody just asked for my shirt. Can you believe that?' Journalists would get involved and headlines such as SECRET FOOTBALLER IN SHIRT-SWAP SNUB would appear and, naturally, I'd have to emigrate. Fear of rejection is a cruel mistress, a great barrier to possibility. I don't have a history of rejection, mind you – perhaps because I never put myself in a position where rejection can occur. In fact, now that I commit these words to print I can see my own ridiculousness. Maybe it's why this very pseudonym exists? Interesting.

Anyhow, by the time all of that has gone through my head most of the shirt swapping has taken place. On one occasion I remember at White Hart Lane, the whistle had gone and the Spurs players were either stripped to the waist with our shirts slung over their shoulders, or had indicated that most annoying of traits, that they would be happy to swap shirts in the tunnel. The swapping of shirts in the tunnel exists because fans and some managers began to get the arse that players cared more about getting a good shirt than they did about winning the match. (Step forward Arsenal's former Brazilian left-back, Santos.) In actual fact all this has done is deprive the watching world of a very public show of sportsmanship, which is a shame, given that the most famous photograph in the history of world football is a picture of Bobby Moore and

Pelé embracing one another having swapped their shirts in an act of utter, unrestrained respect – in a game that England lost, by the way.

Anyhow, over the far side of the White Hart Lane pitch a lamb had strayed from the flock. He looked disheartened with football, with life. He trudged towards the tunnel, which sits between the two dugouts at White Hart Lane, seemingly with the weight of the world on his shoulders. Gareth Bale was radiating the symptoms of a player who, prior to this match, had played his first bunch of games for Tottenham without winning a single one. He had been labelled a curse by the media; his manager Harry Redknapp had himself said that he'd never known anything like it. Spurs had brought Gareth Bale, a left-back wearing the number 3 on his back, to north London from Southampton for a fee of £8.5 million, and right at that moment it looked as if the money would have been better spent as kindling for an enormous and utterly pointless bonfire in the middle of Hackney Marshes.

One second I had, as usual, no plans to swap my shirt, but then seeing Bale completely fed up stirred something in me that a footballer understands only too well. It's a lonely game at times and, right then, Bale was the biggest loner there was. His teammates were scared to death of seeing his name on the teamsheet, and he knew it. The only thing I had in my possession that demonstrated my understanding of where Bale was in his career was my shirt. Gareth Bale was the lowest hanging fruit in football right then.

The tricky part was getting his attention; he didn't know me and I didn't know him. His name didn't lend itself to an easy call either – no 'Hey, Scholesy/Stevie/Lamps/Wazza ...' 'Baley?' No, not that one. 'Hey, Gaz?' No, awful. I'd never heard anyone call him Gaz. What were his teammates calling him during the game? Oh, that's right, they weren't calling him anything, were they? None of them were calling for the ball from him because none of them were giving it to him. Then it came to me, 'Hey, Gareth!'

He swivelled, as if to say, 'Who, me?' I pinched my shirt at the belly between my thumb and forefinger and stretched it outward towards him. 'Fancy a change-up?' I asked.

It isn't an exaggeration to say that at that particular moment I became Gareth Bale's best friend for at least 20 seconds. He appeared to grow right in front of me, by a foot at least, and a grin broke out across his face. 'Yeah, cool, cheers!' he said, and he took his shirt off as we smacked our hands together and wished each other the best for the future. He walked off down the tunnel looking at the shirt I'd just given him, and as I watched him disappear into the darkness I said, under my breath, 'Any time, mate.' Then I turned to applaud our fans, but most of them had already left.

I tell myself that those fans missed the miracle of White Hart Lane; they missed the moment when I turned a diffident, struggling young footballer into the confident player who, at £85 million, would soon become the most expensive signing in the world, merely through an act of extraordinary kindness – and me wanting a Spurs shirt.

I never played for Spurs, but I've done my bit for the club. And just maybe, once a week or so, in a mansion outside Madrid, Gareth Bale glances up at the wall in his lounge where the framed shirts hang and reads, 'Messi 10', 'Ribéry 7' and 'Pirlo 21', and in the middle of them he sees a framed jersey with the name 'TSF' above the number and he bows his head.

'Fancy a change-up?' Whoever he was, English can't have been TSF's first language, he thinks.

WATFORD

I hate Watford. No, that's an exaggeration. I don't like Watford. I have played in teams that have lost to Watford on a regular basis, which ordinarily would be fine, except Watford are the only team where I genuinely don't know how they're doing it.

Well, not entirely. Watford are a team that have the mix of players down to a fine art: they know what players they need, what works. In some years those players are available and within budget and in some years they're not – and if they're not, Watford are wise enough not to go chasing them.

Actually, the catchment area of Watford is huge, for a start: they compete in Hertfordshire, where they are by far and away the biggest club in the county – Stevenage are close, and Luton (in Bedfordshire) are too, but because Watford are the highest-punching club in the Hertfordshire footballing fraternity they also tend to get a lot of the London overspill in terms of players cast off by their Premier League cousins. And their fans are part of the London overspill too – because of that, they're capable of dishing out the abuse.

In recent years, the club have had a great deal of success in kick-starting the careers of striking talent such as Danny Webber, Marlon King and Troy Deeney, to name but three. And every now and again, Watford put the whole thing together and make a bid for an unlikely promotion. They mix the raw ingredients together and come up with an unlikely shot at the Holy Grail. The raw ingredients are simple: power, fight, physicality, strength, will-to-win, skill and pace. Sounds obvious, but the standout point here is that you don't have to employ the very best to be successful.

Pace is interesting. When Ashley Young was a kid playing at Watford he nutmegged me during a game. It was from a throw-in, where the ball dropped down and fell between us; his lightning feet managed to poke the ball between my legs and he was away. At the next throw-in I joked to him, 'If you nutmeg me again, I'll cripple you.' Young laughed. At that point he had a really carefree approach to the game; he was a kid just doing what his youth team manager would have told him to do: 'Just express yourself when you go out there.' That was how he played. When he got to Aston Villa, it was the same. When we lined up for throw-ins I'd say the same thing and he'd laugh – at one point he even tried to nutmeg me deliberately until I grabbed his shirt and pushed his face in the Villa Park soil. Still he took it in good spirits, and we smacked hands as I helped him up.

A couple of years later Manchester United signed Ashley Young for £17.5 million, and I duly turned up to Old Trafford and stood in the same spot on the pitch as both of us had many times before. But this time, there was no laughter from Young – it was as if he had suddenly left the humour at the door. I found it a real shame. It was now all about winning, performing, nothing else. Ashley Young, by virtue of the fact that our careers collided for so many years prior to that moment, came to epitomise the chess-like dullness of top-level football for me. A little bit of my love for the game died on the pitch at Old Trafford that day.

WEST BROMWICH ALBION

The good thing about having played football is that anybody even remotely involved in the game likes to tell you exactly how deep their knowledge of the ins and outs of football is. You don't even have to fish for gossip. You just shoot at the barrel. Good gossip is football's equivalent of being a made guy in the mafia.

Once upon a not very long ago I was engaged with a law firm on a deal that I have to supply brand partners for football clubs – as shirt sponsors, kit manufacturers and stadium-naming rights holders. They're a huge law firm based in London, and what I like about them is that they too know where lots of the bodies are buried. Knowledge is power, my friends.

At one meeting we went through each football club pointing out where we felt that we could add value and pull off the niftiest of commercial deals. We were pretending to be Masters of the Universe. We got to Crystal Palace. 'Of course, you know why they sacked Tony Pulis, don't you?' said the lawyer from behind the desk.

I didn't know, but I was in the market for finding out. I'm a big player, but small when it comes to gossip. 'Well, I know that he likes to spend money on players,' I said, suitably soberly. 'I assumed that Palace didn't want to back him?'

'No, no, no,' said my man, looking perplexed at the thought that he might have taken a fool for a client. 'No, that's not it at all.'

He went on to open a can of worms. 'Mr Pulis had a large payment due to him for keeping Palace in the Premier League. He asked Parish for the payment to be made early, and Parish duly obliged. As soon as the payment was made, Pulis resigned.'

That was very interesting in terms of the owner–manager dynamic it revealed, but not exactly what I'd thought he was going to say. Generally I am all for managers and players coming and going as they see fit. As I've stated, loyalty in football is a mirage. Pulis did the job, a great job in fact. Pulis was owed the money. He got the money. He resigned. So what? 'That's interesting,' I said, in a tone that made it clear to the lawyer that I was a little disappointed in his anecdote, 'but why resign?'

The lawyer stiffened up and bristled a bit. (That's lawyers for you: half-human and half-walrus, if you ask me.) 'He resigned because there are a lot of teams out there these days that will pay you £2 million for keeping them up. In fact, now he's proved how good he is at it, they would probably pay him even more – £3 million? £4 million? The more he does it, the better he gets. What difference does it make if the club gets another year in the Premier League earning £100 million? Money well invested. The thing was that Palace were waking up the morning after, realising they should have got in bed with somebody who had a five-year plan.'

'A keeper?'

'No, a manager! What is wrong with you? Pulis can certainly get more elsewhere now, so why stay? All he had to do was wait for the right club to come along, the sort of club that should stay up but is actually getting a little jumpy. They are the ones who say, "Let's pay £2 million for a clean-up guy to come in here and sort us out and save us." It's a cracking little niche to carve out as a manager.'

As I mentioned earlier, it certainly is; it's genius, in fact. I had heard of this new breed of gun-for-hire manager who floated through the flotsam and jetsam picking up a couple of million here and there for salvage jobs. I was annoyed with myself for having to have it spelled out. It was a cottage industry (except at Fulham, sadly). There comes a time, a tipping point, a Black Monday, when the clubs in the lower half of the Premier League look at the league table and then look at the fixtures they have left to play. Then they look at the collection of highly paid sulkers and bluffers in their dressing room and decide that if they don't do something quickly they are all going to end up as chopped liver.

Pulis has been at eight clubs, from Bournemouth to West Brom (including two spells at Stoke), without ever having had a relegation. West Brom's ruthlessly efficient chairman Jeremy Peace will have spotted that at some point, and he was on to a winner. Peace tried the cheap option with Alan Irvine, and was the last of the Premier League chairmen to throw out the 'wage cap' that West Brom had in place, which around six or seven years ago was £25,000 a week. Pulis plays the percentages on the pitch, while Peace plays them in the boardroom. If you are thinking, as people often do, about what sort of gift to get TSF as a token of thanks for entertaining them and brightening their lives, a season ticket to West Brom might be appropriate. Far from ever worrying about what the point of West Bromwich Albion is – they'll post profits, buy some more good players, get great crowds, play good football on a decent pitch, have players coming through like Saido Berahino, who they can cash in for 30 million quid and then get all sentimental about – I would red-circle them as one of the most interesting clubs in the league. Would you rather be a West Brom fan or an Aston Villa or an Everton fan? West Brom is a fine example of how to run a slowly evolving football club, and how to go from being completely cuddly to being completely ruthless when the occasion demands.

The wage cap was brought in earlier at the Hawthorns than anywhere else in the Premier League, and stuck with for longer. They were looking for that in-house stability which would float them up from the Championship regularly. Since the turn of the century they have had four promotions to celebrate and, of course, the Great Escape of 2005 when they became the first team to avoid relegation having been bottom of the Premier League at Christmas.

And on each of the occasions that they won promotion, they refused to overspend. They stuck with their managers forever, it seemed, and they were gracious about coming back down because they knew that until they had found the financial tipping point, the system worked. And they always felt that they had the manager and the team to bring them straight back up. They went down with teams of strong Championship players and came right back up with them. Jeremy Peace was a little more hardnosed when he took over as the majority shareholder in 2005 and by 2010, when they last celebrated a promotion, you got the impression that Albion had built up enough money through promotions and parachutes to start the process of fielding more of a Premier League-style team, and were willing to try the technique of aiming for 10th place rather than sticking with a plucky Championship side in the Premier League.

It hasn't always worked smoothly, which is why Tony Pulis is there, but the purse strings have loosened because the competition is stronger. Peace recognised that, so guys like Brown Ideye, Callum McManaman and Stéphane Sessègnon have all come in on transfers.

All that and Adrian Chiles and Frank Skinner as their celebrity fans. Forget your meat pies. It's all raw sex at the Hawthorns.

16. CLOSING

So far this retirement lark has been a trip back to the basics. The real world is much like I left it. I've explored it all with the dogs of Her Majesty's revenue service howling as an accompaniment, and I've seen lots of ideas rotting on vines. All the time, I've been promising myself I won't become one of those ex-footballer statistics concerning divorce or bankruptcy. I am too greedy to be a scout, too odd to be a manager, too wired to be a pundit, too beautiful for you not to hate me and so on. It is obvious that I should own a football club. I should create something great in my own image. The game should be the instrument of my genius, the canvas for my vision.

We had been looking through the classifieds for some time hoping to see a football club for sale. Good value, one careful owner; huge dormant following for this sleeping giant, would suit retired player.

The serious side is that having been through every grade of football I have learned a lot of things that are of little use in any other walk of life. Football clubs are different, though.

I have ideas and ideals that I would like to bring to one. I think we could be successful and make a difference. My sense of rejection and failure seems to tail off when I go back to football, looking for a helping hand.

So we looked for a club that I could seduce. And I kept on looking out for my gaggle of young players, anticipating and choosing the right time for each to take flight. Some would be stars, others journeymen, but they were good kids. They needed a guide to help them navigate the jungle they were going to trek through.

Finally, we tracked down a club that fitted the bill perfectly, one that came within our budget. We submitted a proposal to buy the club: £8 million in cash, plus a £2 million package to cover running costs. The club still had its parachute payments, close to £20 million, which made it very buyable. The owners, for their part, did not want to be there; they had been lumbered with the club and didn't know anything about football.

However, there was a broker involved, and he wouldn't budge. He wouldn't submit our offer and he wouldn't return phone calls, even to our lawyer, a very respected commercial lawyer. We just couldn't get past this guy. We knew why – everyone knew why. This was the club I was telling you about earlier with the planning permission for a small town. The land was worth a fortune. In order to buy time between the raising of capital to develop the land and the breaking of ground – somewhere around 12 months – he was fending off all approaches. And then the broker immediately requested that the parachute payments be brought forward by a year. This was something so incredible and surprising that the Premier League agreed to it without, it seemed, asking why.

These things don't happen overnight, though. It takes at least two weeks to draw down the cash. At the same time the broker ran around the world trying to secure a £20 million loan against the club at an extortionate rate of interest, something like 12 per cent.

To our credit we wanted a football club that we could buy and bring into the Premier League, not because we're the last honest men and women in the world but because we have a mixture of people who love sport and who like to swing their dicks, as they say, amongst the elite. That's how clubs are. There aren't many dreamers with their eyes fixed on the stars. Ambition is ambition. Whatever the professional tier of the football club you buy, it's best that your club's needs coincide with the needs and egos of the people buying it, not their financial interests. It's the best side of a not particularly shiny coin. Don't get me wrong – we want to develop the land too – but it is our intention to return the profit to the club's coffers so that we can improve the squad, not to skim the profits off the top and pay huge 'consultancy fees' back to ourselves.

A week in, we tracked down the offices of the owners. They were based on the other side of the world. Worse, they were out of town on business and nobody had any idea where they were. We got the picture. Nobody was telling us exactly where they were.

As the person who had put the consortium together, with the intention of installing myself as chairman, I was responsible. It had taken me a year to get the funds in place through wealthy individuals, one of whom had been adamant that he 'would never touch a football club as long as he lived'. With time running out, the broker got his loan over the line and saddled the club with a £20 million debt, minus the interest, with only three years to pay it back. And as it turned out we wouldn't be able to pay it back with the parachute payments because they were drawn down too and paid back as directors' loans to the owners. The debt in the club was now huge enough for us to predict administration three to four years down the line, by which time the owners would have fucked off back to the other side of the world. You can go to the 'fit and proper persons' department of the Football League, incidentally, and you can air all your grievances about current owners; you can say things like, 'We think this is happening, can you look into it?' But unfortunately it's like going to the police and reporting a missing person within 24 hours.

'Don't worry, we've found her,' you tell the police later that day.

'Great, is she OK?'

'Um ... no, she's dead. That's why we came to you this morning and said that it was completely out of character. But thanks for your help.'

We came in with the intention of bringing life to a club that deserved better times. Now we will have to sit back and watch the chronicle of a death foretold. If we had ploughed on, the inevitable outcome would have been seen as our fault. Checkmate. So the investors pulled out – rightly so – and the deal which had taken a year to put together fell apart like a cheap suit.

There is talking cynically. And there is living cynically.

But it was a pipe dream. It was a pipe dream that we very nearly pulled off, and there will be other times to buy a football club – maybe not quite as good as that opportunity, but something somewhere will crop up. However, despite telling myself that it was a blue-sky venture, I find myself bitterly disappointed because I allowed myself to act out in my head exactly what I would do and what an incredible achievement it would be to buy a football club and become the chairman.

Life goes on. I have a head that doesn't like time spent in the sidings. Life goes on because I need to earn money. I need to do things. I either work and engage or I sit around in the darkness with the damp, black sack of depression as a hoodie.

The strange thing about retirement is that I've never been busier. Three months after I brought the curtain down on a gloriously average football career, I took a call from a TV producer, a man behind a clutch of great comedy shows, who asked me if I'd like to consult on his latest idea about a Premier League footballer who is always injured. Six months earlier I had written a comedy script about a Premier League footballer who had retired through depression – stay with me, that's not the funny bit – and returned home to be around the familiar surroundings of his parents' house and the friends he used to work with and play pub football with.

Gradually his friends win him round and he starts to play pub football with them again and he starts to enjoy himself and the comedy follows. If I do say so, my script is fucking hilarious and maybe if I don't get a call from the great and the good of TV comedy when this book comes out, I'll publish it online for the hell of it. Come on Netflix, maybe I'll call it *Game of Drones*?

The producer's idea was that he wanted a 'make-believe' Premier League player who was always injured. He wondered how the player would deal with that and what would happen if he introduced a mate, a sidekick, who appeared to have his footballer friend's best interests at heart but, in reality, did nothing but fuck things up and whose wife is struggling to move clubs, away from her support network (sound familiar?). The TV producer is on to something because this dynamic exists. I've witnessed it.

I saw one of my very good friends, a centre-half, completely fleeced by the hangers-on around him. I tried. I really did. But when a player is in the moment, being told what a great player he is and what a fantastic man he is, and how they love it when he buys champagne and gets them into clubs, well, I defy most people not to feel as if they are king of the world. Needless to say, that player has now declared himself bankrupt.

But providing that you have some idea of who is trying to fleece you, and that you are fully aware of the fact your career is going over a cliff, then there are roles in football that need to be filled. The role of the agent is most sought-after, least understood and, financially at least, the most uplifting.

The crop of kids had asked me to become their agent, but I had a slight hurdle to overcome. I'd never sat the agency exam, and suddenly the kids were being offered contracts with their club. No problem. Let me show you how easy it is to register a football agency and what you do if time is of the essence. My very good friend, 'the lawyer' who works in the City as a partner at one of the world's largest law firms, has helped with the Secret Footballer brand in many ways, bringing in investment and know-how. Over too many bottles of Sauvignon Blanc – his favourite tipple – on a glorious evening on the company's balcony overlooking St Paul's Cathedral, we discovered a loophole in the agency world that allowed lawyers to represent footballers. Less than 24 hours later, 'the lawyer' had drafted a handwritten letter to the FA to confirm his intention to become a football agent. He also sent an email version to a general address, which I found on the FA's website. Two minutes later he received the following email response.

Dear Mr ******

I have the pleasure of confirming your registration as a 'Registered Lawyer' with the Football Association. Your registration number is *******.

You are now entitled to operate throughout the FA's jurisdiction; however, please note that you are not permitted to refer to yourself as an 'FA licensed agent' or words to that effect, nor are you entitled to use or reproduce the FIFA or FA logos. You are permitted to refer to yourself as a 'registered lawyer under the FA Football Agents Regulations'.

Your registered status remains subject to your adherence to the rules and regulations of both the FA and FIFA. Failure to comply with these requirements, and in particular with the FA's Football Agents Regulations, may result in your registration being suspended or withdrawn. We would therefore refer you to the FA's website www.thefa.com/thefa/ rulesandregulations/agents where you will find the FA's rules and regulations as well as additional information relevant to agents, such as guidance notes to the regulations. You are under an obligation to ensure that you know, understand, and act in accordance with the rules and regulations that apply to you.

In accordance with your obligations under rhe FA Football Agents Regulations, you are required to supply copies of any and all representation contracts that you have entered into in respect of any transaction in which you have acted on behalf of: i) any club based in England or ii) any player whose registration was held by any club based in England immediately prior to or after the transaction or iii) any player intending to transfer to any club based in England. If these documents have not already been provided, please supply them within 14 days of the date of this email. You are reminded that originals of such contracts are also required to be submitted to the FA upon renewal.

> Please also note that you are under a duty to inform me of any changes to your contact details or circumstances as soon as possible.
>
> Kind Regards

And that, dear reader, providing you set up a company with a good lawyer – or a shit one – who acts as a director and knows how to use email, is how easy it is to become a football agent. Unbelievable. Before the rules changed regarding representation in the agency world, I still didn't hold an agency licence. But it hasn't stopped any league club from doing business with me. I'm not bragging; I'm just highlighting a stark fact. Why sit an exam for a qualification that I don't actually need? If I fail, then I can't sit the exam for another year, so what becomes of my players? I'll tell you what becomes of them: they get snapped up by the big agencies that have the FA 'on toast', as we say in the trade.

But for all that, you need talent through the door – and other people's interest.

The length of a player's contract is critical in transfers because it directly affects the transfer fee for the player. Think about Robin van Persie: Arsenal were forced to sell him for a cut price £19 million to an archrival in Manchester United. It was either that or lose him for nothing the following summer. If he'd had five years left on his contract Arsenal wouldn't have had to sell. The same applies further down the leagues, only more so. Money is tight. The short contract not only triggers interest, it keeps clubs with reasonable means believing that they are in with a chance of signing a good young player. If the kid has a long contract, he is tied to his current club and his cost will become prohibitive.

I point all this out to the gifted kid I represent, and to his dad, over lunch. This is the way the world of football works. To be a success as a player (or as a club) the coins have to keep coming up heads as you spin them. Five heads in a row. Ten heads in a row. It's a tall order. All you can do for protection is plan for the day when a tail comes up and think of some way of staying in the game and hoping for another run. The kid sees it. His dad doesn't.

The kid's dad has been becoming more of a problem the more things go on. He is overprotective and he has that little bit of knowledge that is a dangerous thing. He has that little bit of knowledge that comes from too many people pouring poison in his ear. As he sees it, the nice club down the road have offered his son a perfectly good contract and his son is being told not to sign it. Over dinner at their house, I tell him the reasons for not signing, something that very few agents would take the time to do. (Most would suggest meeting in a service station and even then it would be a ball ache for the agent.) I have spent six months pushing the numbers of his contract north to four times the amount of any other player at his level. By now the phone calls have started coming in from big clubs casting envious glances towards this kid. There is a buzz. Between us we have put him in a great position, holding all the cards.

It's a nice situation. So forget the contract offer – things are moving elsewhere. The Championship, as I've outlined, is the next obvious move for him. No good can come of being hidden away with the training cones at United or Chelsea. He wants games. He needs games.

There is a growing tension between his dad and me, though. Dad is keen to take the first bus that pulls up at any stop – we've been through the Republic of Ireland situation, and now he should be signing the first contract that his current club has put in front of him. There is no long game for the dad. Get everything now in case it ends tomorrow. I'm the guy who keeps coming to dinner and, believe me, it isn't for the fucking curries. Except now he thinks of me as an agent, and if I am an agent I must have cloven feet and a little tail. But in an attempt to show my human traits, I pay the £2,000 that it costs for a complete set of new boots. Nobody else does that. Nobody. It is a sign of my belief and dedication to the kid that I sort this out.

'Hmmm,' says the dad, and narrows his eyes. He's not happy over the Irish under-21s, and he doesn't like the advice about moving on to a bigger club next summer, and making that move more possible by not signing up to a bigger contract where we are now. He doesn't like it, because he doesn't understand it. And why would he? That's why players have agents.

I have been telling the dad for a long time what the kid's current club will do. They will hope to divide and conquer in order to get him to sign this deal and ward off the

Championship big boys. They will try everything to get you to do this deal yourself, I tell him. They will invite you into the boardroom before the game and pour cheap wine down your throat and down your wife's throat. They'll tell you how much they love your son. How it's one big family at the club. Speaking of family, they'll say, 'Do you know that you can do the deal yourself as the legal guardian? Why do you need an agent? At that age? At a family club? You don't need an agent! Silly! We're all friends here, right? We want the same things, right? Agents are so unpleasant. These forms are standard.'

It's underhand, it's deceitful, it's an out-and-out lie. It's clever, though. And the fact is that, as a parent, it is so short-sighted to try to do a deal yourself. The agency regulations changed in March 2015, which means that anybody can now represent a player as an intermediary. They don't need contracts between themselves and the players. This is dangerous. This is opening up the Wild West. It will mean that people will enter into the football world and get fucked over, which inevitably means a young player getting fucked over. The big agencies have moved to address this issue. Living cynical, as they say. The big agencies are now paying the best friend or the father of a player a six-figure salary as a kind of entry-level legal bribe in order to keep the best players on their books. 'You do the deal. We are here if you want to reference or use our expertise. We are all one big family.'

They are employing Daddy (or the best friend) as the agent on a salary-only basis. The actual agency fee goes to the agency itself. It's clever. Bring in the dad and the kid goes nowhere. In 100 out of 100 cases, the dads know nothing about how this side of football works, and more often than not they are working men on £30,000 or £40,000 a year. But this is more like £100,000 a year and to a working man – to any man – that's a lot of dough. To a big football agency it's nothing. They'll move the kid or sign a new deal every three years and take a £500,000 payday each time. The sums add up.

Unsurprisingly, the clubs have clocked this and are doing the same thing. Including the club that I'm now embroiled with. My goal is to get this kid out in the summer. It's easy – he has a year left on his deal and his value, with add-ons, is £250,000, tops. Most of the teams in the Championship are able and willing to pay that level of fee for a player who they can sell on for anywhere between £4 million and £6 million. £250,000 is their punt level. Beyond that, the transfer fee only increases if you are a seasoned professional.

But I'm getting nervous. My last call to Dad has been blanked. That's a warning sign. I know the club are playing on Saturday, and I fully expect the chief executive to slap on the Old Spice and make another run at Dad. 'Cut the agent out,' he'll say. 'He's taking money off your son's plate. You know he's fucked a load of people over before, right? You do know that about him, don't you? He will ruin your son's career. Why take the chance? This is your son we're talking about.'

All true. Careers have been ruined. Money has been snatched off plates. But not by me. By the chief executive. Cynical bastard. By the club. Built in his image. Not by me.

BLACK TUESDAY

Yesterday the deal to buy the football club that we were interested in officially went up in smoke. Today I get a phone call. It's the dad, and I know what's coming because he blanked me again when I rang him last Friday just to check in. 'I've got some news that you might not like,' he says. 'We went down to the club on Sunday and we've signed the deal. And, furthermore, I'll be representing my son going forward.' I can still hear the laughter of the chief executive in the boardroom. The biggest mistake anybody outside of football can make is to think that they can do this themselves. It is a minefield where people will fuck you over at every opportunity. And the dad and his kid, and me – but I'm not important – have been fucked over.

I draw a deep breath before looking out of my window at the river that runs past my house. I see a beautiful swan flapping its wings. It's not dying, but I could really do with kicking it. That's what Dad has done to his son. Kicked him so he can't fly away.

'Listen,' I say. 'I'm just going to tell you honestly and openly what I think about this, and I fully expect you to take your medicine here, then hang up and never bother me again. But please try to listen to what I'm saying to you, because it's important.

'Let me start with the facts. When nobody was interested in your son, I coached him because I believed in him – just me, nobody else. I didn't have to do that, but I did. He asked me to be his agent, not the other way around. I drove the value of his contract up to four times that of anybody else, and you just came in at the back end once all the heavy lifting was done, and signed it. You got a buzz, and now you think you're an agent. You just made a massive, massive mistake. All you have achieved in signing that deal is to handcuff your son to that club for another four years. He would have moved to the Championship this summer and now he won't because the transfer fee will be too high.

'You have just put another £750,000 on his transfer fee and now the clubs that were interested can't afford him because £1 million is outside of their payment strategy for players of that age. But you didn't know that, because you're not an agent. You have no knowledge of the implications of the decision that you just made.

'Furthermore, you've been extremely deceitful. I came to your house half a dozen times, and you kept saying to me that this is all about trust, and I agreed. Everything that I said would happen to your son has happened. Everything that I said I was going to achieve for your son, I have achieved. So let me tell you what has happened. You have Googled the world of the football agent, and you have read horror stories, but you've also seen how much money you can make. You've seen pound signs and you have become greedy.

'But it's important to remember that a good agent has contacts and is respected in the game. I can get to every single manager and scout in the country, and they will take my call. What are you going to do? Phone customer services at Manchester United? And even if you get into the room to discuss a deal they will have your pants down because this is a small world and they will know that you were the guy who fell for the oldest trick in the book and signed this contract. Will you even know how much money to ask for? You may well have just cost your own son a chance of playing in the Premier League, but you have definitely just ensured that he is never paid what he's worth. If I was the chief executive at a club, and the player's dad walks in to represent him, I would think all my Christmases had just come at once.

'The fact is that you need a job to do and you think that this is it. But you know nothing about the industry that you're going into, and people who do that make mistakes. So, for all that, do you know what the worst part of all of this is? That you've been prepared to risk all that at the expense of your own son. That is something that I will never be able to get my head around. Your ambitions to be an agent – something you don't know a thing about – have totally fucked your own son. You'd have had a better chance of being successful if you'd driven him to training while wearing a blindfold with both arms tied behind your back. Good luck, because you will definitely, definitely need it.'

'OK,' he said, and put the phone down.

Later that afternoon, a friend from the club rang me and confirmed my suspicions. The chief executive had indeed told the dad over a number of weeks that I had screwed over a load of people in football, including players, and that I would stab his son in the back the first chance I got, and that I was just out to make money.

It's funny, because the image that popped into my head was one of myself and the kid on the training pitch, when everyone else had gone home, practising ball control while it was pissing down with rain. I didn't see anybody else back then, just me, and I certainly wasn't getting paid for it. But then my mate at the club really stuck the knife in: 'He [the chief executive] also called a meeting with the entire youth team and all the first year pros and told them that if they sign with you as their agent they won't get a professional contract with the club.' Uncalled for, but I know why he did that. He did that because he knows that I was absolutely right in my dealings with my player. He knows that my advice was absolutely right and proper and that my player should never have signed a new contract because he was too good to be taken hostage by this nasty little club. The plan to take him to the Championship was totally correct and the chief executive would have done exactly the same thing and provided the same advice if the boot was on the other foot. I ran an honest race, and I'd run him bloody close, and it had scared the life out of him.

I liked the kid. Still do. All the best to him with Ireland and with getting out of the new contract he has cuffed himself to. He has made the wrong moves but for now he feels like he is winning, and for most footballers that's enough on any given day. The true cost of bad decision-making only ever reveals itself in times of hardship, be that financial or the sudden realisation that the career you'd expected to materialise hasn't. And by then, it's too fucking late.

17. A-Z TERMINUS

WEST HAM UNITED

You won't like hearing this, West Ham fans, but if there is one club that all footballers feel is out of touch with what it can deliver and what its fans expect, it's West Ham United. Every manager I've had, indeed every manager that my friends have ever had, will say the same thing on rocking up to play West Ham at the Boleyn Ground: 'West Ham's fans will win us this match. We just have to keep them quiet for 15 minutes.' And it's true – almost the second that the big hand has aligned with the hour hand at a quarter past three, West Ham's fans start groaning. Seriously, I've been on the pitch and experienced it, and I've been on the bench and experienced it. In fact, never have I heard so much abuse directed at players from their own fans as I have at West Ham, and that was when they were 1–0 up.

I'm not entirely sure as to the reason for this. It could be some kind of reluctance to let the past go. The 'we won the World Cup' stench is still all around the Boleyn Ground, and it's a nice line to trot out as banter, but somewhere along the way it seems to have become enshrined in the West Ham constitution, regarded as fact. Geoff Hurst, Martin Peters and, in particular, Bobby Moore are legends of the game and rightly so, but they certainly weren't alone. It's as if all the '66 business has curtailed the desperately needed reality check that most clubs, at some point in their existence, go through.

Recently David Sullivan, the co-chairman of West Ham, met with fans outside the Hawthorns having just lost 4–0 to West Brom in the FA Cup. He was absolutely abused, with people asking him for 'proper answers' – someone pointing out that they had 'been stuck on the motorway where someone died' on the way to the game. It turned out that three West Ham fans had died that day, but tragic though that undeniably was, quite how that related to David Sullivan is a mystery to me. The point is that at the time, the Hammers were in eighth place in the Premier League, eight points off a Champions League place in mid-February, having not lost in six games. A week earlier they'd lost their talismanic striker, Andy Carroll, to a knee injury for the rest of the season. All these things that you do, West Ham fans, all these things make you weaker; they make managers tell us players that you will win us the game. Ultimately, they make your team beatable.

But that said, sometimes West Ham play well and some-times they even get a helping hand from the rest of us. It was at Upton Park, as it was called then, sitting on the bench, where I witnessed one of the most bizarre moments of my football career. We weren't playing well. West Ham had flown out of the traps, and any hopes that we harboured of winning the game now seemed to hinge on soaking up the pressure and hitting the Hammers on the counterattack. We had the players to do it – well, we did before one of them got sent off in a moment of pure 'head loss'. Midway through the first half one of our defenders got himself into a mix-up and tore his knee ligaments, but the game continued as the ball hadn't gone out of play. Struggling to get back into position, one of the West Ham players saw our defender hobbling back and flighted a perfect pass over his head to Carlton Cole, who duly scored. That's how good you have to be to play Premier League football – you have to be able to see things like that as a player, especially a midfielder; you have to be able to take advantage in an instant of anything that presents itself. Carlton Cole didn't just wander into that position by accident. He had sussed the opportunity.

Unfortunately, our striker was less observant and hadn't seen that the defender had injured himself in the build-up. He thought that our defender had simply lost position and been too lazy to get back into shape. He began shouting at our defender, who had clearly had enough and strode purposefully down the pitch to confront him. I thought that was odd, and immediately stood up to get a view of the conversation. As they got closer, our striker started waving his arms and pointing to the goal, then kept turning his back as if to illustrate that our defender had been caught on the wrong side of the player with his back to play, which was true enough. The problem is that when you injure your ligaments you can't turn your body in the conventional way; you turn it in the direction of least pain. At no point did our defender point to his knee, which I thought was both admirable and stupid. The two players got closer before, bang, the striker hit our defender clean in the face. On the pitch our players looked disgusted with our striker – he'd let us all down, and we all showed it visibly. And yet in the changing room, after we'd lost the game, only one person said anything – and that was because he took offence at our manager saying, 'I know you hate him right now.' The player retorted, 'No, we don't hate him, gaffer. "Hate" is a strong word. We don't hate him, but he's fucking let us down and dropped us right in the shit and made us look like cunts.' All of which was true. But the vigour with which our manager defended our striker, our best source of goals, was startling. Our striker had hit one of his own players and yet here we were being asked not to hate him, to forgive him and concentrate on the next game. Two things happened after that. Firstly, our striker never apologised to us on the bus, which he should have. And, secondly, that defender never played another game for us again. When that happened I lost every ounce of respect I had for that manager, but now I realise he was just displaying the ultimate selfishness, the same selfishness that Fergie had. It is often said in football that to be a manager you are either the best friend of the players, or you are successful. It was a big lesson.

I used to debate this point with my best friends. We're a little foursome that goes way back. One of them is a big West Ham fan, who was in the stadium that day, while the other two support Arsenal and Tottenham, respectively. Every year we bet £10 on which of our teams will finish highest. Historically, this has generally become a case of handing over cash immediately to the Arsenal fan, although recently things have become more interesting. Two years ago 'Scott', as we'll call him, bet me that West Ham would beat Spurs home and away. He duly won, and in the middle of that he also bet that the Hammers would beat Spurs in their Capital One Cup match. They did. Good year for Scott. Cue mass hysteria at West Ham and the ordering of 10,000 Fruit of the Loom T-shirts to commemorate something for which there is no trophy. Although, I may just be a bitter Spurs fan.

However, last year wasn't such a good one for Scott, and he owed me a tenner for West Ham's defeat to Spurs in August. But I haven't exactly got time to turn up at Scott's door and start demanding a tenner, have I? Moreover, since my retirement, I've been busier than ever and getting the four of us together has been tough – and in every case it has been because I just couldn't find the time. Text message between TSF and Scott, 29 July 2014:

Scott: 'All right, pal? When you were suffering with depression what was the medication you were on?'

TSF: 'Citalopram.'

Scott: 'Just been put on it tonight.'

TSF: 'Good. You'll feel much better soon.'

Scott: 'Cheers, pal. Been at rock bottom for a while. Me and the missus going through a mutual break-up, both unhappy. Doc reckons these will help. Hardest step getting to the doctor's, so hopefully things will start to change.'

TSF: 'Fair enough, mate. You gotta do what's right.'

Scott: 'Obviously not easy though coz of the boys, so took a lot of thinking, etc. But they'll have a happier daddy now, over the coming weeks/months.'

TSF: 'It's all about the kids, mate.'

Scott: 'Absolutely, pal. Kids are the most important thing in all of it.'

The above is a word-for-word exchange of texts, and as you can see from my bluntness that I was absolutely flat out working on books and getting my shit together after retirement. I was dealing with my club to make sure that they paid me what we'd agreed. (Don't ever think that the club will just pay you. 'Oh, you didn't get it? Sorry, not sure what happened there. We'll look in to it, it must be HSBC's fault. Maybe they fucked up?' Yeah ... that must be it.) I was also fighting to get the bank off my back, who wanted to know what I was going to do now and that the severance money from the club I'd just left should by rights belong to them. Never happening.

But even so, for a subject such as depression – something that I know rather a lot about – I was a fucking disgrace in helping Scott. He had reached out and I was nowhere to be found. Instead, I was completely wrapped up in my own little world, struggling to meet the deadline for my previous book, *The Secret Footballer's Guide to the Modern Game*. That

Saturday night he invited the three of us, plus a few others, up to a restaurant close to where we're all from. I could have gone, I really could have, but I didn't. I saw the pictures of them all on Facebook the following day, having a nice meal, smiling and laughing together. And I felt a little guilty, to be honest – but no more so than normal. There'd be other times, after all.

The next day we all went about our business. I went to training, the brothers went to work, and so did Scott, digging a trench to lay a gas pipe in a town close to where all of us grew up. At 11.30 a.m. Scott threw down his shovel and turning to his workmate said, 'Fuck this, let's call it a day.' Not wanting to turn his nose up at the possibility of a half-day, Scott's workmate agreed and offered to drive the van home, dropping Scott off two miles down the road at his mum and dad's house, both of whom were at work. Scott took the spare key from his pocket and opened the front door. He walked into the hallway and threw his bag down before taking a left turn into the adjoining garage where he hanged himself. He left behind his wife and my godchildren, two little boys, both of whom are absolutely football mad and crazy about West Ham United.

Now, whenever a journalist I know asks me the question, 'So, how many people know that you are TSF?' the answer is easy: one less than before. Sometimes I feel him. I don't know what it is, but as I'm writing this, I feel him. I know he's looking at me and I don't want to look up from my laptop because I don't want to see him looking at me.

After he was buried I just couldn't deal with it – it was too much. Sometimes when I'm standing on the station platform with the King's Cross express approaching at full speed, I think about the day that a little village church was taken over by 600 people wearing claret and blue, standing room only, with 'I'm Forever Blowing Bubbles' playing over the sound system. I think about the difference between the expectation and the reality of life, and how out of sync they can sometimes be, and I use the time to draw a comparison between the West Ham fans and my friend, because in the time that it takes me to do that, the train has passed.

I think about him every day.

EPILOGUE

As for me. Welcome back to the world of football. I had forgotten that this is how it really works: deals to buy clubs going wrong, dads of players getting above their station, two years down the fucking pan in the world of living cynically.

Time to take stock. Let's put what we're usually told about football into perspective, because it is the sort of shit that I have tried, through these books, to show up for what it is. Are we better off for knowing that Alex Ferguson thinks Wayne Rooney is a baby? Probably not. Are we better off for knowing that Wayne Rooney has had a hair transplant (and will need another in the next three years)? Probably not. Are we better off knowing that Luis Suárez is a racist or that David Beckham has OCD to the point where he has to face the brand names of products outwards when he assembles them in the fridge? Probably not. Even so, many of you out there paid your hard-earned money to read about all of the above.

It was this bullshit as much as anything else that I wanted to put in its place by writing about the game as the game deserves to be written about. And it is also the same bullshit

– the circus around football – that I now need a break from. I love playing football, but all the peripheral shit has curbed my appetite for it considerably. I've been involved in this game every day for nearly 15 years. It has been an eye-opener and, more and more, an inconvenience. There is no memorabilia in my house; there is nothing to suggest that I ever played football – if I were selling my home and you came to view it you'd guess that an architect, a designer or an artist lived there. The idiosyncrasies in football have become a form of torture for me; the characteristics that define football, especially in this country, are the same characteristics that bring on the red mist.

When a player shoots and the ball flies over the goal, I just want to punch the grown men in the crowd who can't wait to leap up with their arms in the air. The same too for the referees who look past you into space without saying a word, even though I'm only a yard away trying to make a point about an incident in the game. Elsewhere, I don't want a man who knows less than me about football to tell me what time I have to be somewhere and where I have to go, especially when it involves me wearing a silly, cheap-looking tracksuit. I'm a grown man.

I stopped reading the football section of my newspaper many years ago, but it's impossible to avoid when I'm out and about and the back page has been left unfurled on the train. I hate it. I hate reading about it. I hate seeing the name of my former team on the map of Great Britain every time the fucking weather comes on after the BBC news – it reminds me of shit times, depressing times. I fucking hate the way, when a player scores a goal, that the opposition fans will rush down to the front of the stands and hurl the most obscene amounts of abuse at him for doing his job well, but make out that the three-foot-high advertising hoarding is somehow insurmountable, preventing them from getting on to the pitch. Seriously, you see grown men with one leg hanging over the hoarding as if that was as far as they could get, the other leg planted in the stands. I'm willing them to hurdle the barrier, just so I can see what will actually happen … but they never do.

I hate catching a glimpse of John Terry's face in the newspaper left on the train. I'm sick to fucking death of seeing Wayne Rooney's grin on an advertising board. I hate seeing some of the idiots involved in punditry. When I first saw Thierry Henry on Sky Sports I couldn't believe how bad he was, let alone that Sky were paying him. I can't take another instance of watching Tim Sherwood throw his fucking stupid gilet down (you're either not in control of yourself or you're trying to show the fans how much you care – the former is lamentable, the latter means you're a cunt). I can't take seeing another 'couldn't give a fuck' performance from Emmanuel Adebayor, a player who had everything – and I mean everything – and traded it in for the good life.

And that's the reality of football. Nothing changes. Unless you leave the life. Then, of course, everything changes. When I think back to the game, the game that I love, I can't stop the hairs on the back of my neck from standing up – and not in a huge European game or World Cup final, but in the most insignificant moments of a match between a non-league hopeful and a Premier League big boy in an FA Cup third-round tie, say. If I'm in a bar and a game is on then, of course, I kick the balls that need to be kicked and I head the balls that need to be headed. I don't mean to – I have no affinity with either team – but I instinctively do it. I can't help myself because I've been doing it since I was old enough to walk. If you put a Coke can, a pebble, or John Terry in front of me, I'll kick them.

Football is the greatest game on the face of the earth; the greatest game ever invented. I love it, I love football. At one point in my life I used to be able to play it, and I was good. Actually, I wasn't just good, I was very fucking good. Of all those who have ever come out against the Secret Footballer, not one of them has ever denied that.

In the words of Johnny Rotten, 'Ever get the feeling you've been cheated? Goodnight.'

INDEX